Fodor's In Focus

BARBADOS & ST. LUCIA

1st Edition

Where to Stay and Eat
for All Budgets

Must-See Sights
and Local Secrets

Ratings You Can Trust

Fodor's Travel Publications   New York, Toronto, London, Sydney, Auckland
www.fodors.com

FODOR'S BARBADOS & ST. LUCIA

Series Editor: Douglas Stallings
Editor: Paula Margulies
Editorial Production: Carolyn Roth
Editorial Contributor: Jane E. Zarem
Maps & Illustrations: David Lindroth, *cartographer*; Bob Blake, Rebecca Baer, and William Wu, *map editors*
Design: Fabrizio LaRocca, *creative director*; Guido Caroti, *art director*; Ann McBride, *designer*; Melanie Marin, *senior picture editor*
Cover Photo (Anse l'Ivrogne and Gros Piton, Soufrière, St. Lucia): Greg Johnston/Danita Delimont
Production/Manufacturing: Matthew Struble

SPECIAL SALES

This book is available for special discounts for bulk purchases for sales promotions or premiums. Special editions, including personalized covers, excerpts of existing books, and corporate imprints, can be created in large quantities for special needs. For more information, write to Special Markets/Premium Sales, 1745 Broadway, MD 6-2, New York, NY 10019, or e-mail specialmarkets@randomhouse.com.

AN IMPORTANT TIP & AN INVITATION

Although all prices, opening times, and other details in this book are based on information supplied to us at press time, changes occur all the time in the travel world, and Fodor's cannot accept responsibility for facts that become outdated or for inadvertent errors or omissions. **So always confirm information when it matters,** especially if you're making a detour to visit a specific place. Your experiences—positive and negative—matter to us. If we have missed or misstated something, **please write to us.** We follow up on all suggestions. Contact the Barbados & St. Lucia editor at editors@fodors.com or c/o Fodor's at 1745 Broadway, New York, NY 10019.

PRINTED IN THE UNITED STATES OF AMERICA

10 9 8 7 6 5 4 3 2 1

Be a Fodor's Correspondent

Your opinion matters. It matters to us. It matters to your fellow Fodor's travelers, too. And we'd like to hear it. In fact, we *need* to hear it. When you share your experiences and opinions, you become an active member of the Fodor's community. Here's how you can help improve Fodor's for all of us.

Tell us when we're right. We rely on local writers to give you an insider's perspective. But our writers and staff editors also depend on you. Your positive feedback is a vote to renew our recommendations for the next edition.

Tell us when we're wrong. We update most of our guides every year. But things change. If any of our descriptions are inaccurate or inadequate, we'll incorporate your changes in the next edition and will correct factual errors at fodors.com *immediately*.

Tell us what to include. You probably have had fantastic travel experiences that aren't yet in Fodor's. Why not share them with a community of like-minded travelers? Share your discoveries and experiences with everyone directly at fodors.com. Your input may lead us to add a new listing or a higher recommendation.

Give us your opinion instantly at our feedback center at www.fodors.com/feedback. You may also e-mail editors@fodors.com with the subject line "Barbados & St. Lucia Editor." Or send your nominations, comments, and complaints by mail to Barbados & St. Lucia Editor, Fodor's, 1745 Broadway, New York, NY 10019.

Happy Traveling!

Tim Jarrell, Publisher

CONTENTS

ABOUT THIS BOOK

Our Ratings

We wouldn't recommend a place that wasn't worth your time, but sometimes a place is so experiential that superlatives don't do it justice: you just have to be there to know. These sights, properties, and experiences get our highest rating, **Fodor's Choice**, indicated by orange stars throughout this book. Black stars highlight sights and properties we deem **Highly Recommended**, places that our writers, editors, and readers praise again and again for consistency and excellence.

Credit Cards

Want to pay with plastic? **AE, D, DC, MC, V** after restaurant and hotel listings indicate whether American Express, Discover, Diners Club, MasterCard, and Visa are accepted.

Restaurants

Unless we state otherwise, restaurants are open for lunch and dinner daily. We mention dress only when there's a specific requirement and reservations only when they're essential or not accepted—it's always best to book ahead.

Hotels

Unless we tell you otherwise, you can assume that the hotels have private bath, phone, TV, and air-conditioning. We always list facilities but not whether you'll be charged an extra fee to use them, so when pricing accommodations, find out what's included.

Many Listings

★	Fodor's Choice
★	Highly recommended
✉	Physical address
✛	Directions
⌂	Mailing address
☎	Telephone
🖷	Fax
⊕	On the Web
✆	E-mail
✍	Admission fee
☉	Open/closed times
Ⓜ	Metro stations
🖭	Credit cards

Hotels & Restaurants

🏨	Hotel
↳	Number of rooms
☖	Facilities
❨❩	Meal plans
✕	Restaurant
⚖	Reservations
⊽	Smoking
⚐	BYOB
✕🏨	Hotel with restaurant that warrants a visit

Outdoors

🏌	Golf
⛺	Camping

Other

☾	Family-friendly
⇨	See also
✉	Branch address
☞	Take note

UNITED
STATES

Miami

Key West

Nassau

The Bahamas

Havana

Cuba

Turks and
Caicos Islands

George
Town

*Little
Cayman*

*Cayman
Brac*

Puerto Plata

*Grand
Cayman*

Haiti *Hispaniola*

Montego Bay

Ocho Rios

Port-au-Prince

Santo
Domingo

Jamaica

Kingston

GREATER

Caribbean   Sea

0   200 mi

0   200 km

Cartagena

Maracaibo

COLOMBIA

PANAMA

The Caribbean

ATLANTIC OCEAN

Dominican Republic

LEEWARD ISLANDS

St. John
St. Thomas
Tortola
Virgin Gorda
San Juan
St. Maarten/
St. Martin
Anguilla
St. Barthélemy
Saba
Barbuda
Puerto Rico
St. Eustatius
St. Croix
St. Kitts
Antigua
Nevis
Montserrat
Guadeloupe
Marie Galante

ANTILLES

Dominica
Martinique
Fort-de-France
St. Lucia
Barbados
Bridgetown
St. Vincent
Bequia
The Grenadines
Carriacou
St. George's
Grenada

WINDWARD ISLANDS

LESSER ANTILLES

Aruba
Curaçao
Bonaire
Willemstad
Islas Los Roques
Tobago
Port of Spain
Trinidad
La Guaira
Caracas

VENEZUELA

WHEN TO GO

The Caribbean high season is traditionally from December 15 through April 15—when northern weather is at its worst. During this season you're guaranteed that all hotels and restaurants will be open and busy. It's also the most fashionable, the most expensive, and the most popular time to visit. British tourists in particular come to both Barbados and St. Lucia for two or three weeks during the high season. If you wait until mid-May or June, prices may be 20% to 50% less, and this is particularly true of Barbados; however, some hotels close, particularly later in the summer and early fall. The period from mid-August through late November is typically the least busy time in both Barbados and St. Lucia.

Climate

The Caribbean climate is fairly constant. Summer, however, can bring somewhat higher temperatures and more humidity because the trade winds slow. The Atlantic hurricane season begins on June 1 and stretches all the way through November 30. While heavy rains can happen anytime throughout the year, it's during this six-month period when tropical fronts are most likely. Major hurricanes are a relatively rare occurrence in Barbados because the island is 100 mi farther east

than the rest of the Lesser Antilles chain (giving hurricanes less chance to gain in strength from the warm Caribbean waters).

Forecasts **National Weather Service** (⊕www.wrh.noaa.gov). **Weather Channel** (⊕www.weather. com).

Bridgetown, Barbados

Castries, St. Lucia

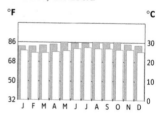

Barbados

WORD OF MOUTH

". . . [B]arbados is good for the first-timer, as it has some of everything the Caribbean has to offer . . . except a volcano."

— xkenx

"Nowhere have we found the people more enchanting, the place more inviting, or the culture more interesting."

— Cwalker

By Jane E. Zarem

THE NUMBER OF TIMES I'VE ARRIVED at Barbados's Grantley Adams International Airport reaches well into the double digits. Recently, something new caught my eye—besides the stunning reconstruction of the airport itself. On the east side of the terminal, the 28,000-square-foot, $3.5-million Barbados Concorde Experience showcases one of seven supersonic airliners retired from the British Airways fleet. The new attraction is certainly fitting. After all, a retirement home in Barbados—a British outpost and holiday destination for nearly four centuries—is the dream (and, in fact, the reality) for many Brits. Moreover, Barbados was Concorde's only Caribbean destination during the iconic jetliner's lofty heyday, delivering the well-heeled to their tropical holidays at Mach 2 speed.

Without question, Barbados is the most "British" island in the Caribbean. In contrast to the turbulent colonial past experienced by neighboring islands, which included repeated conflicts between France and Britain over dominance and control, British rule in Barbados carried on uninterrupted for 340 years—from the first established British settlement in 1627 until independence was granted in 1966. That's not to say, of course, that there weren't significant struggles in Barbados, as elsewhere in the Caribbean, between the British landowners and their African-born slaves and other indentured servants.

With that unfortunate period of slavery relegated to the history books, the British influence on Barbados can still be felt today in local manners, attitudes, customs, and politics—tempered by the characteristically warm nature of the Bajan people. ("Bajan," pronounced *bay*-jun, derives phonetically from the British pronunciation of "Barbadian.") In keeping with British traditions, many Bajans worship at the Anglican church; afternoon tea is a ritual; cricket is the national pastime (a passion, most admit); dressing for dinner is a firmly entrenched tradition; and patrons at some bars are as likely to order a Pimm's Cup as a rum and Coke. And yet, Barbados is hardly stuffy—this is still the Caribbean, after all.

The long-standing British involvement is only one of the unique attributes that distinguishes Barbados from its island neighbors. Geographically, Barbados is a break in the Lesser Antilles archipelago, the chain of islands that stretches in a graceful arc from the Virgin Islands to Trinidad. Isolated in the Atlantic Ocean, Barbados is 100 mi (160 km) due east of St. Lucia, its nearest neighbor. And

BARBADOS TOP 5

■ Great resorts run the gamut—from unpretentious to knock-your-socks-off—in terms of size, intimacy, amenities, and price. Choose one on the lively south coast or the ritzy west coast.

■ Golfers can play on some of the best championship courses in the Caribbean—including a public course on the south coast with very reasonable greens fees.

■ Great food includes everything from street-party barbecue to international cuisine that rivals the finest dining found anywhere in the world.

■ With a wide assortment of land and water sports, sightseeing options, historic sites, cultural festivities, and nightlife, there's always plenty to do and see in Barbados.

■ Bajans are friendly, welcoming, helpful, and hospitable. You'll like them; they'll like you.

geologically, while most of the Lesser Antilles are the peaks of a volcanic mountain range, Barbados is the top of a single, relatively flat protuberance of coral and limestone—the source of building blocks for many a plantation manor. (Many of those historic greathouses, in fact, have been carefully restored. Some are open to visitors.)

Bridgetown, both the capital city and the commercial center, is on the southwest coast of pear-shaped Barbados. Most of the 280,000 Bajans live and work in and around Bridgetown, in St. Michael Parish, or along the idyllic west coast or busy south coast. Others reside in tiny villages that dot the interior landscape. Broad sandy beaches, craggy cliffs, and picturesque coves make up the coastline, while the interior features forested hills and gullies and acre upon acre of sugarcane.

Tourist facilities are concentrated on the west coast in the St. James and St. Peter parishes (appropriately dubbed the Platinum Coast) and on the south coast in Christ Church Parish. Traveling along the west coast to historic Holetown, the site of the first British settlement, and continuing to the northern city of Speightstown, you can find posh beachfront resorts, luxurious private villas, and fine restaurants enveloped by lush gardens and tropical foliage. The trendier, more commercial south coast offers more competitively priced hotels and beach resorts, and its St. Lawrence Gap area is jam-packed with shops, restaurants, and nightlife. The relatively wide-open spaces along the southeast coast are proving ripe for development, and some wonderful inns and hotels already take advantage of the intoxicatingly beautiful ocean vistas. For their own holidays, though, Bajans escape to the rugged east coast, where the Atlantic surf pounds the dramatic shoreline with unrelenting force.

All in all, Barbados is a sophisticated tropical island with rich history, lodgings to suit every taste and pocketbook, and plenty to pique your interest both day and night—whether you're British or not!

EXPLORING BARBADOS

The terrain changes dramatically from any one of the island's 11 parishes to the next, and so does the pace. Bridgetown, the capital, is a rather sophisticated city. West-coast resorts and private estates ooze luxury, whereas the small villages and vast sugar plantations found through-out central Barbados reflect the island's rich history. The relentless Atlantic surf shaped the cliffs of the dramatic east coast, and the northeast is called Scotland because of its hilly landscape. Along the lively south coast, the daytime hustle and bustle produce a palpable energy that continues well into the night, at countless restaurants, dance clubs, and nightspots.

ABOUT THE HOTELS

Prices in Barbados can be twice as high in peak season (December 15 to April 15) as during the quieter months. Most hotels do not include meals in their rates, but some will offer breakfast or a meal plan. Others require you to purchase a meal plan during high season, and a few offer all-inclusive packages.

Families and long-term visitors can choose from a wide variety of villas and condos—everything from an individual luxury villa overlooking the sea or nestled in the hill-side to busy villa complexes with resort-style amenities. A few small, cozy inns are found along the east, southeast, and northwest coasts. They can be ultra-luxurious, fairly simple, or something in between.

Assume that all hotels operate on the European Plan (**EP**—with no meals) unless we specify that they use the Conti-nental Plan (**CP**—with a Continental breakfast), Breakfast Plan (**BP**—with full breakfast), or the Modified American Plan (**MAP**—with breakfast and dinner). Other hotels may

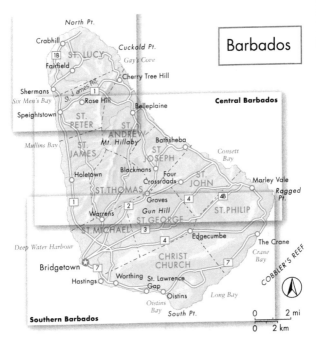

North Pt.
Crabhill
ST. LUCY
Cuckold Pt.
Fairfield
Gay's Cove
Cherry Tree Hill
Shermans
St. James Rd.
Six Men's Bay
Rose Hill
Belleplaine
Speightstown
ST.
PETER
ST.
ANDREW
Mt. Hillaby
Bathsheba
Mullins Bay
ST.
JAMES
ST.
JOSEPH
Consett
Bay
Holetown
Blackmans
Four
ST.
JOHN
Marley Vale
Crossroads
Ragged
Pt.
ST.THOMAS
Groves
ST.PHILIP
Warrens
Gun Hill
ST.GEORGE
ST.MICHAEL
Edgecumbe
The Crane
Deep Water Harbour
CHRIST
CHURCH
Crane
Bay
COBBLER'S REEF
Bridgetown
Hastings
Worthing
St. Lawrence
Gap
Oistins
Long Bay
Oistins
Bay
South Pt.

Barbados

Central Barbados

Southern Barbados

0   2 mi
0   2 km

offer the Full American Plan (**FAP**—including all meals but no drinks) or may be All-Inclusive (**AI**—with all meals, drinks, and most activities.)

ABOUT THE RESTAURANTS

First-class restaurants and hotel dining rooms serve sophisticated cuisine—often prepared by chefs with international experience—which can rival that served in the world's best restaurants. Most menus include seafood, prepared every way imaginable. Expect dorado (also known as mahimahi or dolphin—the fish, not the mammal), kingfish, snapper, and flying fish, which is so popular that it has officially become a national symbol. Shellfish also abounds, as do steak, pork, and local black-belly lamb.

Local specialty dishes include *buljol* (a cold salad of pickled codfish, tomatoes, onions, sweet peppers, and celery) and *conkies* (cornmeal, coconut, pumpkin, raisins, sweet potatoes, and spices, wrapped in a banana leaf and steamed). *Cou-cou,* often served with steamed flying fish, is a mixture of cornmeal and okra, usually topped with a spicy

PERFECT DAYS & NIGHTS

Barbados from Bottom to Top. You can't come to Barbados and not visit Harrison's Cave. The underground tram will thrill the whole family. Afterward, visit Flower Forest and Orchid World, two beautiful gardens that also have snack bars where lunch is available. Stop at Gun Hill Signal Station on the way home.

A Day in the Wild Wild East. Plan a day-trip to the rugged east coast. From Speightstown, you'll head east to Farley Hill and the Barbados Wildlife Reserve before continuing on to St. Nicholas Abbey (a lovely great house that's worth a stop). Cherry Tree Hill, a panoramic view of the whole Atlantic coast, is a definite photo op. The ride along the coastal road is particularly scenic. Stop for a Bajan buffet lunch at one of the Cliffside inns before heading back through the center of the island. From south coast hotels, do the trip in reverse.

A Day of Shopping. Take the free shopping shuttle from your hotel to Bridgetown to see the sights and do some shopping. The major stores are on Broad Street and on the side streets heading toward the water. Plan to have an alfresco lunch—perhaps a flying-fish sandwich and a Banks beer—at the Waterfront Café on the Careenage. Make time to visit Pelican Craft Centre, a 10-minute walk north of downtown, where you can see artisans at work.

A Day at the Gap. Spend a day on the south coast. Visit the Graeme Hall Nature Sanctuary in Worthing. Then escape the hot sun at the Barbados Museum in the Garrison and the George Washington House in Bush Hill. Stroll along St. Lawrence Gap and choose a place for lunch. On weekend nights, stick around for the Oistins Fish Fry—a street party with barbecued chicken and fish, cold drinks, music, and lots of people.

A Day (and Evening) on the West Coast. Spend a beach day on the west coast. At Mullins Beach, near Speightstown, water-sports equipment and beach chairs may be rented, and Mannie's Suga Suga serves all-day refreshments. At night, head for First and Second streets in Holetown. Pick any restaurant—they're all good—and end the evening at Lexy's Piano Bar.

Creole sauce made from tomatoes, onions, and sweet peppers. Bajan-style pepperpot is a hearty stew of oxtail, beef chunks, and "any other meat" in a rich, spicy gravy that's simmered overnight.

For lunch, restaurants often offer a traditional Bajan buffet of fried fish, baked chicken, salads, macaroni pie (macaroni and cheese), and a selection of steamed or stewed local roots and vegetables. Be cautious with the West Indian condiments—like the sun, they're hotter than you think. Typical Bajan drinks, besides Banks Beer and Mount Gay Rum, are *falernum* (a liqueur concocted of rum, sugar, lime juice, and almond essence) and *mauby* (a nonalcoholic drink made by boiling bitter bark and spices, straining the mixture, and sweetening it). You're sure to enjoy the fresh fruit or rum punch.

The dress code for dinner in Barbados is conservative, casually elegant, and, on occasion, formal—a jacket and tie for gentlemen and a cocktail dress for ladies in the fanciest restaurants and hotel dining rooms, particularly during the winter holiday season. Jeans, shorts, and T-shirts (either sleeveless or with slogans) are always frowned upon at dinner. Beach attire is appropriate only at the beach. And any form of camouflage—even a baby's T-shirt—may not be worn anywhere in Barbados and will be confiscated by the police.

WHAT IT COSTS IN U.S. DOLLARS				
$$$$	$$$	$$	$	¢
RESTAURANTS				
over $30	$20–$30	$12–$20	$8–$12	under $8
HOTELS*				
over $350	$250–$350	$150–$250	$80–$150	under $80
HOTELS*				
over $450	$350–$450	$250–$350	$125–$250	under $125

*EP, BP, CP **AI, FAP, MAP Restaurant prices are for a main-course, excluding the customary 10% service charge. Hotel prices are for two people in a double room in high season, excluding the 7½% VAT, customary 10% service charge, and meal plans (except at all-inclusive hotels).

IF YOU LIKE

Beaches. Let's face it, everyone visiting the Caribbean expects great beaches. Some islands have better beaches than others, of course, but Barbados has its share of fabulous ones—pure white sand, turquoise sea, gentle surf for swimmers, rough and windy conditions for surfers. There are busy beaches with lots of water sports and secret coves for romantic picnics. The west coast beaches are narrower than those on the south coast, particularly in the fall when summer storms can erode the coastline. South-coast beaches are broad and powdery, with gentle surf that becomes rougher as you approach the island's windy southern point. Windsurfers love that area, however, while surfers congregate at Bathsheba Soup Bowl on the wild and woolly east coast, which is otherwise not recommended for swimming.

Gardens. Beautiful flowers are a given in the Caribbean, where the bountiful sunshine and 'tropical showers help all plants to thrive. Barbados has a wealth of privately owned gardens that are open to the public and showcase local ferns and flowers, as well as orchids and other exotic plants. In addition to the joy of walking along their lush pathways and seeing nature's beauty up close, visitors find these gardens a wonderfully quiet place for peaceful repose.

History. The most British of Caribbean islands—a British colony for 340 years until it became independent in 1966—Barbados has a lot of well-documented history to share. The Barbados Museum is a wonderful place for the whole family to find out about the old days, but touring some of the well-preserved "great houses" provides a vivid picture of how the plantation owners lived back in the day.

Rum. Barbados is "where de rum come from," and visitors all seem to enjoy a distillery tour and tasting—Mount Gay or Malibu just north of Bridgetown or Foursquare Plantation in the center of the island. A visit to the Frank Hutson Sugar Museum is a good place to start, though, because sugar, after all, is "where de rum *really* come from."

TIMING

Barbados is busiest in the high season, which extends from December 15 through April 15. Off-season hotel rates can be half what they are during this busy period. During the high season, too, a few hotels may require you to buy some kind of meal plan, which is not usually required in the low season. As noted in the listings, some hotels close in September and October, the slowest months of the off-season, for annual renovations. Some restaurants may close for brief periods within that time frame, as well.

In mid-January the **Barbados Jazz Festival** is a weeklong event jammed with performances by international artists, jazz legends, and local talent.

In February the weeklong **Holetown Festival** is held at the fairgrounds to commemorate the date in 1627 when the first European settlers arrived in Barbados.

Gospelfest occurs in May, and hosts performances by gospel headliners from around the world.

Dating from the 19th century, **Crop Over,** a monthlong festival similar to Carnival that begins in July and ends on **Kadooment Day** (a national holiday), marks the end of the sugarcane harvest.

BRIDGETOWN

This bustling capital city is a major duty-free port with a compact shopping area. The principal thoroughfare is Broad Street, which leads west from National Heroes Square.

Numbers in the margin correspond to points of interest on the Bridgetown map.

WHAT TO SEE

❷ **The Careenage.** Bridgetown's natural harbor and gathering place is where, in the early days, schooners were careened (turned on their sides) to be scraped of barnacles and repainted. Today the Careenage serves as a marina for pleasure yachts and excursion boats. A boardwalk skirts the north side of the Careenage; on the south side, a lovely esplanade has pathways and benches for pedestrians and a statue of Errol Barrow, the first prime minister of Barbados. The city's two bridges, the Chamberlain and the Charles Duncan O'Neal, span the harbor.

❸ **National Heroes Square.** Across Broad Street from the Parliament Buildings and bordered by High and Trafalgar streets, this triangular plaza marks the center of town. Its monument to Lord Horatio Nelson (who was in Barbados only briefly in 1777 as a 19-year-old navy lieutenant) pre-

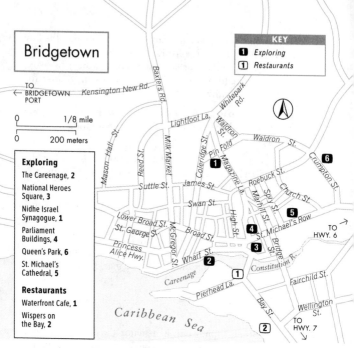

TO
← BRIDGETOWN
PORT

Exploring

The Careenage, **2**

National Heroes
Square, **3**

Nidhe Israel
Synagogue, **1**

Parliament
Buildings, **4**

Queen's Park, **6**

St. Michael's
Cathedral, **5**

Restaurants

Waterfront Cafe, **1**

Wispers on
the Bay, **2**

dates Nelson's Column in London's Trafalgar Square by
36 years. Also here are a war memorial and a fountain that
commemorates the advent of running water on Barbados
in 1865.

❶ **Nidhe Israel Synagogue.** Providing for the spiritual needs
of one of the oldest Jewish congregations in the western
hemisphere, this synagogue was formed by Jews who left
Brazil in the 1620s and introduced sugarcane to Barbados. The adjoining cemetery has tombstones dating from
the 1630s. The original house of worship, built in 1654,
was destroyed in an 1831 hurricane, rebuilt in 1833, and
restored with the assistance of the Barbados National Trust
in 1987. Friday-night services are held during the winter
months, but the building is open to the public year-round.
Shorts are not acceptable during services but may be worn
at other times. ⊠*Synagogue La., St. Michael* ☎*246/426–
5792* 🕮*Donation requested* ☉*Weekdays 9–4.*

❹ **Parliament Buildings.** Overlooking National Heroes Square
in the center of town, these Victorian buildings were
constructed around 1870 to house the British Commonwealth's third-oldest parliament. A series of stained-glass

CLOSE UP

1

Errol Barrow, National Hero

Errol Barrow (1920–1987), trained in Britain as a lawyer and economist, led his native Barbados to independence in 1966 and became the island nation's first prime minister. During his initial tenure, which lasted through 1976, Barrow expanded the tourist industry, reduced the island's dependence on sugar, introduced national health insurance and social security, and extended free education to the community college level. Barrow was reelected prime minister in 1986 but collapsed and died at his home a year later. He is honored as a national hero and the "Father of Independence," and his birthday—January 21—is celebrated as a national holiday. On that day in 2007, a 9-foot-tall statue of Errol Barrow was erected on the esplanade along the Careenage, picturesquely sited between the city's two bridges and facing Parliament.

windows depicts British monarchs from James I to Victoria. ⊠*Broad St., St. Michael* ☎*246/427–2019* ✉*Donations welcome* ⊙*Tours weekdays at 11 and 2, when Parliament isn't in session.*

❻ Queen's Park. Northeast of Bridgetown, Queen's Park contains one of the island's two immense baobab trees. Brought to Barbados from Guinea, in West Africa, around 1738, this tree has a girth of more than 51 feet. Queen's Park Art Gallery, managed by the National Culture Foundation, is the island's largest gallery; exhibits change monthly. Queen's Park House, the historic home of the British troop commander, has been converted into a theater, with an exhibition room on the lower floor and a restaurant. ⊠*Constitution Rd., St. Michael* ☎*246/427–2345 gallery* ✉*Free* ⊙*Daily 9–5.*

❺ St. Michael's Cathedral. Although no one has proved it conclusively, George Washington is said to have worshipped here in 1751, on his only trip outside the United States. The original structure was nearly a century old by then. Destroyed twice by hurricanes, it was rebuilt in 1784 and again in 1831. ⊠*Spry St., east of National Heroes Sq., St. Michael.*

RENTING A CAR. If you're staying on the remote southeast or east coasts, you may want to rent a car for your entire stay. In more populated areas, where taxis and public transportation are readily available, you might rent a car or minimoke (a tiny, open-sided beach buggy) for a day or two of exploring on your own. Rates are about $55 per day during the high season.

SOUTHERN BARBADOS

Christ Church Parish, which is far busier and more developed than the west coast, is chockablock with condos, high- and low-rise hotels, and beach parks. It is also home to the St. Lawrence Gap, with its many places to eat, drink, shop, and party. As you move southeast, the broad, flat terrain comprises acre upon acre of cane fields, interrupted only by an occasional oil rig and a few tiny villages. Along the byways are colorful chattel houses, the property of tenant farmers. Historically, these typically Barbadian, ever-expandable homes were built to be dismantled and moved as required.

☙ **Barbados Concorde Experience.** Opened to the public in April 2007, the Concorde Experience revolves around the British Airways Concorde G-BOAE (Alpha Echo, for short), a supersonic aircraft that flew between London and Barbados for many years and now makes its permanent home here. In addition to being able to board the aircraft, you'll learn how its technology was developed and how it differed from other jets. You may or may not have been able to fly the Concorde when it was still traversing the Atlantic, but this is your chance to experience some ultramodern history. ✉*Grantley Adams International Airport, Christ Church* ☎*246/253–6257* ⊕*www.barbadosconcorde.com* ✉*$17.50* ☉*Daily 9*AM*–5*PM.

Barbados Military Cemetery (✉*Graves End, Needham's Point, St. Michael* ☎*245/426–0982* ✉*Free* ☉*Daily 8*AM*–4*PM) is situated near the shore behind historic St. Ann's Fort. First used in 1780, when the area was pretty much marshland, the dead were placed in shallow graves or simply left on top of the ground where many were absorbed, within a few short days, into the swamp. In the early 20th century, a number of the remaining graves were dug up to provide room for oil storage tanks; the salvaged headstones were placed on a cenotaph, erected in 1920–24. A "Cross of Sacrifice" was erected in 1982 to honor all the military dead, and a second cenotaph, erected in 2003, honors the Barbadian merchant seamen who died in World War II.

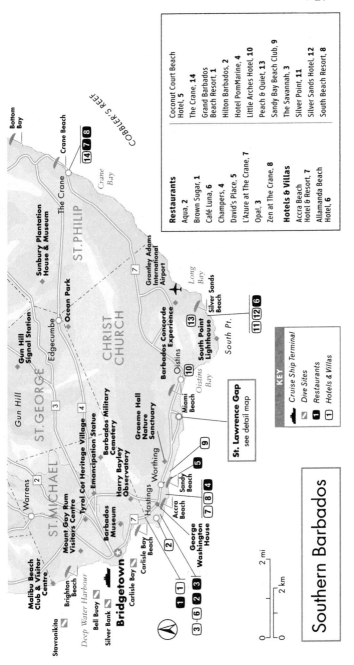

Southern Barbados

Restaurants
Aqua, 2
Brown Sugar, 1
Café Luna, 6
Champers, 4
David's Place, 5
L'Azure at The Crane, 7
Opal, 3
Zen at The Crane, 8

Hotels & Villas
Accra Beach Hotel & Resort, 7
Allamanda Beach Hotel, 6
Coconut Court Beach Hotel, 5
The Crane, 14
Grand Barbados Beach Resort, 1
Hilton Barbados, 2
Hotel PomMarine, 4
Little Arches Hotel, 10
Peach & Quiet, 13
Sandy Bay Beach Club, 9
The Savannah, 3
Silver Point, 11
Silver Sands Hotel, 12
South Beach Resort, 8

KEY
🚢 Cruise Ship Terminal
⬜ Dive Sites
1 Restaurants
① Hotels & Villas

🕐 **Barbados Museum.** This intriguing museum, established in
★ 1933 in the former British Military Prison—which dates
back to 1815—in the historic Garrison area, has artifacts
from Arawak days (around 400 BC) and galleries that depict
19th-century military history and everyday life. You can
see cane-harvesting tools, wedding dresses, ancient (and
frightening) dentistry instruments, and slave sale accounts
kept in a spidery copperplate handwriting. The museum's
Harewood Gallery showcases the island's flora and fauna;
its Cunard Gallery has a permanent collection of 20th-cen-
tury Barbadian and Caribbean paintings and engravings;
and its Connell Gallery features European decorative arts.
Additional galleries include one for children. The Shilstone
Memorial Library houses rare West Indian documenta-
tion—archival documents, genealogical records, photos,
books, and maps—dating back to the 17th century. The
museum also has a gift shop and a café. ✉*Hwy. 7, Garrison Savannah, St. Michael* ☎*246/427–0201 or 246/436–
1956* ⊕*www.barbmuse.org.bb* 💲*$5.75* 🕐*Mon.–Sat. 9–5,
Sun. 2–6; library, Mon.–Fri. 9–1.*

Codrington Theological College. An impressive stand of royal
palms lines the road leading to the coral-stone buildings
and serene grounds of Codrington College, an Anglican
seminary opened in 1745 on a cliff overlooking Consett
Bay. You're welcome to tour the buildings and walk the
nature trails. Keep in mind, though, that beachwear is
not appropriate here. ✉*Sargeant St., Consett Bay, St.
John* ☎*246/423–1140* ⊕*www.codrington.org* 💲*$2.50*
🕐*Daily 10–4.*

Emancipation Statue. This powerful statue of a slave—whose
raised hands, with broken chains hanging from each wrist,
evoke both contempt and victory—is commonly referred
to as the Bussa Statue. Bussa was the man who, in 1816,
led the first slave rebellion on Barbados. The work of Barbadian sculptor Karl Brodhagen, the statue was erected in
1985 to commemorate the emancipation of the slaves in
1834. The statue, in the middle of a busy intersection east
of Bridgetown, used to overlook a broad cane field—a setting that made the depiction of Bussa all the more poi-
gnant. Today the cane field is rapidly being subdivided into
housing lots. Nevertheless, the statue remains a moving
reflection of a particularly painful period in island—if not
world—history. ✉*St. Barnabas Roundabout, intersection
of ABC Hwy. and Hwy. 5, Haggatt Hall, St. Michael.*

George Washington House. George Washington slept here! This carefully restored and refurbished 18th-century plantation house in Bush Hill is the only place where the future first president of the United States actually slept outside of North America. Teenage George and his older half-brother Lawrence, who was suffering from tuberculosis and seeking treatment on the island, rented this house overlooking Carlisle Bay for two months in 1751. Opened to the public in December 2006, the lower floor of the house and the kitchen have period furnishings; the upper floor is a museum with both permanent and temporary exhibits that display artifacts of 18th-century Barbadian life. The site includes an original 1719 windmill and bathhouse, along with a stable added to the property in the 1800s and, of course, a gift shop and small café. Guided tours begin with an informative, 15-minute film appropriately called *George Washington in Barbados.* ⊠*Bush Hill, The Garrison, St. Michael* ☎*246/228–5461* 🖃*$12.50* ☺*Mon.–Sat. 9–4:30.*

☾ **Graeme Hall Nature Sanctuary.** This 35-acre oasis, a Barba-
★ dos National Environmental Heritage Site, sits smack in the middle of the busy commercial area of the south coast. Saved from almost-certain development as a golf course or other commercial use, the sanctuary includes the island's largest inland lake along with ponds and wading pools, swampy marshes and mangroves, observation huts, horticulture exhibits, and two enormous walk-through aviaries filled with brilliantly colored parrots, macaws, flamingos, and ibis. It's interesting, educational, peaceful, and delightful for both adults and kids. ⊠*Main Rd., Worthing, Christ Church* ☎*246/435–9727* ⊕*www.graemehall.com* 🖃*$12.50* ☺*Daily 8–6.*

☾ **Harry Bayley Observatory.** The Barbados Astronomical Society's headquarters since 1963, the observatory has a Celestron 14-inch reflector telescope—the only one in the eastern Caribbean. Visitors can view the moon, stars, planets, and astronomical objects that may not be visible from North America or Europe. ⊠*Off Hwy. 6, Clapham, St. Michael* ☎*246/426–1317 or 246/422–2394* 🖃*$5* ☺*Fri. 8:30 PM–11:30 PM.*

☾ **Ocean Park.** View stingrays, sharks, moray eels, spiny lobsters, and other marine life up close and personal at this fun-for-all marine park. Throughout the day, informative talks and feeding demonstrations teach visitors about the underwater creatures on exhibit in the touch pools, mega-tanks, living reef display, mangrove swamp, and freshwater falls. An additional family-fun feature is the adjacent miniature golf course ($2.50 extra). ⊠*Hwy. 6, Balls Complex, Christ Church* ☎*246/420–7405* ⊕*www.oceanparkbarbados.com* 🖃*$17.50* ☉*Daily 9–6.*

Ragged Point (⊠*Marley Vale, St. Philip*) is the easternmost point of Barbados and the location of East Coast Light, one of four strategically placed lighthouses on the island. While civilization in the form of new homes is encroaching on this once remote location, the view of the entire Atlantic coastline of Barbados is still spectacular—and the cool ocean breeze is beautifully refreshing on a hot, sunny day.

South Point Light (⊠*Atlantic Shores, Christ Church*) is the oldest of four lighthouses on Barbados. Assembled on the island in 1852, after being shown at London's Great Exhibition the previous year, the landmark lighthouse is located just east of Miami Beach and marks the southernmost point of land on Barbados. The 89-foot tower, with its distinguishing red and white horizontal stripes, is closed to the public, but visitors may freely walk about the site, take photos, and enjoy the view.

★ **Sunbury Plantation House & Museum.** Lovingly rebuilt after a 1995 fire destroyed everything but its thick flint-and-stone walls, Sunbury offers an elegant glimpse of the 18th and 19th centuries on a Barbadian sugar estate. Period furniture, old prints, and a collection of horse-drawn carriages lend an air of authenticity. Two nights a week, a five-course candlelight dinner is served at the 200-year-old mahogany table in the Sunbury dining room ($47.50 per person, reservations required). A buffet luncheon is served daily in the courtyard for $17.50 per person. ⊠*Off Hwy. 5, Six Cross Roads, St. Philip* ☎*246/423–6270* ⊕*www.barbadosgreat house.com* 🖃*$7.50* ☉*Daily 10–5.*

☾ **Tyrol Cot Heritage Village.** This coral-stone cottage just south of Bridgetown was constructed in 1854 and has been preserved as an example of period architecture. In 1929 it became the home of Sir Grantley Adams, the first premier of Barbados and the namesake of its international airport. Part of the Barbados National Trust, the cottage is now filled with the late Sir Grantley and Lady Adams's antiques and memorabilia. It's also the centerpiece of an outdoor "living museum," where artisans and craftsmen have their workshops in a cluster of traditional chattel houses. The crafts are for sale, and refreshments are available at the "rum shop." ✉*Rte. 2, Codrington Hill, St. Michael* ☎*246/424–2074 or 246/436–9033* 🖼*$6* ⊙*Weekdays 9–5.*

CENTRAL BARBADOS

On the west coast, in St. James Parish, Holetown marks the center of the Platinum Coast—so called for the vast number of luxurious resorts and mansions that face the sea. Holetown is also where British captain John Powell landed in 1625 to claim the island for King James. On the east coast, the crashing Atlantic surf has eroded the shoreline, forming steep cliffs and prehistoric rocks that look like giant mushrooms. Bathsheba and Cattlewash are favorite seacoast destinations for locals on weekends and holidays. In the interior, narrow roads weave through tiny villages and along and between the ridges. The landscape is covered with tropical vegetation and is riddled with fascinating caves and gullies.

CUBAN MONUMENT. On October 6, 1976, Cubana Airlines Flight 455, a DC-8 aircraft en route to Cuba from Barbados, was brought down by a terrorist bombing attack, killing all 73 people on board. The aircraft crashed into the sea off Paynes Bay on the West Coast of Barbados. Four anti-Castro Cuban exiles were arrested for the crime. Two were sentenced to 20-year prison terms; one was acquitted; the fourth was held for eight years awaiting sentencing and later fled. A pyramid-shaped granite monument dedicated to the victims was installed along Highway 1 at the approximate location where the wreckage was brought ashore; it was unveiled during a 1998 visit by Cuban president Fidel Castro.

★ **Andromeda Botanic Gardens.** Beautiful and unusual plant specimens from around the world are cultivated on six acres of gardens nestled among streams, ponds, and rocky outcroppings overlooking the sea above the Bathsheba coastline. The gardens were created in 1954 with flowering plants collected by the late horticulturist Iris Bannochie. They're now administered by the Barbados National Trust. The Hibiscus Café serves snacks and drinks. ✉*Bathsheba, St. Joseph* ☎*246/433–9384* 🖼*$8.75* ⊙*Daily 9–5.*

Banks Brewery Visitor Centre. Banks is the home brew of Barbados and a very good brew, at that. After a short audio-visual presentation in the Brewseum, which is actually

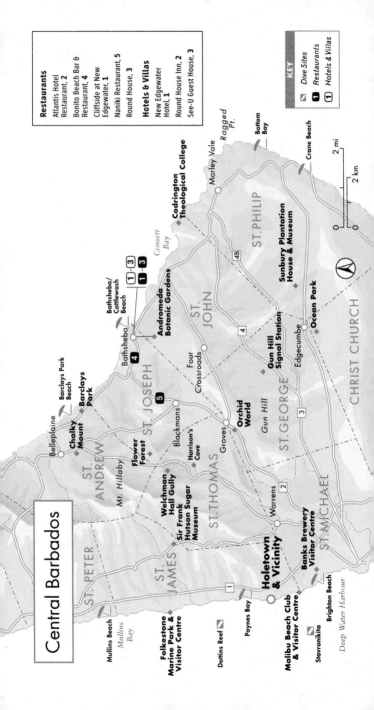

Central Barbados

KEY

☑ Dive Sites
❶ Restaurants
① Hotels & Villas

ST. PETER

ST. ANDREW

ST. JAMES

ST. THOMAS

ST. JOSEPH

ST. JOHN

ST. GEORGE

ST. MICHAEL

ST. PHILIP

CHRIST CHURCH

Mullins Beach

Mullins Bay

Belleplaine

Barclays Park Beach

Barclays Park

Chalky Mount

Mt. Hillaby

Flower Forest

Welchman Hall Gully

Sir Frank Hutson Sugar Museum

Harrison's Cave

Blackmans

Bathsheba/Cattlewash Beach

Codrington Theological College

Consett Bay

Ragged Pt.

Marley Vale

Bottom Bay

Crane Beach

Bathsheba

Andromeda Botanic Gardens

Four Crossroads

Gun Hill Signal Station

Gun Hill

Orchid World

Groves

Edgecumbe

Sunbury Plantation House & Museum

Ocean Park

Folkestone Marine Park & Visitor Centre

Paynes Bay

Dottins Reef

Holetown & Vicinity

Warrens

Banks Brewery Visitor Centre

Malibu Beach Club & Visitor Centre

Stavronikita

Brighton Beach

Deep Water Harbour

0   2 mi

0   2 km

Holetown Landing

On May 14, 1625, English Captain John Powell anchored his ship off the west coast of Barbados and claimed the island on behalf of King James I. He named his landfall Jamestown. Nearly two years later, on February 17, 1627, Captain Henry Powell landed in Jamestown with a party of 80 settlers and 10 slaves. They used a small channel, or "hole," near the settlement to offload and clean ships, so Jamestown soon became known as Holetown. Today Holetown is a vibrant town with shopping centers, restaurants, nightspots, and, of course, hotels and resorts. It is also the site of the annual Holetown Festival—a week of parades, crafts, music, and partying—held in mid-February each year to commemorate the first settlement. The celebration begins at the Holetown Monument in the center of town.

the Old Brewhouse, see the original copper brewing kettles that have since been replaced by modern stainless steel vats. Watch the computerized brewing, bottling, and crating process as it occurs in the New Brewhouse and Bottling Hall, then visit the Beer Garden for a sample or two. The souvenir shop sells Banks logo gear. The tour lasts an hour; reservations are required. ✉ *Wildey, St. Michael* ☎ *246/228–6486* ⊕ *www.banksbeer.com* 🖃 *$6; $16 includes round-trip transportation* ☾ *Weekdays 10, 12, and 2.*

Barclays Park. Straddling the Ermy Bourne Highway on the east coast, just north of Bathsheba, this public park was donated by Barclays Bank (now First Caribbean International Bank). Pack a picnic or stop at the popular snack bar and enjoy lunch with a gorgeous ocean view.

Chalky Mount. This tiny east-coast village is perched high in the clay-yielding hills that have supplied local potters for 300 years. A number of working potteries are open daily to visitors. You can watch as artisans create bowls, vases, candleholders, and decorative objects—which are, of course, for sale.

★ **Flower Forest.** It's a treat to meander among fragrant flowering bushes, canna and ginger lilies, puffball trees, and more than 100 other species of tropical flora in a cool, tranquil forest of flowers and other plants. A ½-mi-long (1-km-long) path winds through the 50-acre grounds, a former sugar plantation. It takes about 30 to 45 minutes to follow the path, or you can wander freely for as long as you wish. Benches located throughout the forest give you a place to pause and reflect. There's also a snack bar, a gift shop, and a beautiful view of Mt. Hillaby. ⊠ *Hwy. 2, Richmond Plantation, St. Joseph* ☎ *246/433–8152* 🖃 *$10* ⊙ *Daily 9–5.*

🖰 **Folkestone Marine Park & Visitor Centre.** On land and off-★ shore, the whole family will enjoy this park just north of Holetown. The museum and aquarium illuminate some of the island's marine life; for some firsthand viewing, there's an underwater snorkeling trail around Dottin's Reef (glass-bottom boats are available for nonswimmers). A barge sunk in shallow water is home to many fish, making it a popular dive site. ⊠ *Church Point, Holetown, St. James* ☎ *246/42–2314* 🖃 *Free* ⊙ *Daily 9–5; museum, weekdays 9–5.*

🖰 **Gun Hill Signal Station.** The 360-degree view from Gun Hill, ★ 700 feet above sea level, was what made this location of strategic importance to the 18th-century British army. Using lanterns and semaphores, soldiers based here could communicate with their counterparts at the Garrison, on the south coast, and at Grenade Hill, in the north. Time moved slowly in 1868, and Captain Henry Wilkinson whiled away his off-duty hours here by carving a huge lion from a single rock, which is on the hillside just below the tower. Come for the short history lesson—but mainly for the view; it's so gorgeous, military invalids were once sent here to convalesce. ⊠ *Gun Hill, St. George* ☎ *246/429–1358* 🖃 *$4.60* ⊙ *Weekdays 9–5.*

★ Fodor'sChoice **Harrison's Cave.** This limestone cavern, complete 🖰 with stalactites, stalagmites, subterranean streams, and a 40-foot waterfall, is a rare find in the Caribbean—and one of Barbados's most popular attractions. The cave reopened in 2007, following extensive renovations including a new visitor center with interpretative displays, life-size models and sculptures, a souvenir shop, improved restaurant facilities, and access for people with physical disabilities. The one-hour tours are conducted via electric trams, which fill up fast; reserve ahead of time. ⊠ *Hwy. 2, Welchman Hall, St. Thomas* ☎ *246/438–6640* ⊕ *www.harrisonscave.com* 🖃 *$20* ⊙ *Daily 9–6; last tour at 4.*

Malibu Beach Club & Visitor Centre. The fun-loving Malibu Rum people encourage those taking the distillery tour at this club just north of Bridgetown to make a day of it. The beach—which has a variety of water-sports options—is adjacent to the visitor center. Lunch and drinks are served at the beachside grill. ⊠*Black Rock, Brighton, St. Michael* ☎*246/425–9393* ⊕*www.malibu-rum.com* ⌑*$7.50, $27.50 with lunch, $37.50 day pass* ⊙ *Weekdays 9–5.*

★ **Mount Gay Rum Visitors Centre.** On this popular 45-minute tour you learn the colorful story behind the world's oldest rum, made in Barbados since the 18th century. Although the actual distillery is in the far north, in St. Lucy Parish, tour guides explain the rum-making procedure in detail. Both historic and modern equipment is on display, and row after row of barrels are stored here. The tour concludes with a tasting and an opportunity to buy bottles of rum and gift items—and even have lunch. ⊠*Spring Garden Hwy., Brandons, St. Michael* ☎*246/425–8757* ⊕*www.mountgay. com* ⌑*$6, $27.50 with lunch* ⊙ *Weekdays 9–4.*

Orchid World. Follow meandering pathways through tropical gardens filled with thousands of colorful orchids. You'll encounter Vandaceous orchids attached to fences or wire frames, Schomburgkia and Oncidiums on mahogany trees, Aranda and Spathoglottis orchids growing in a grotto, and Ascocendas suspended from netting in shady enclosures. You'll find seasonal orchids, scented orchids, multicolored Vanda orchids . . . and more. Benches are well placed for stopping for a little rest, admiring the flowers, or simply taking in the expansive view of the surrounding cane fields and distant hills of Sweet Vale. Snacks, cold beverages, and other refreshments are served in the café. ⊠*Hwy. 3B, Groves, St. George* ☎*246/433–0306* ⌑*$10* ⊙ *Daily 9–5.*

Welchman Hall Gully. This 1-mi-long (2-km-long) natural gully is really a collapsed limestone cavern, once part of the same underground network as Harrison's Cave. The Barbados National Trust protects the peace and quiet here, making it a beautiful place to hike past acres of labeled flowers and stands of trees. You can see and hear some interesting birds—and, with luck, a native green monkey. ⊠*Welchman Hall, St. Thomas* ☎*246/438–6671* ⌑*$5.75* ⊙*Daily 9–5.*

NORTHERN BARBADOS

Speightstown, the north's commercial center and once a thriving port city, now relies on quaint local shops and informal restaurants. Many of Speightstown's 19th-century buildings, with typical overhanging balconies, have been or are being restored. The island's northernmost reaches,

CLOSE UP

Where de Rum Come From

For more than 300 years, a daily "tot" of rum (2 ounces) has been duly administered to each sailor in the British Navy—as a health ration. At times, rum has also played a less appetizing—but equally important—role. When Admiral Horatio Nelson died in 1805 aboard a ship during the Battle of Trafalgar, his body was preserved in a cask of his favorite rum until he could be properly buried.

Few Caribbean islands are without a locally made rum, but Barbados is truly "where de rum come from." Mount Gay, the world's oldest rum distillery, has continuously operated on Barbados since 1703, according to the original deed for the Mount Gay Estate, which itemized two stone windmills, a boiling house, seven copper pots, and a still house. The presence of rum-making equipment on the plantation at the time suggests that the previous owners were actually producing rum in Barbados long before 1703.

Today much of the island's interior is still planted with sugarcane—where the rum really does come from—and several great houses, situated on historic sugar plantations, have been restored with period furniture and are open to the public.

To really understand rum, however, you need to delve a little deeper than the bottom of a glass of rum punch. Mount Gay offers an interesting 45-minute tour of its Bridgetown plant, followed by a tasting. You'll learn about the rum-making process from cane to cocktail, hear more rum-inspired anecdotes, and have an opportunity to buy bottles of its famous Eclipse or Extra Old rum at duty-free prices. Bottoms up!

St. Peter and St. Lucy parishes, have a varied topography and are lovely to explore. Between the tiny fishing towns along the northwestern coast and the sweeping views out over the Atlantic to the east are forest and farm, moor and mountain. Most guides include a loop through this area on a daylong island tour—it's a beautiful drive.

☺ **Animal Flower Cave.** Small sea anemones, or sea worms, resemble jewel-like flowers when they open their tiny tentacles. They live in small pools—some large enough to swim in—in this cave at the island's northernmost tip. The view of breaking waves from inside the cave is magnificent. ⊠*North Point, St. Lucy* ☎*246/439–8797* ⊴*$2* ⊙*Daily 9–4.*

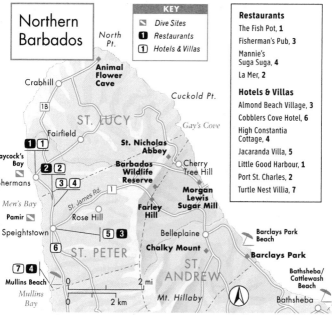

Northern Barbados	North Pt.	**KEY**

KEY
- Dive Sites
- 1 Restaurants
- ① Hotels & Villas

Restaurants
The Fish Pot, **1**
Fisherman's Pub, **3**
Mannie's
Suga Suga, **4**
La Mer, **2**

Hotels & Villas
Almond Beach Village, **3**
Cobblers Cove Hotel, **6**
High Constantia
Cottage, **4**
Jacaranda Villa, **5**
Little Good Harbour, **1**
Port St. Charles, **2**
Turtle Nest Villia, **7**

☾ **Barbados Wildlife Reserve.** The reserve is the habitat of her-
★ ons, innumerable land turtles, screeching peacocks, shy
deer, elusive green monkeys, brilliantly colored parrots (in
a large walk-in aviary), a snake, and a caiman. Except for
the snake and the caiman, the animals run or fly freely—so
step carefully and keep your hands to yourself. Late afternoon is your best chance to catch a glimpse of a green monkey. ⊠*Farley Hill, St. Peter* ☎*246/422–8826* ☎*$11.50*
☾*Daily 10–5.*

Farley Hill. At this national park in northern St. Peter, across
the road from the Barbados Wildlife Reserve, the imposing
ruins of a plantation great house are surrounded by gardens and lawns, along with an avenue of towering royal
palms and gigantic mahogany, whitewood, and casuarina
trees. Partially rebuilt for the filming of *Island in the Sun,*
the classic 1957 film starring Harry Belafonte and Doro-
thy Dandridge, the structure was later destroyed by fire.
Behind the estate, there's a sweeping view of the Scotland
region, named for its rugged landscape. ⊠*Farley Hill,
St. Peter* ☎*246/422–3555* ☎*$2 per car, pedestrians free*
☾*Daily 8:30–6.*

Sir Frank Hutson Sugar Museum. The Sugar Museum is located in an old boiling house in the yard of the Portvale Sugar Factory, one of two sugar refineries in operation in Barbados. The museum has a collection of original machinery, old photographs, and other implements used to refine sugar and make molasses. A video presentation explains the production process from cutting the cane to sweetening your coffee and, of course, making rum. During the grinding season (February through May), you can also tour the modern factory to see how sugar is produced today. ✉*Hwy. 2A, Rock Hall, St. Thomas* ☎*246/432–0100* 💲*$4; $7.50 includes factory tour* ⊗*Mon.–Sat. 9–5.*

⏱ **Morgan Lewis Sugar Mill.** Built in 1727, the mill was operational until 1945. Today it's the only remaining windmill in Barbados with its wheelhouse and sails intact. No longer used to grind sugarcane, except for occasional demonstrations, it was donated to the Barbados National Trust in 1962 and eventually restored to its original working specifications in 1998 by millwrights from the United Kingdom. The surrounding acres are now used for dairy farming. ✉*Cherry Tree Hill, St. Andrew* ☎*246/422–7429* 💲*$5* ⊗*Weekdays 9–5.*

★ **St. Nicholas Abbey.** There's no religious connection here at all. The island's oldest great house (circa 1650) was named after the original British owner's hometown, St. Nicholas Parish near Bristol, and its neighbor Bath Abbey. Its stone-and-wood architecture makes it one of only three original Jacobean-style houses still standing in the western hemisphere. It has Dutch gables, finials of coral stone, and beautiful grounds that include an old sugar mill. The first floor, fully furnished with period furniture and portraits of family members, is open to the public. Fascinating home movies, shot by a previous owner's father, record Bajan life in the 1930s. ✉*Cherry Tree Hill, St. Peter* ☎*246/422–5357* 💲*$12.50* ⊗*Weekdays 10–3:30.*

CHERRY TREE HILL. The cherry trees for which this spot was named have long since disappeared, but the view from Cherry Tree Hill, just east of St. Nicholas Abbey, is still one of the most spectacular in Barbados. While only about 850 feet above sea level, it is one of the highest points on the island and affords a broad view of the rugged east coast and the entire Scotland District—so named because its rolling hills resemble the moors of Scotland.

CLOSE UP

Sugar: How Sweet It Is . . .

Sugarcane was introduced to Barbados in the 1630s. Considered "white gold" by the original plantation owners, sugar production relied on forced labor (African slaves) and indentured servants (white civilians who wanted to emigrate overseas, kidnapped individuals, and convicted criminals dubbed "Red Legs," presumably because of the chaffing marks that the chains made on their white legs). Slavery was abolished in 1834, yet records show that Barbados still had 491 active sugar plantations in 1846, along with 506 operating windmills. And until 1969, when the mechanical harvester was introduced in Barbados,

cane was cut by manual labor. Nowadays, few people want the backbreaking job of cutting cane, so nearly all cane grown anywhere is cut mechanically. Today in Barbados, some 1,500 small farms (about 200 acres each) produce about 60,000 tons of sugar annually, but only one operating windmill remains and just two companies refine sugar. Unfortunately, small farms and hilly terrain make mechanization less efficient. So while sugar remains an important agricultural product in Barbados, its value to the local economy has declined relative to tourism and other business interests.

Today, when approaching from the west, you drive through a majestic stand of mature, leafy mahogany trees.

WHERE TO EAT

The largest concentration of restaurants on the west coast is in Holetown, particularly on First and Second streets, where you'll find everything from poached fish to pizza, barbecue to bistro, curry to stir-fry. Many more excellent restaurants are scattered along Highway 1 south of Holetown—including some of the finest ones on the island. A handful of others are in Speightstown, in the far northwest. And don't dismiss the hotel restaurants, many of which are quite fabulous. On the south coast, the St. Lawrence Gap area is chockablock with popular restaurants—at least 17 at last count. Seafood served at water's edge is a highlight, but you'll also find restaurants offering Mexican, Greek, Italian, Asian Fusion, and, of course, Bajan cuisine. Some of the local favorites, where businesspeople come for the daily Bajan buffet luncheon, are in or closer to Bridgetown.

A few small inns perched on cliffs overlooking the east coast offer lunch—often a Bajan buffet—and beautiful ocean views to individuals and groups touring that rugged side of the island.

BRIDGETOWN

Bridgetown restaurant locations are plotted on the Bridgetown map.

CARIBBEAN/SEAFOOD

$$ ✕**Waterfront Cafe.** This friendly bistro alongside the Careenage is the perfect place to enjoy a drink, snack, or meal—and to people-watch. Locals and tourists alike gather for all-day alfresco dining on sandwiches, salads, fish, pasta, pepperpot stew, and tasty Bajan snacks such as buljol, fish cakes, and plantation pork (plantains stuffed with spicy minced pork). The panfried flying-fish sandwich is especially popular. In the evening you can gaze through the arched windows while savoring nouvelle Caribbean cuisine, enjoying cool trade winds, and listening to live jazz. There's a special Caribbean buffet and steel-pan music on Tuesday night from 7 to 9. ⊠*The Careenage, Bridgetown, St. Michael* ☎*246/427–0093* ▭*AE, DC, MC, V* ⊘*Closed Sun.*

ECLECTIC

$$$$ ✕**Wispers on the Bay.** Pass through the large wooden doors from the street and enter into a lush inner courtyard with gardens, walkways, small shops, a waterfall, and sitting areas. The restaurant itself is seaside, with wispy white curtains and crisp white tablecloths and seat covers. Dine outdoors on the breezy deck or inside in air-conditioned comfort. In terms of ambience, think Miami's South Beach transported to the Caribbean. At lunch, enjoy homemade soups, fresh salads, or a variety of entrées that might include pear and cheese tortellini, West Indian curried chicken, or steamed New Zealand mussels. Dinner menu choices range from charbroiled tuna or Angus tenderloin broiled to perfection to vanilla-scented salmon braised with lemon rice and herb-roasted rack of lamb. The catch of the day is served with steamed vegetables and pesto mashed potatoes and drizzled with pink grapefruit vinaigrette. Lunch is à la carte; the fixed-priced dinner menu includes an appetizer, entrée, and dessert. ⊠*Old Bayshore/Arawak Beach Complex, Bay St., Bridgetown, St. Michael* ☎*246/826–5222* ⌂*Reservations essential* ▭*AE, D, DC, MC, V* ⊘*No lunch Sat.–Sun; no dinner Mon.*

SOUTHERN BARBADOS

Restaurant locations in southern Barbados are plotted on the Southern Barbados and St. Lawrence Gap maps.

ASIAN

$$$–$$$$ ✕**Zen at The Crane.** Thai and Japanese specialties reign supreme in a magnificent setting overlooking Crane Beach. The centerpiece of the sophisticated, Asian-inspired decor is a 12-person sushi bar, where chefs prepare exotic fare before your eyes. Try sizzling lobster kabayaki served in a cast-iron grill pan, teriyaki beef or chicken, tempura prawns, stir-fried meats and vegetables in oyster sauce, or a deluxe bento box. An extensive menu of Thai appetizers, soups, noodles, fried rice, and chef's specials and main courses from the wok are noted as being spicy, spicier, and spiciest. Choose to dine in the tatami room for a traditional Japanese dining experience. ⊠*The Crane, Crane Bay, St. Philip* ☎246/423–6220 ⚄*Reservations essential* ⊟*AE, MC, V* ⊘*Closed Tues.*

CARIBBEAN

$$$$ ✕**Aqua.** Sophisticates and trendsetters come to this chic spot for lunch with a view or an exotic cocktail before dining by candlelight on modern Caribbean fare—or what Chef Michael Hinds, formerly executive sous chef at Sandy Lane Hotel, calls "Bajan Fusion" cuisine. That translates as combining premier food and cosmopolitan flavors with local traditions. For example, lunch may include fish-and-chips with seaweed salad, stir-fried beef and tiger prawns with Oriental noodles, linguini with forest mushrooms and bush basil, or West Indian chicken curry with lemongrass sauce. Or choose a not-so-simple sandwich: tomato and garlic foccacia with provolone cheese, roast chicken, grilled pepper wrap, and tomato relish; or parma ham and mozzarella panini with pesto and arugula salad. At dinner, try grilled kingfish with "soused" breadfruit and local beans, five-spice braised short ribs of beef with whipped market vegetables, or crusted red snapper with eggplant caponata and basil-puréed potatoes. Prefer something light to match the cool blue decor and cooling ocean breeze? Aqua offers an extensive sushi menu as an option at both lunch and dinner. In any case, save room for dessert. The rum and pineapple tarte tatin with Madras curry ice cream or the spiced banana spring rolls with fried coconut ice cream and brandy caramel coulis just might entice you. ⊠*Main Rd., Hastings, Christ Church* ☎246/420–2995 ⚄*Reservations essential* ⊟*AE, MC, V* ⊘*No lunch Sat.*

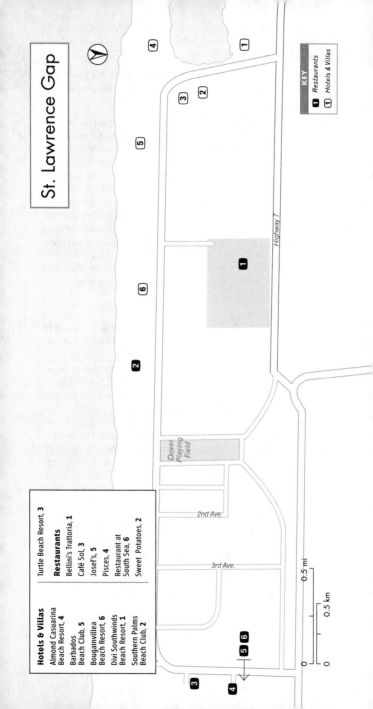

St. Lawrence Gap

Hotels & Villas

Almond Casuarina
Beach Resort, **4**

Barbados
Beach Club, **5**

Bougainvillea
Beach Resort, **6**

Divi Southwinds
Beach Resort, **1**

Southern Palms
Beach Club, **2**

Turtle Beach Resort, **3**

Restaurants

Bellini's Trattoria, **1**

Café Sol, **3**

Josef's, **5**

Pisces, **4**

Restaurant at
South Sea, **6**

Sweet Potatoes, **2**

Dover Playing Field

2nd Ave.

3rd Ave.

Highway 7

0   0.5 km

0   0.5 mi

KEY

🔲 *Restaurants*

🔲 *Hotels & Villas*

$$$ ✕**David's Place.** Come here for sophisticated Bajan cuisine in a prime waterfront location on St. Lawrence Bay. Waves gently lap against the pilings of the open-air deck—a rhythmic accompaniment to the soft classical background music. Owner David Trotman personally keeps an eye on every detail. For starters, the pumpkin soup is divine, and the spicy fish cakes are classic. Specialties such as grilled flying fish, pepperpot stew, and Creole shrimp all come with a selection of local vegetables and a choice of rice and peas, macaroni pie, or cou-cou—and delicious homemade cheddar-cheese bread. The menu always includes two or three vegetarian dishes, as well, such as lemon-tossed linguini or vegetable crepes with a tomato-cream sauce. Dessert might be bread pudding, carrot cake with rum sauce, or coconut cream pie. Complement your meal with a glass of wine from the extensive list. ⊠*St. Lawrence Main Rd., Worthing, Christ Church* ☎*246/435–9755* ⌖*Reservations essential* ▭*AE, MC, V* ⊘*Closed Mon. No lunch.*

$$–$$$ ✕**Brown Sugar.** Set back from the road in an old traditional
★ home, the lattice-trimmed dining patios here are filled with ferns, flowers, and water features. Brown Sugar is a popular lunch spot for local businesspeople, who come for the nearly 30 delicious local and Creole dishes spread out at the all-you-can-eat, four-course Bajan buffet. Here's your chance to try local specialties such as flying fish, cou-cou, buljol, souse, fish cakes, and pepperpot. In the evening, the à la carte menu has dishes such as fried flying-fish, coconut shrimp, and plantain-crusted mahimahi; curried lamb, filet mignon, and broiled pepper chicken; and seafood or pesto pasta. Bring the kids—there's a special children's menu with fried chicken, fried flying-fish fingers, and pasta dishes. Save room for the warm *paw paw* (papaya) pie or Bajan rum pudding with rum sauce. ⊠*Bay St., Aquatic Gap, St. Michael* ☎*246/426–7684* ⌖*Reservations essential* ▭*AE, MC, V* ⊘*No lunch Sat.*

$$–$$$ ✕**Sweet Potatoes.** "Good Old Bajan Cooking" is the slogan at this popular restaurant in the Gap, and that's what you can expect. Of course, you'll want to start everything off with a chilled rum punch. Then whet your appetite with some favorite local appetizers such as buljol (marinated codfish seasoned with herbs and onions), sweet plantains stuffed with minced beef, pumpkin and spinach fritters, or deep-fried fish cakes. A selection of Bajan appetizers will make a good, filling lunch, as well. The dinner menu highlights flying fish stuffed with local vegetables, grilled

chicken breast in a Malibu rum sauce, catch of the day bathed in a Creole sauce, and jerk pork. Rum cake, flambéed banana, and bread pudding with rum sauce are traditional desserts. ⊠*St. Lawrence Gap, Dover, Christ Church* ☎*246/420–7668* ⌂*Reservations essential*ß ⊟*AE, DC, MC, V.*

CONTINENTAL

★ **Fodor's**Choice ✕**Restaurant at South Seas.** In this stylish water-
$$$$ front establishment celebrated as one of the best restaurants on Barbados—certainly on the south coast—Chef Barry Taylor creates a tempting menu of dishes. Raised in both Barbados and Rio and educated in the United States, Taylor cooks with an international flair. Appetizers might include rosemary-scented roasted elk or snow crab and yellowfin tuna cakes. Main courses range from USDA prime beef tenderloin or Peking duckling cooked two ways to Arborio-crusted Vietnamese shrimp or panfried New Bedford scallops. The dining veranda overlooks a quiet cove on one side and beautiful landscaped gardens on the other. The restaurant has one of the most extensive wine, brandy, and vintage rum collections on the island. There's even a cigar menu featuring a dozen Cubans, plus selections from Barbados, Honduras, and the Dominican Republic. Dining here is a very special experience. ⊠*St. Lawrence Gap, Dover, Christ Church* ☎*246/420–7423* ⌂*Reservations essential* ⊟*AE, MC, V* ⊘*No lunch; closed Sun.*

ECLECTIC

$$$–$$$$ ✕**Café Luna.** The sweeping view of pretty Enterprise Beach from Café Luna, the alfresco dining deck on top of the Mediterranean-style Little Arches Hotel, is spectacular at lunchtime and magical in the moonlight. At lunch, sip on crisp white wine or a fruity cocktail while you await your freshly made salad, pasta, or sandwich. At dinner, owner and executive chef Mark de Gruchy prepares contemporary favorites from around the world, including fresh Scottish salmon grilled to perfection, oven-roasted New Zealand rack of lamb, fettuccine with fresh seafood, and local chicken breast with mango chutney. ⊠*Little Arches Hotel, Enterprise Beach, Christ Church* ☎*246/428–6172* ⌂*Reservations essential* ⊟*MC, V.*

$$$–$$$$ ✕**Champers.** In 2006 owner Chiryl Newman relocated
★ her popular restaurant and watering hole to elegant new digs—an old Bajan home renovated into a snazzy seaside restaurant—on a quiet lane just off the main South Coast

Road in Rockley. Luncheon guests—about 75% local businesspeople—enjoy repasts such as char-grilled beef salad, Champers fish pie, grilled barracuda, or chicken and mushroom fettuccine in a creamy chardonnay sauce. Dinner guests swoon over dishes such as the roasted rack of lamb with spring vegetables and mint-infused jus, the sautéed sea scallops with stir-fried vegetables and noodles with red Thai curry sauce, and the Parmesan-crusted barracuda with whole-grain mustard sauce. But this isn't nouvelle cuisine. The portions are hearty and the food is well seasoned with Caribbean flavors, "just the way the locals like it," says Newman. The cliff-top setting overlooking Accra Beach offers diners a panoramic view of the sea and a relaxing atmosphere for daytime dining. At night, particularly at the bar, there's a definite buzz in the air. Nearly all the artwork gracing the walls is by Barbadian artists and may be purchased through the on-site gallery. ⊠*Skeetes Hill, Rockley, Christ Church* ☎*246/434–3464* ⚓*Reservations essential* ⊟*AE, D, DC, MC, V* ☺*Closed Sun.*

GREEK

$$–$$$$ ✕**OPA!** If you're in the mood for an authentic souvlaki, moussaka, or gyros dinner—or simply a delicious Greek salad or personal Greek pizza—this family-run Greek restaurant, specializing in traditional dishes, is the place for you. Sitting on the dining deck overlooking the sea, you'll begin to wonder if you're staring at the Caribbean or the Aegean. Never mind—sit back, sip your ouzo, and nibble on a plate of *dolmades avgolemono* (stuffed grape leaves), spanakopita (spinach and feta cheese wrapped in buttery phyllo), or fried calamari (tender rounds of squid). ⊠*Shak Shak Complex, Main Rd., Hastings, Christ Church* ☎*246/435–1234* ⚓*Reservations essential* ⊟*AE, D, MC, V* ☺*No lunch Sat.–Sun.*

ITALIAN

$$–$$$ ✕**Bellini's Trattoria.** Classic northern Italian cuisine is the specialty at Bellini's, on the main floor of the Little Bay Hotel. The atmosphere here is smart-casual—and is as appropriate for a family meal as for a romantic dinner for two. Toast the evening with a Bellini cocktail (ice-cold sparkling wine with a splash of fruit nectar) and start your meal with bruschetta, an individual gourmet pizza, or perhaps a homemade pasta dish with fresh herbs and a rich sauce. If you're not already stuffed, move on to the signature garlic shrimp entrée or the popular chicken parmigiana—then top it all off with excellent tiramisu. We recommend making your reservations

early; request a table on the Mediterranean-style veranda to enjoy one of the most appealing dining settings on the south coast. ⊠ *Little Bay Hotel, St. Lawrence Gap, Dover, Christ Church* ☎ *246/435–7246* ⚖ *Reservations essential* ⊟ *AE, MC, V* ⊘ *No lunch.*

MEXICAN

$$-$$$ ✕ **Café Sol.** Enjoy Tex-Mex nachos, tacos, burritos, and tostadas in this Mexican bar and grill in the heart of busy St. Lawrence Gap. Or choose a burger, honey-barbecue chicken, or flame-grilled steak from the Gringo menu. Add helpings of Spanish rice and beans, a Corona, and plenty of jalapeño peppers, guacamole, and salsa to give everything a Mexican feel. Some people come just for the margaritas— 15 fruity varieties rimmed with Bajan sugar instead of salt. Café Sol has two happy hours every night. ⊠ *St. Lawrence Gap, Christ Church* ☎ *246/426–7655* ⊟ *AE, MC, V* ⊘ *No lunch Mon.*

SEAFOOD

$$$-$$$$ ✕ **Josef's Restaurant.** The signature restaurant of Austrian restaurateur Josef Schwaiger, in a cliff-side Bajan dwelling surrounded by gardens, is one of the most upscale seaside dining spots on the south coast. Josef's cuisine fuses Asian culinary techniques and Caribbean flavors. Fruits of the sea—seared yellowfin tuna with mango-cilantro sauce or catch of the day with tomato fondue and creamed potatoes, for instance—are prominent, and the wine list is extensive. Try shredded duck with herbed hoisin pancakes as an innovative starter, or let the free-range chicken teriyaki with stir-fry noodles tingle your taste buds. Pasta dishes assuage the vegetarian palate. ⊠ *Waverly House, St. Lawrence Gap, Dover, Christ Church* ☎ *246/435–8245* ⚖ *Reservations essential* ⊟ *AE, MC, V* ⊘ *No lunch.*

$$$-$$$$ ✕ **Pisces.** For seafood lovers, this is nirvana. Prepared here ★ in every way—from charbroiled to gently sautéed—seafood specialties may include conch strips in tempura, rich fish chowder, panfried fillets of flying fish with a toasted almond crust and a light mango-citrus sauce, and seared prawns in a fragrant curry sauce. Landlubbers in your party can select from a few chicken, beef, and pasta dishes on the menu. Whatever you choose, the herbs that flavor it and the accompanying vegetables will have come from the chef's own garden. Save room for the bread pudding, yogurt-lime cheesecake, or homemade rum-raisin ice cream. Twinkling white lights reflect on the water as you dine. ⊠ *St. Law-*

rence Gap, Dover, Christ Church ☎*246/435–6564* ⚓*Reservations essential* ═*AE, MC, V* ◎*No lunch.*

$$$ ╳**L'Azure at The Crane.** Perched on an oceanfront cliff, L'Azure is an informal luncheon spot by day that turns elegant after dark. Enjoy seafood chowder—prepared with lobster, shrimp, dorado, local vegetables, and a dash of sherry—or a light salad or sandwich while absorbing the breathtaking view. At dinner, candlelight and soft guitar music enhance a fabulous Caribbean lobster seasoned with herbs, lime juice, and garlic butter and served in its shell; if you're not in the mood for seafood, try the perfectly grilled filet mignon. Sunday is really special, with a Gospel Brunch at 10 AM and a Bajan Buffet at 12:30 PM. ⊠*The Crane, Crane Bay, St. Philip* ☎*246/423–6220* ⚓*Reservations essential* ═*AE, MC, V.*

EAST COAST

Restaurant locations on the east coast are plotted on the Central Barbados map.

CARIBBEAN

$$–$$$ ╳**Atlantis Hotel Restaurant.** People have been stopping by for lunch with a view here since 1945, when Mrs. Enid Maxwell bought this property, a quaint, 19th-century seaside hotel. New owners have kept up Mrs. Maxwell's tradition—all Bajan cuisine that complements the natural environment. Each Wednesday and Sunday the enormous buffet includes pumpkin fritters, rice and peas, breadfruit casserole, steamed fish creole, oven-barbecued chicken, pepperpot, macaroni pie, ratatouille, and more. Homemade coconut pie tops the dessert list. The Atlantis is a lunch stop for organized day tours, so it sometimes gets crowded. ⊠*Atlantis Hotel, Tent Bay, Bathsheba, St. Joseph* ☎*246/433–9445* ═*AE, MC, V.*

$$–$$$ ╳**Cliffside Restaurant.** The outdoor deck of this restaurant in the New Edgewater Hotel provides one of the prettiest, breeziest ocean views in all of Barbados and, therefore, is a good stop for lunch when touring the East Coast. From noon to 3, choose the Bajan buffet or select from the menu. Either way, you might enjoy fried flying fish, roast or stewed chicken, local lamb chops, rice and peas, steamed root vegetables, sautéed plantains, and salad. Afternoon tea with scones, pastries, and sandwiches is served from 3:30 to 6. Dinner is also served, but mostly to hotel guests and local

residents, who are better able to find their way home in the dark on the neighborhood's winding, often unmarked roads. ⊠ *Bathsheba Beach, Bathsheba, St. Joseph* ☎ *246/433–9900* ⚱ *Reservations essential* ⊟ *AE, MC, V.*

\$\$–\$\$\$ ✕ **Naniki Restaurant.** Rich wooden beams and stone tiles, clay
★ pottery, straw mats, colorful dinnerware, and fresh flowers from the adjacent anthurium farm set the style here. Huge picture windows and outdoor porch seating allow you to enjoy the exhilarating panoramic view of surrounding hills and—when making the alfresco choice—a refreshing breeze along with your lunch of exquisitely prepared Caribbean standards. Seared flying fish, grilled dorado, stewed *lambi* (conch), curried chicken, and jerk chicken or pork are accompanied by cou-cou, peas and rice, or salad. On Sunday, lunch is a Caribbean buffet. Vegetarian dishes are always available. ⊠ *Suriname, St. Joseph* ☎ *246/433–1300* ⊟ *AE, DC, MC, V* ⊗ *Closed Mon. No dinner.*

\$ ✕ **Bonito Beach Bar & Restaurant.** The Bonito's wholesome
☾ West Indian home cooking has soothed the hunger pangs of many folks who find themselves on the east coast at lunchtime. The view of the Atlantic from the second-floor dining room is striking, and the Bajan buffet lunch includes fried fish and baked chicken accompanied by salads and vegetables fresh from the garden. Beer, rum punch, fresh fruit punch, and lime squash are refreshing choices to accompany your meal. ⊠ *Coast Rd., Bathsheba, St. Joseph* ☎ *246/433–9034* ⊟ *AE, D, DC, MC, V* ⊗ *Closed Sun.*

SEAFOOD

\$\$–\$\$\$ ✕ **Round House.** Owners Robert and Gail Manley oversee an extensive menu for guests staying in their inn, tourists enjoying the east coast, and Bajans dining out. The lunch menu includes homemade soups and quiches, sandwiches, salads, and pasta. Dinner choices—served in the moonlight—extend from shrimp scampi, oven-baked dolphin steak, or grilled flying-fish fillet to baked ham, sirloin steak, or homemade pasta specials. Some people come just for the flying-fish paté. Rolls and breads (whether for sandwiches or dessert), along with apple and coconut pies, are personally made by the owners. The Round House is an ocean-facing manse-turned-inn built in 1832. The view of the rugged coastline from the outside dining deck is mesmerizing. ⊠ *Bathsheba Beach, Bathsheba, St. Joseph* ☎ *246/433–9678* ⚱ *Reservations essential* ⊟ *AE, D, MC, V* ⊗ *No dinner Sunday, except for inn guests.*

WEST COAST

If you are looking for a quick bite, Chefette is the island's homegrown fast-food restaurant chain. You can get bagels for breakfast and chicken, burgers, pizza, rotis, ice cream, and more all throughout the afternoon and evening. Chefette has more than a dozen outlets strategically located throughout Barbados, including one at the airport. One of the nicest is in Holetown, where you can eat your take-out meal at a picnic table on a seaside boardwalk.

Restaurant locations on the west coast are plotted on the Central Barbados and Northern Barbados maps as well as on the Holetown & Vicinity map.

CARIBBEAN

$$–$$$ ✕**Angry Annie's.** You can't miss this place. Outside and inside, everything's painted in cheerful Caribbean pinks, blues, greens, and yellows—and it's just steps from the main road. The food is just as lively: great barbecued "jump-up" ribs and chicken, grilled fresh fish or juicy steaks, "Rasta pasta" for vegetarians, and several spicy curries. Eat inside on gaily colored furniture, outside under the stars, or take it away with you. Fun for people of all ages, Angry Annie's has a vibrant atmosphere and serves satisfying meals. ⊠*1st St., Holetown, St. James* ☎*246/432–2119* ▭*AE, DC, MC, V* ⊘*No lunch.*

$$–$$$ ✕**Mannie's Suga Suga.** The beach crowd comes for all-day dining—breakfast, lunch, and beach-served snacks and drinks—at Barbados's trendiest beach bar on one of the island's finest strips of sand. Owner/manager Mannie Ward oversees a varied menu of international and Bajan favorites that includes soups, salads, cutters (sandwiches), hot dogs and hamburgers, and barbecued pork, beef, chicken, or fish—and a long list of sides such as fish cakes, rice and peas, fried plantains, potato or breadfruit chips, pumpkin or conch fritters, deep-fried eggplant or zucchini, and garlic bread. Some people change out of their bathing suits and return for the Japanese and Thai cuisine served at dinner, especially on Monday nights when there's a cabaret show. ⊠*Mullins Beach, Speightstown, St. Peter* ☎*246/419–4511* ▭*MC, V* ⊘*No dinner Thurs. and Sun.*

$$–$$$ ✕**Ragamuffins.** The only restaurant on Barbados in an authentic chattel house, Ragamuffins is tiny, funky, lively, and informal. The menu offers seafood, perfectly broiled T-bone steaks, West Indian curries, and vegetarian dishes

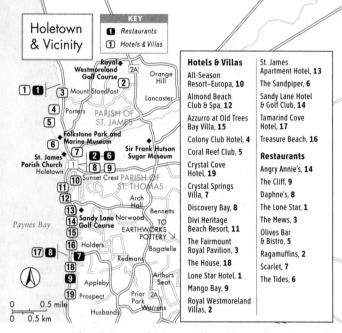

Holetown & Vicinity

KEY
1 Restaurants
1 Hotels & Villas

Hotels & Villas

All-Season Resort-Europa, **10**

Almond Beach Club & Spa, **12**

Azzurro at Old Trees Bay Villa, **15**

Colony Club Hotel, **4**

Coral Reef Club, **5**

Crystal Cove Hotel, **19**

Crystal Springs Villa, **7**

Discovery Bay, **8**

Divi Heritage Beach Resort, **11**

The Fairmount Royal Pavilion, **3**

The House, **18**

Lone Star Hotel, **1**

Mango Bay, **9**

Royal Westmoreland Villas, **2**

St. James Apartment Hotel, **13**

The Sandpiper, **6**

Sandy Lane Hotel & Golf Club, **14**

Tamarind Cove Hotel, **17**

Treasure Beach, **16**

Restaurants

Angry Annie's, **14**

The Cliff, **9**

Daphne's, **8**

The Lone Star, **1**

The Mews, **3**

Olives Bar & Bistro, **5**

Ragamuffins, **2**

Scarlet, **7**

The Tides, **6**

such as Bajan stir-fried vegetables with noodles. Dine inside or out. The kitchen is within sight of the bar—which is a popular meeting spot most evenings for vacationers and locals alike. ⊠*1st St., Holetown, St. James* ☎*246/432–1295* ⌂*Reservations essential* ▭*AE, D, MC, V* ⊙*No lunch.*

$$–$$$ ✕**Scarlet.** When you see a bright red building on the side of the road, you'll know you've found Scarlet. Movers and groovers come here in the evening to chill over a martini and share nibbles, such as a plate of flying-fish lollipops; or settle in after cocktails for a burger with sophisticated toppings, Bajan ham with corn pancakes, or perhaps Baxter's Road chicken. Enjoy your meal sitting at the large bar—the centerpiece of this casual but stylish watering hole—or at a nearby table. Specialty of the house: Scarlet Rocks (vodka, raspberry schnapps, strawberries, cranberry juice, basil, and black pepper!). ⊠*Hwy. 1, Paynes Bay, St. James* ☎*246/432–3663* ⌂*Reservations essential* ▭*AE, MC, V* ⊙*No lunch; closed Mon.*

¢–$ ✕**Fisherman's Pub.** This is as local as local gets! For years, fishermen and other locals have come here daily for the inexpensive, authentic Creole buffet served at lunchtime. For $10 or less, you can soak up the atmosphere and fill your plate with fried flying fish, stewed chicken or pork, curried goat or lamb, macaroni pie, fried plantain, cou-cou, and crisp green salad. In the evening, choose from the bar menu and dance (or simply listen) to catchy calypso music. Fisherman's Pub is an open-air, waterfront restaurant built on stilts just a stone's throw from the Speight-stown fish market. ⊠*Queen's St., Speightstown, St. Peter* ☎*246/422–2703* ⌚*No reservations accepted* ▭*MC, V.*

CONTINENTAL

$$$$ ✕**The Tides.** Enter into a pretty courtyard, and have a
★ cocktail at the cozy bar or the coral stone lounge before proceeding to your seaside table in this former private mansion. Perhaps the most intriguing feature of this stunning setting—besides the sound of waves crashing onto the shore just feet away—are the row of huge tree trunks growing right through the dining room. The food is equally dramatic. Chef Guy Beasley and his team give a contemporary twist to fresh seafood, filet of beef, rack of lamb, and other top-of-the-line main courses by adding inspired sauces and delicate vegetables and garnishes. Local residents and repeat visitors agree that The Tides is one of the island's best restaurants. ⊠*Hwy. 1, Holetown, St. James* ☎*246/432–8356* ⌚*Reservations essential* ▭*MC, V* ⊘*No lunch Sat.–Sun.*

$$$–$$$$ ✕**The Mews.** Dining at The Mews is like being invited to
★ a very chic friend's home for dinner. This once was, in fact, a private home. The front room is now an inviting bar, and the interior courtyard is an intimate, open-air dining area. The second floor is a maze of small dining rooms and dining balconies, but you've come for the food, after all. International cuisine is presented with contemporary flair. A plump chicken breast, for example, will be stuffed with cream cheese, smoked salmon, and herb pâté and served on a garlic and chive sauce. A braised lamb shank is presented on a bed of cabbage with a port-thyme jus and creamed potatoes. And fillet of mahimahi is poached in a lemongrass, ginger, and cilantro broth. The warm molten chocolate cake is a must for dessert. Some call the atmosphere avant-garde; others call it quaint. Everyone calls the food delicious. But don't stop at dinner—at about 10 PM the bar begins to bustle. And on weekends, the fun spills out into the street. ⊠*2nd St., Holetown, St. James* ☎*246/432–1122* ⌚*Reservations essential* ▭*AE, MC, V* ⊘*No lunch; closed Sun.*

ECLECTIC

★ **Fodor's**Choice ✕**The Cliff.** Chef Paul Owens' mastery is the
$$$$ foundation of one of the finest dining experiences in the
Caribbean, with prices to match. Steep steps hug the cliff
on which the restaurant sits to accommodate those arriving by yacht, and every candlelit table has a sea view.
Starters include smoked salmon ravioli with garlic sauce
and grilled portobello mushroom on greens with truffle
vinaigrette; for the main course, try Caribbean shrimp
with a Thai green-curry coconut sauce, veal chop with
a mustard and tarragon sauce, or red-snapper fillet on a
baked potato cake. Dessert falls into the sinful category,
and service is impeccable. The prix-fixe menu will set you
back $93 per person for a two-course meal (starter–main
course or main course–dessert) or $110 per person for a
three-course meal. Reserve days or even weeks in advance
to snag a table at the front of the terrace for the best view.
⊠*Hwy. 1, Derricks, St. James* ☎*246/432–1922* ⚓*Reservations essential* ⊟*AE, DC, MC, V* ⊗*Closed Sun. Apr.
15–Dec. 15. No lunch.*

$$$$ ✕**The Lone Star.** In the 1940s this was the only commercial
garage on the west coast; today it's the snazzy restaurant in
the tiny but chic Lone Star Hotel, where top chefs in the open-
plan kitchen turn the finest local ingredients into gastronomic
delights. The menu is extensive but pricey, even for lunch.
All day, such tasty dishes as fish soup with rouille, Caesar
or Thai chicken salad, tuna tartare, rotisserie chicken, and
linguine with tomato-basil sauce and feta cheese are served
in the oceanfront beach bar. At sunset, the casual daytime
atmosphere turns trendy. You might start with an Oriental
tasting plate or a half-dozen oysters, followed by crispy roast
duckling, grilled fish of the day, or lamb cutlets—or choose
from one of dozens of other tasty land, sea, and vegetarian
dishes. ⊠*Lone Star Hotel, Hwy. 1, Mount Standfast, St.
James* ☎*246/419–0599* ⊟*AE, MC, V.*

$$$ ✕**La Mer.** Enjoy dinner with a view overlooking the pretty,
man-made lagoon at Port St. Charles, a tony villa com-
munity that particularly appeals to boating enthusiasts.
Fresh fish from Six Men's Bay, just up the road, and ten-
der cuts of meat are seared on either of two grills—wood
or lava-rock—while vegetarian dishes are stirred up at the
wok station. This is a perfect place for a light meal, Sunday
brunch, or—with the moonlight reflecting on the lagoon—
a romantic dinner. ⊠*Port St. Charles, Speightstown, St.*

Peter ☎246/419–2000 ⚒Reservations essential ☰AE, MC, V ☉Closed Mon.; no dinner Sun.

ITALIAN

\$\$\$\$ ✕**Daphne's.** Wedged between the Tamarind Cove Hotel
★ and its sister hotel, The House, Daphne's is the chic and glamorous Caribbean outpost of the famed London eatery. The chef whips up contemporary versions of classic Italian dishes. Grilled mahimahi, for example, becomes "modern Italian" when combined with Marsala wine, peperonata, and zucchini. Perfectly prepared pappardelle with braised duck, red wine, and oregano is a sublime pasta choice. Light meals, salads, and half-portions of pasta are available at lunch. The extensive wine list features both regional Italian and fine French selections. ⊠Paynes Bay, St. James ☎234/432–2731 ⚒Reservations essential ☰AE, D, MC, V.

MEDITERRANEAN

\$\$\$–\$\$\$\$ ✕**The Fish Pot.** Just north of the little fishing village of Six
★ Men's Bay, toward the far northern west coast of Barbados, this attractive seaside restaurant serves excellent Mediterranean cuisine and the freshest fish. Gaze seaward through windows framed with pale green louvered shutters while lunching on a seafood crepe or pasta with seafood or puttanesca sauce. In the evening, the menu may include panfried red snapper with caper-and-thyme mashed potatoes, seared herb-crusted tuna on garlic and spinach polenta, sun-dried tomato risotto tossed with vegetables, and lamb shank braised in red wine. Bright and cheery by day and relaxed and cozy by night, the Fish Pot offers a tasty dining experience in a setting that's more classy than its name might suggest. ⊠Little Good Harbour, Shermans, St. Peter ☎246/439–3000 ⚒Reservations essential ☰MC, V.

\$\$\$ ✕**Olives Bar & Bistro.** This intimate restaurant, a quaint
★ Bajan residence in the center of Holetown, is a favorite west-coast dining spot of local professionals and visitors alike. Mediterranean and Caribbean flavors enliven inventive thin-crust pizzas and tasty salads at lunch; the dinner menu often includes fresh seafood, such as seared yellowfin tuna with ratatouille or pan-seared sea scallops with basmati rice and steamed greens. Vegetarian selections are always available. Dine inside, accompanied by the hint of soothing light jazz music, or in the courtyard; the upstairs bar is a popular spot to mingle over coffee, refreshing drinks, or snacks (pizza, pastas, and salads). ⊠2nd St., Holetown, St. James ☎246/432–2112 ☰AE, MC, V.

WHERE TO STAY

Most visitors stay on either the fashionable west coast, north of Bridgetown, or on the action-packed south coast. On the west coast, the beachfront resorts in St. Peter and St. James parishes are mostly luxurious, self-contained enclaves. Highway 1, a two-lane road with considerable traffic, runs past these resorts, which can make casual strolling to a nearby bar or restaurant difficult. Along the south coast, in Christ Church Parish, many hotels are clustered near the busy strip known as St. Lawrence Gap, convenient to dozens of small restaurants, bars, and night-clubs. On the much more remote east coast, a few small inns offer oceanfront views, cool breezes, and get-away-from-it-all tranquillity.

The lodgings listed below all have air-conditioning, telephones, and TVs in guest rooms unless otherwise noted.

VILLA & CONDO COMPLEXES

Villa communities and condominium complexes, which are continually cropping up along the south and west coasts of Barbados, can be an economical option for families, groups, or couples vacationing together. Vacationers can rent individual units directly from property managers, the same as reserving hotel accommodations. Units with fully equipped kitchens, two to six bedrooms, and as many baths run $200 to $2,500 per night in the off-season—double that in winter.

PRIVATE VILLAS & CONDOS

Local real-estate agencies will arrange holiday rentals of privately owned villas and condos along the west coast in St. James and St. Peter. All villas and condos are fully furnished and equipped, including appropriate staff depending on the size of the villa or unit—which can range from one to eight bedrooms. The staff usually works six days a week. Most villas have TVs, DVDs and/or VCRs and CD players; all properties have telephones, and some have Internet access and/or fax machines. Telephones are usually barred from making overseas calls; plan to use a phone card or calling card. Vehicles are generally not included in the rates, but rental cars can be arranged and delivered to the villa upon request. Linens and basic supplies (e.g., bath soap, toilet tissue, dishwashing detergent) are included.

Units with one to six bedrooms and as many baths run $200 to $2,500 per night in summer, and double that in winter. Rates include utilities and government taxes. The only additional cost is for groceries and staff gratuities. A security deposit is required upon booking and refunded seven days after departure less any damages or unpaid miscellaneous charges.

VILLA RENTAL AGENCIES

Altman Real Estate (⊠ *Hwy. 1, Derricks, St. James* ☎ *246/432–0840 or 866/360–5292* ⊕ *www.aaaltman.com*)

Bajan Services (⊠ *Newton House, Battaleys, St. Peter* ☎ *246/422–2618 or 866/978–5239* ⊕ *www.bajanservices.com*)

Island Villas (⊠ *Trents Bldg., Holetown, St. James* ☎ *246/432–4627* ⊕ *www.island-villas.com*)

PRIVATE APARTMENT RENTAL SOURCES

Apartments are available for holiday rentals in buildings or complexes that can have as few as three or four units or as many as 30 to 40 units—or even more. Prices range from $30 to $300 per night. The **Barbados Tourism Authority** (☎ *246/427–2623* ⊕ *www.barbados.org*) on Harbour Road in Bridgetown has a listing of apartments in prime resort areas on both the south and west coasts, complete with facilities offered and rates.

SOUTH COAST

Hotel locations in southern Barbados are plotted on the Southern Barbados map as well as The St. Lawrence Gap map.

HOTELS

$$$$ ⊞ **Almond Casuarina Beach Resort.** Frequent visitors to the ♺ south coast of Barbados have fond memories of the Casuarina Beach Club, famous for being the first hotel on the island to win a "Green Globe" award by the Green Hotels Association. Completely renovated, refurbished, and expanded by new owner Almond Resorts, which operates two other resorts in Barbados and two in St. Lucia, this south coast landmark reopened as Almond Casuarina Beach Resort in early 2008. In almost every way, it is still as "green" as ever. Operations will continue to be environmentally sound, and the lush 8-acre garden of mature bamboo, palm, and fruit trees (and a few resident green monkeys) that takes up the entire central courtyard remains beautifully intact. The main difference is that this

is no longer a self-catering establishment but, instead, an elegant all-inclusive resort. Accommodations are in blocks that surround the garden. Rooms in a newly constructed building on the beachfront offer mesmerizing views of the sea all day long. Almond Casuarina offers enough opportunities for dining, socializing, relaxing, water sports, and land sports to keep you occupied as much or as little as you wish. And everything is included in the room rate—even windsurfing or sailing lessons and an all day, every day, Kids' Club that organizes age-appropriate entertainment and educational activities for children of all ages. Guests of Almond Casuarina also have full access to all the dining, recreational, and entertainment facilities at the partner hotels on the west coast—Almond Beach Village in Speightstown and Almond Beach Club in St. James—including shuttle transportation. **Pros:** Great beach and beautiful garden, every amenity you could imagine, wonderful for kids. **Cons:** Lots of good restaurants to try in nearby St. Lawrence Gap, but you've paid for an all-inclusive resort. ⊠*St. Lawrence Gap, Dover, Christ Church* ☎*246/428–3600* ⊕*almondresorts.com* ⌑*260 rooms, 7 suites* ⌂*In-room: safe, refrigerator. In hotel: 3 restaurants, room service, bars, pools, gym, spa, beachfront, water sports, no elevator, children's programs (ages infant–17), concierge, laundry facilities, public Internet:* ⊟*AE, D, MC, V* ⊺◖*AI.*

$$$$ ▥**The Crane.** Originally built in 1887 on a seaside bluff on
★ the southeastern coast in order to catch the cooling Atlantic breezes, the Crane is the island's oldest hotel in continuing operation. Today, that original coral-stone building is the centerpiece of a luxurious, 40-acre villa complex that combines the character and ambience of the 19th century with the comforts and amenities expected today. Step back in time and stay in a Historic Hotel Apartment decorated with original antiques; corner suites have walls of windows and wraparound patios or balconies with panoramic ocean views. Alternatively, the upscale Private Residences—in five modern but architecturally compatible high-rise buildings—are spacious, individually owned condo-style villas with hardwood floors, hand-carved four-poster beds, multiple bathrooms with spa showers, fully equipped kitchens, entertainment centers, objets d'art, and private plunge pools. Expansion plans in coming years will add another high-rise building, low-rise townhouses, a spa, gym, and town square with shops, a deli, a jazz bar, an Italian restaurant (in addition to Zen, L'Azure, and a poolside café), and

1

a conference facility. The Crane's original pool is a frequent backdrop for photo shoots, while a huge pool complex nearer the villas includes a spa pool, built in a clifftop ruin with a 360-degree view, and a half-dozen connecting pools and other water features. The adjacent old stable serves as a pool bar. Reef-protected, pink-sand Crane Beach is 98 steps (or an elevator ride) down the cliff. The Crane is a perfect choice for anyone seeking tranquillity, elegance without ostentation, gracious informality, and every modern convenience. Plan to rent a car, though, if you expect to spend much time away from the resort grounds. The minimum stay is seven nights in high season; three nights during the rest of the year. **Pros:** Enchanting view, lovely beach, fabulous suites, great restaurants. **Cons:** Remote location, rental car recommended, service tends to be aloof. ⊠*Crane Bay, St. Philip* ☎*246/423–6220* 🖷*246/423–5343* ⊕*www.thecrane.com* 🖘*4 rooms, 14 suites, 184 villas* ♿*In-room: no a/c (some), safe, kitchen (some), refrigerator, DVD (some), VCR (some), ethernet, Wi-Fi (some). In-hotel: 3 restaurants, room service, 2 bars, tennis courts, pools, gym, spa, beachfront, laundry facilities (some), laundry service, concierge, public Internet, public Wi-Fi* ⊟*AE, MC, V* ⦿*EP.*

DID YOU KNOW? Portuguese explorer Pedro a Campos is credited with naming Barbados. In 1536, when he stopped by the island en route to Brazil, he and his crew were intrigued by the bearded appearance of the indigenous fig trees. "Os Barbados," or "the bearded ones," he proclaimed—and the name stuck.

$$$$ ▣**Divi Southwinds Beach Resort.** The all-suites Divi Southwinds is uniquely situated on 20 acres of lawn and gardens that are bisected by the action-packed St. Lawrence Gap. The bulk of the suites are north of the Gap in a large, unspectacular three-story building offering garden and pool views. The property south of the Gap wraps around a stunning half-mile of Dover Beach, where 16 beach villas provide an intimate setting steps from the sand. Whichever location you choose, all suites have separate bedrooms, sofa beds in the sitting room, and full kitchens. The rambling resort has many amenities and is within walking distance of lots of shops, restaurants, and nightspots, so it appeals equally to families with kids and fun-loving couples or singles. Kids under 15 stay free in their parents' suite. **Pros:** Beautiful beach—so opt for a beach villa. **Cons:** Few water sports available and none included, some rooms aching for renovations, too pricey for the value received. ⊠*St. Lawrence Main Rd., Dover, Christ Church* ☎*246/428–7181* 🖷*246/420–2673* ⊕*www.diviresorts.com* ⇩*121 1-bedroom suites, 12 2-bedroom suites* ⌂*In-room: kitchen. In-hotel: 2 restaurants, bars, tennis courts, pools, gym, beachfront, no elevator, laundry facilities, public Internet* ⊟*AE, D, DC, MC, V* ⑩⑪*EP.*

$$$$ 🖳**Hilton Barbados.** Beautifully situated on the sandy Need-
☾ ham's Point peninsula, the luxurious Hilton Barbados is
★ just minutes from Bridgetown. All 350 rooms and suites in this high-rise have private balconies overlooking either the ocean or Carlisle Bay; 77 rooms are on executive floors, with a private lounge and concierge services. Meetings are big business here, as the property has the largest hotel meeting space in Barbados. The broad white-sand beach, the sprawling bi-level pool complex, and a host of activities on land and sea make this a hit with vacationing families, as well. Children under 18 stay free in a room with adults, children ages five to 12 get a break on meals, and children under five eat for free—and parents get one complimentary night of babysitting with a three-night stay! **Pros:** Convenient location, beautiful beach, excellent accommodations, lots of services and amenities. **Cons:** Huge business meeting venue, lack of intimacy, could be anywhere. ⊠*Needham's Point, Aquatic Gap, St. Michael* ☎*246/426–0200* 🖷*246/434–5770* ⊕*www.hiltoncaribbean.com/barbados* ⇩*317 rooms, 33 suites* ⌂*In-room: safe, ethernet, dial-up. In-hotel: 3 restaurants, room service, bars, tennis courts, pools, gym, beachfront, water sports, children's programs (ages 4–12), laundry service, concierge, executive floor, public Wi-Fi, some pets allowed, no-smoking rooms* ⊟*AE, D, DC, MC, V* ⑩⑪*EP.*

$$$$ 🖳**Turtle Beach Resort.** Families flock to Turtle Beach because
☾ it offers large, bright suites and enough activities for everyone to enjoy—all the time and all included. The Tommy Turtle Kids Club keeps children busy with treasure hunts, supervised swims, games, and other activities from 9 AM to 9 PM each day. That gives parents a chance to play tennis, learn to windsurf or sail, relax at the beach, join the daily shopping excursion to Bridgetown, or enjoy a quiet dinner for two at Asagio's Restaurant. Families also have good times together—cooling off in the three pools, riding the waves on boogie boards, searching for baby turtles hatching on the beach, dining buffet style at open-to-the-view Chelonia Restaurant, or having a casual meal at the

Waterfront Grill. **Pros:** Perfect for family vacations, nice pools, roomy accommodations, lots of services and amenities. **Cons:** Beach is fairly narrow and congested compared to other south coast resorts, open vent to hallway can be noisy at night. ⊠*St. Lawrence Gap, Dover, Christ Church* ☎*246/428–7131* 🖷*246/428–6089* ⊕*www.turtle beachresortbarbados.com* ➷*161 suites* ♿*In-room: safe, refrigerator, ethernet. In-hotel: 3 restaurants, room service, bars, tennis courts, pools, gym, spa, beachfront, diving, water sports, bicycles, children's programs (ages 3–12), laundry service, concierge, public Internet* ▭*AE, D, DC, MC, V* ⊚*AI.*

$$$–$$$$ 🖾**Barbados Beach Club.** Designed with families in mind, this �8 four-story hotel (with elevators) sits on a beautiful stretch of south-coast beach—and it offers tremendous value. For the price of your room, you get everything from beach volleyball to miniature golf and nature walks. If you like real golf, special packages are offered in conjunction with the nearby Barbados Golf Club. So grab a boogie board or a kayak and hit the water or take a scuba-diving lesson in the pool. Join the aerobics class in the pool or in the gym. Or sit by one of three pools (one for kids) and socialize while working on your tan. Meals are leisurely and informal at the Poolside Restaurant. At night the Sea Rocks Restaurant specializes in Caribbean seafood with a Mediterranean influence, while Veneto's is pure Italian. Children can eat early and a staff member will watch the kids if parents want a special dinner alone at one of the restaurants. **Pros:** Great beach, good value, wonderful for kids, golf package. **Cons:** Limited access to fine-dining restaurants. ⊠*Maxwell Coast Rd., Maxwell, Christ Church* ☎*246/428–9900* ⊕*www.barbadosbeachclub.com* ➷*105 rooms, 2 penthouse suites* ♿*In-room: safe, refrigerator, Wi-Fi. In-hotel: 3 restaurants, bars, tennis court, pool, gym, beachfront, diving, water sports, laundry service, children's program (ages 4–11), concierge, public Internet, public Wi-Fi, no-smoking rooms* ⊚*AI.*

$$$–$$$$ 🖾**Little Arches Hotel.** Off the beaten track just east of the ★ picturesque fishing village of Oistins, this classy boutique hotel has a perfect vantage point overlooking the sea and is just 100 yards from pretty, palm-lined Miami Beach. The small hotel has a distinctly Mediterranean ambience; beautifully appointed rooms are decorated with Italian fabrics, local pottery, and terrazzo flooring. Bathrooms have showers only but feature locally made earthenware sinks and

fluffy robes. The pool is on the roof, alongside the open-air Café Luna restaurant. Each unit has a unique layout and is named for a different Grenadine island. The Union Island and Palm Island suites each have a kitchen and a large, oceanfront patio with a private hot tub. Guests who book a 10-day stay are entitled to a choice of a complimentary round of golf at the Barbados Golf Club, an in-room champagne breakfast and massage, or a fully catered day sail aboard the hotel's 42-foot monohull yacht, *Soul Venture*, or 44-foot catamaran, *Silver Moon*. We recommend you leave the kids home if you're staying here, as Little Arches offers pure romance. **Pros:** Stylish accommodations, great restaurant, across from fabulous Miami Beach. **Cons:** Fairly remote, rental car advised. ✉*Enterprise Beach Rd., Enterprise, Christ Church* ☎*246/420–4689* 🖷*246/418–0207* ⊕*www.littlearches.com* ⇨*8 rooms, 2 suites* ⚄*In-room: safe, kitchen (some), dial-up. In-hotel: restaurant, bar, pool, bicycles, no elevator, laundry service, public Internet* ▭*MC, V* ⍟*EP.*

$$$ 🏨 **Bougainvillea Beach Resort.** Attractive seaside villas are
☾ situated around the pool or face the beachfront like a private town-house community with separate entrances. In this time-share property operated as a hotel, the suites are huge (compared to hotel suites in this price category) and decorated in appealing Caribbean pastels. Depending on the room category, rooms either have a sitting area or a separate sitting room, with a pullout sofa—great for families with small kids. This is, in fact, a very family-oriented resort, although it is just as popular for honeymoons and weddings. All suites have balconies or terraces that overlook either the pool and gardens or the sea. St. Lawrence Gap, with all its restaurants and excitement, is a 15-minute westward stroll along the beach or a 20-minute walk along the road. The picturesque fishing village of Oistins is about the same distance in the opposite direction. A supermarket is about a mile from the resort, and there is a small grocery store very close to the property. Alternatively, guests can have groceries delivered to their room or prestocked before arrival. You can even arrange a private cook, who will prepare and serve Bajan specialties—and clean up the dishes. Children under 12 stay free when sharing a room with adults. The minimum stay in high season is seven nights. **Pros:** Big suites, good value, great for families. **Cons:** Bathrooms need updating, sea can be rough for swimming. ✉*Maxwell Coast Rd., Maxwell, Christ Church*

☎246/418–0990 ⊕*www.bougainvillearesort.com* ⤳*138*
suites ♿*In-room: dial-up. In-hotel: 2 restaurants, room ser-*
vice, bars, tennis court, pools, gym, spa, beachfront, water
sports, no elevator, children's program (ages 3–12), laundry
service, public Internet, public Wi-Fi ▤*MC, V* ♡*EP.*

$$$ ▦**The Savannah.** Convenient, comfortable, and particu-
larly appealing to independent travelers who don't expect
or want organized entertainment and group activities, the
Savannah is a hotel rather than a resort. Nevertheless, it's
perfectly situated for walks to the Garrison historic area,
the Barbados Museum, the racetrack, and the Graeme Hall
Nature Centre—and it's minutes from Bridgetown by car or
taxi. Two modern wings spill down to the beach from the
main building, once the historic Sea View Hotel. Definitely
opt for a room in one of the modern wings, which overlook
a lagoon-style pool that flows between them in graduated
steps, from a waterfall at the higher end to a more tradi-
tional pool by the beach. The oceanfront duplex suites at
each end are the cat's meow. A favorite of local business-
people, Boucan Restaurant is a buzz of activity at lunch-
time. **Pros:** Right on the beach, interesting pool, convenient
to Bridgetown and sites. **Cons:** Not a good choice for kids,
rooms could use some sprucing up. ✉*Garrison Main
Rd., Hastings, Christ Church* ☎*246/435-9473* 🖷*246/
435-8822* ⊕*www.gemsbarbados.com* ⤳*90 rooms, 8
suites* ♿*In-room: safe, refrigerator, VCRs (some), dial-up.
In-hotel: 2 restaurants, bars, pools, gym, spa, beachfront,
no elevator, laundry service, public Internet, airport shut-
tle, no-smoking rooms* ▤*AE, D, DC, MC, V* ♡*CP.*

$$$ ▦**Southern Palms Beach Club.** Pretty in pink, you might say.
☻ The pink, plantation-style main building opens onto an
inviting pool area and 1,000 feet of white sandy beach.
Rooms and suites are attractive and spacious. The duplex
suites are a good choice for families, as kids under 12 stay
free. All accommodations have either a balcony or patio,
where you can enjoy the ocean breeze or simply stare out
to sea. Friendly, low-key, and peaceful are good descriptions of the day-to-day atmosphere. Play miniature golf or
shuffleboard with the kids, learn to windsurf, take a scuba
lesson in the pool, join a beach volleyball game, grab a
boogie board or perhaps a tennis racquet, or hit the gym—
you choose. In the evening, live local bands entertain the
after-dinner crowd, and a steel band accompanies the Sunday buffet lunch. **Pros:** Friendly and accommodating staff,
close to lots of restaurants and entertainment, nice beach.

Cons: Rooms are dated but are large and clean, beach vendors can be a nuisance (not the hotel's fault) ⊠*St. Lawrence Gap, Dover, Christ Church* ☎*246/428–7171* ⊕*www.southernpalms.net* ☞*72 rooms, 20 suites* ♿*In-room: safe, kitchen (some), Wi-Fi. In-hotel: restaurant, room service, bar, tennis courts, pools, gym, beachfront, water sports, no elevator, laundry facilities, laundry service, public Internet, public Wi-Fi* ⊟*AE, MC, V* ⑩*EP.*

$$–$$$ 🏨**Allamanda Beach Hotel.** Located just opposite Hastings ☾ Plaza, a shopping center that has some duty-free shopping and a few eateries, all rooms at Allamanda Beach Hotel accommodate up to three people; the one-bedroom suites accommodate three adults or two adults and two children. All 50 units have good-sized kitchenettes for preparing meals, making this a great choice for families. Units all have balconies with an ocean view, and most also overlook the pool. Guests may use the gym and spa at Amaryllis Beach Resort, a sister property just three minutes away in the Garrison area via the hotel's free shuttle. That resort also offers scuba diving, snorkeling, and non-motorized water sports on beautiful Palm Beach that guests may use in addition to the pool and rather rocky beach at Allamanda. Guests can purchase one of the resort's meal plans, which range from a continental or full breakfast each day to the full American plan (three meals a day) with or without beverages included. Those on a meal plan can also enjoy meals at Amaryllis at no extra charge. **Pros:** Inexpensive, self-catering option, friendly atmosphere. **Cons:** Rooms (especially the kitchenettes) are rather worn and ready for some attention, beach is better at sister hotel. ⊠*Main Rd., Hastings, Christ Church* ☎*246/438–1000* ⊕*www.allamandabeach.com* ☞*48 rooms, 2 suites* ♿*In-room: kitchen, Wi-Fi. In-hotel: restaurant, room service, bar, pool, beachfront, no elevator, laundry facilities, concierge, public Internet, public Wi-Fi* ⊟*AE, MC, V* ⑩*EP.*

$$ 🏨**Accra Beach Hotel & Resort.** One of the best choices for vacationers preferring a full-service resort in the middle of the busy south coast, Accra is large, it's modern, it faces a great beach, and it's competitively priced. Six duplex penthouse suites—the priciest accommodations—face the sea. Most rooms overlook the large cloverleaf-shaped pool or the beach—and some of the oceanfront suites have hot tubs on the balconies. The budget-minded can opt for the less expensive "island view" rooms, which face the street. It's not unusual to witness a local couple being married

1

here, and the hotel is a popular meeting venue for businesspeople. That shouldn't interrupt your day lazing on the beach, mingling at the poolside swim-up bar, or dining sumptuously at Wytukai (pronounced Y2K)—the island's only (so far) Polynesian restaurant. **Pros:** Right on a great beach, terrific value, friendly staff. **Cons:** Standard rooms are fairly ordinary, opt for a newer one or choose a suite. ⊠*Hwy. 7, Box 73W, Rockley, Christ Church* ☎*246/435–8920* ㊙*246/435–6794* ⊕*www.accrabeachhotel.com* ⤵*109 rooms, 37 suites* ⌂*In-room: safe, refrigerator (some), ethernet (some), dial-up. In-hotel: 3 restaurants, room service, bars, pool, gym, beachfront, water sports, laundry service, concierge, public Internet, no-smoking rooms* ▤*AE, D, MC, V* ⏲◎*EP.*

$$ ▣**Coconut Court Beach Hotel.** This resort is popular among ☺ families, particularly British families, who especially love the welcoming atmosphere, the Coco Kids Club, and the fact that children under 16 stay free (but a maximum of three people to a room). This is a family-run operation, after all. What this hotel really has going for it, though, is its marvelous location. Rooms stretch right along the beach, so the views and ocean breezes from the private balconies—all day and into the evening—are nothing short of spectacular. Accommodations are designated either rooms or studios—the main difference being that the rooms have a fridge, microwave, toaster, and electric kettle, while the studios have a full kitchenette with all the accouterments found in the rooms plus an oven and stove. Be sure to request a room or studio with a TV, if you wish, and air conditioning, as a handful of the yet-to-be-refurbished ones still rely on fans—and those ocean breezes. **Pros:** Beautiful beachfront, lots of activities for kids, the piña coladas for adults. **Cons:** Not all rooms have air-conditioning, room refurbishment is proceeding rather slowly. ⊠*Main Rd., Hastings, Christ Church* ☎*246/427–1655* ⊕*www.coconut-court.com* ⤵*82 rooms* ⌂*In-room: no a/c (some), no TV (some), safe, refrigrators (some), kitchens (some). In-hotel: restaurant, bars, pool, beachfront, no elevator, children's program (ages 4–12), concierge, laundry service* ▤*AE, MC, V* ⏲◎*EP.*

$$ ▣**Grand Barbados Beach Resort.** Particularly geared to business travelers, this high-rise hotel is close to Bridgetown and offers executive rooms, abundant business services, and extensive meeting facilities. Leisure travelers also appreciate the comfortable rooms and attentive service—and espe-

cially enjoy the hotel's location on beautiful Carlisle Bay. Broad beaches on either side of the building are great for swimming and sunbathing, with powdery white sand and calm water. From guest-room balconies—especially those in the corner rooms—the panoramic view is spectacular. At the far end of a 260-foot-long Victorian pier, five unique suites with over-water patios are a tempting choice for a romantic getaway; the pier is also a perfect spot to watch the sunset. Children under 12 stay free with their parents. **Pros:** Caters to business travelers, beautiful beach, close to Bridgetown, comfortable rooms. **Cons:** Caters to business travelers, hard to compete with newer Hilton Barbados next door. ⌂*Box 639, Aquatic Gap, St. Michael* ☎*246/426–4000* ⎙*246/429–2400* ⊕*www.grandbarbados. com* ⊷*128 rooms, 5 suites* ⌂*In-room: safe, dial-up, Wi-Fi. In-hotel: 2 restaurants, bars, pool, gym, beachfront, diving, water sports, laundry service, concierge, executive floor, public Internet, public Wi-Fi* ▭*AE, DC, MC, V* ⦿*EP.*

$$ ▦**Hotel PomMarine.** And now for something completely different—Hotel PomMarine is part of the Hospitality Institute of Barbados Community College and staffed by its students. The 20 simple yet comfortable rooms and one self-catering suite here are obviously a popular choice of visiting parents, but also of local businesspeople who know value when they see it. You're wondering about the unusual name? The hotel sits on the former site of the Marine and Pomeroy hotels. The goal in building it was to combine hands-on student training with a functioning hotel, and so Hotel PomMarine opened in 1997. Plans are underway to add another 40 rooms. Enjoy the pool, tennis court, a light meal at the Golden Apple Cafe', exquisite dining at Muscovado Restaurant—and perhaps observe students working in a demo kitchen. Hastings Beach is across the street. **Pros:** Cooking demonstrations, great restaurant, a whole different hotel experience. **Cons:** Five-minute walk to the beach, rooms are rather ordinary, no "vacation" atmosphere. ⌂*Barbados Community College, Hastings, Christ Church* ☎*246/228–0900* ⊕*www.pommarine.com* ⊷*20 rooms, 1 suite* ⌂*In-room: safe, kitchen (one). In-hotel: 2 restaurants, bars, pool, tennis court, public Internet* ▭*AE, D, DC, MC, V* ⦿*EP.*

$$ ▦**Sandy Bay Beach Club.** Broad Sandy Beach is the main attraction here, along with the resort's close proximity to south-coast shops, restaurants, nightspots, and attractions. The hotel is within walking distance of St. Lawrence Gap and the Graeme Hall Nature Sanctuary. Guest rooms are in three buildings, arranged in a horseshoe around a large freshwater pool. Most rooms have an ocean view; end units face the broad white-sand beach and have an extraordinary view of the sea. The beach is protected by an offshore reef, so the sea is usually very calm. A full-time activities director will make sure you have plenty to do—or you can opt to have do nothing but relax and soak up the sun. Guests have breakfast, lunch, and dinner at The Quartermaster, a casual restaurant by day and informal eatery at night. In addition, they may reserve one dinner per week at Hidden Treasure, which offers an à la carte menu of international cuisine and Bajan specialties. Sandy Bay is on a main bus route, making it easy to get to Bridgetown and back or to any spot along the south coast. The hotel's parent company is part-owner of the Barbados Golf Club, an 18-hole public golf course that's a 12-minute drive from Sandy Bay, and guests get a discount on greens fees. The nine-hole Rockley Golf Course, however, is just two minutes away. **Pros:** On one of the best south-coast beaches, plenty of water sports, golf discounts, interesting sightseeing within walking distance. **Cons:** Limited access to fine-dining restaurant, definitely don't confuse this hotel with Sandy Lane! ⊠*Main Rd., Worthing, Christ Church* ☎*246/435–8000* ⊕*www. sandybaybeachclub.com* ⇆*41 rooms, 89 suites* ⚬*In-room: safe, refrigerator, kitchen (some), data-port. In-hotel: 2 restaurants, bars, pool, beachfront, water sports, no elevator, public Internet* ⊟*AE, MC, V* ⦿*AI.*

$$ 📺**Silver Sands Hotel.** The sometimes congested lobby is a little deceiving, for Silver Sands sprawls out over 12 acres of gardens and along a significant strip of Silver Sands Beach. But back to the busy lobby—British tour groups of 100 or more arrive twice a month for two-week holidays. This is also a favorite layover hotel for the airlines, because it's so convenient to the airport. So even though the accommodations themselves are rather ordinary, the hotel is often full of guests—who all seem to be enjoying themselves to the fullest. It's a rather young, beach-loving crowd. Many younger guests come here for the nearby windsurfing. Families, however, enjoy the suites and studios, because they have kitchens and kids under 12 share the accommodations for free. Guests can purchase a SmartCard to use in the restaurants, bar, beauty salon, boutique, and minimart. **Pros:** Tour groups and young people love this place, great windsurfing venue, nice pool and beach. **Cons:** Basic commodations, very busy place. ✉*Silver Sands, Christ Church* ☎*246/428–6001* ⊕*www.silversandsbarbados.com* ⇆*41 rooms, 89 suites* ⌂*In-room: kitchen (some). In-hotel: 2 restaurants, bar, tennis court, pools, gym, beachfront, no elevator, laundry facilities, public Internet, public Wi-Fi* ▭*AE, MC, V* ⦿*EP.*

$$ ⊞**South Beach Resort.** The entrance here is certainly dra-
☾ matic—and very much the South Beach style. To enter the sleek lobby, guests cross a double-wide lap pool via a footbridge. This resort is actually a time-share vacation club, but it's run like a hotel—a very cool hotel indeed. Rooms are decorated with quality furniture and fabrics, and the bathrooms are ultramodern. All rooms and suites have an eating area and a pullout sofa in the sitting area, making the accommodations suitable for parents and a couple of kids. Children under 12 are free when staying in the same room as adults. Accra (Rockley) Beach is just across the street, where beach chairs, water-sports equipment, and other beach toys—as well as drinks and snacks—can be rented or purchased. The restaurant at South Beach serves breakfast only—either indoors or poolside. For other meals, the surrounding area is filled with restaurants offering everything from fast food to fine dining. And, of course, each unit has a kitchen. **Pros:** Beautiful bathrooms, Accra Beach is great for families, Wi-Fi everywhere. **Cons:** More a hotel than a resort, on-site restaurant only serves breakfast, beach is across the street. ✉*Main Rd., Rockley, Christ Church* ☎*246/435–8561* ⊕*www.southbeachbarbados.com* ⇆*22 rooms, 25 suites* ⌂*In-room: kitchen, VCR, Wi-Fi. In-hotel: restaurant, room service, bar, pool, laundry facilities, concierge, public Internet, public Wi-Fi, no-smoking rooms* ▭*AE, MC, V* ⦿*EP.*

★ Fodor'sChoice ⊞**Peach & Quiet.** Perhaps Barbados's best-kept
$ secret, this small seaside inn on the southeast coast is the sweetest deal we've found on the entire island. Forego the flashy accoutrements of a resort and, instead, claim one of these stylish suites as your own. With no in-room noisemakers (that is, no TV or radio) and no children around, the only sounds you will hear are the gentle surf and your own conversations. Hands-on British owners Adrian and Margaret Loveridge purchased Peach, the first hotel designed by noted architect Ian Morrison, in 1988. In 2004 they renovated and refurbished the entire property. Decor in the spacious suites, arranged in whitewashed Mykonos-inspired buildings, is elegantly spare. Cooled by ceiling

1

fans, each suite also has a large terrace or balcony and a stocked bookshelf; bathrooms have showers only. Besides lazing in the freshwater pool and windsurfing at nearby beaches (a five-minute walk), guests enjoy swimming and snorkeling among 120 noted varieties of tropical fish in a "rock pool" naturally created by the sea, joining 5-mi (8-km) early-morning or late-afternoon walks, and stargazing at night. You're advised to rent a car. **Pros:** Peace and quiet, adults-only environment, engaging owners, stargazing and nature walks are special treats. **Cons:** Inn is closed half of the year, remote location requires a rental car. ⊠*Inch Marlow Main Rd., Inch Marlow, Christ Church* ☎*246/428–5682* ☎*246/428–2467* ⊕*www.peachandquiet.com* ⌇*22 suites* ⌂*In-room: no a/c, no phone, safe, refrigerator, no TV. In-hotel: restaurant, bar, pool, water sports, no elevator, no kids under 16* ▤*MC, V* ⊘*Closed May–Oct.* ⦿*EP.*

VILLA & CONDO COMPLEXES

$$-$$$ ⛶**Silver Point.** The old Silver Rock Hotel, a haven for windsurfers, has metamorphosed into a trendy boutique villa-hotel. New owners turned the property into a gated community of modern condos that are managed and operated as a hotel. Phase I of the transformation, completed in summer 2006, resulted in 15 one-bedroom, oceanview suites decorated in sleek neutral colors and dark mahogany furniture; along with a café-style restaurant, pool, and lounging area. Phase II, completed in early 2008, added 40 hotel rooms and studios, 22 one-bedroom suites, three two-bedroom suites, and a spa, gym, and two-story open-deck restaurant with a rooftop martini bar. Each unit has coral stone accents, cedar closets, and a combination radio/iPod station; suites have granite and marble countertops in both kitchen and bath. Silver Point is perfect for worldy travelers who enjoy something chic yet fairly remote and secluded—and for those who know that Silver Rock–Silver Sands Beach is the best place for windsurfing and kitesurfing. The hotel, which overlooks the beach, offers a special windsurfing package that includes lessons and plenty of time on the water—hanging on for dear life, we might add. **Pros:** Classy suites, perfect location for windsurfers, gated community. **Cons:** Not within walking distance of anything, sea can be rough for swimming, rental car recommended. ⊠*Silver Sands, Christ Church* ☎*246/420–4416* ⊕*www.silverpointhotel.com* ⌇*40 rooms, 40 suites* ⌂*In-room: kitchen (some), DVD, VCR, Wi-Fi. In-hotel: 2 restaurants, bar, pools, gym, spa, beachfront, water sports,*

no elevator, laundry facilities, laundry service, concierge, public Internet, public Wi-Fi, no-smoking rooms, ⊟*AE, MC, V* ⦿*EP.*

CENTRAL BARBADOS

Hotel locations in central Barbados are plotted on the Central Barbados map.

HOTELS

★ Fodor'sChoice ⊡**Coral Reef Club.** Owned and operated by the
$$$$ O'Hara family since the 1950s, the upscale Coral Reef Club offers the elegance and style of Sandy Lane with less formality. Spend your days relaxing at the beach or around the pool, taking time out for afternoon tea. Individually designed and beautifully decorated suites are in pristine coral-stone manses and cottages scattered over 12½ acres of flower-filled gardens; the public areas ramble along the waterfront. Garden rooms suit one or two guests and have a small patio or balcony, while junior suites have sitting areas and larger patios or balconies. Luxury cottage suites each have a plunge pool, bedroom, and separate living room with a sofa bed, making them perfect for families. Be advised, though, that after 7:30 PM kids are not welcome in the dining room. They can have their evening meal served on the veranda of your suite. The five pricey Plantation suites and two villas have spacious living rooms, private sundecks and plunge pools, and stereos—and are the only accommodations here that come with TVs (other guests can watch TV in the lounge or request one in-room for an added charge). Catch a breeze while mingling at the bar before or after dining in Coral Reef's excellent terrace restaurant. **Pros:** Absolutely delightful, elegant yet informal, beautiful suites with huge verandas, delicious dining, six computers available to guests for free Internet access. **Cons:** No room TVs (if that matters), narrow beach sometimes disappears depending on the weather. ⊠*Hwy. 1, Holetown, St. James* ☎*246/422–2372* 🖷*246/422–1776* ⊕*www.coralreefbarbados.com* ⟿*29 rooms, 57 suites, 2 villas* ⌂*In-room: safe, refrigerator, no TV (some), dial-up, Wi-Fi. In-hotel: restaurant, room service, bar, tennis courts, pools, gym, beachfront, diving, water sports, no elevator, children's programs (ages 2–8), public Internet, no kids under 12 Jan. 15–Mar. 15* ⊟*AE, MC, V* ⊘*Closed June* ⦿*BP.*

$$$$ ⓣ**Lone Star Hotel.** Now here's an idea—British owners transformed this 1940s-era service station into a sleek four-suite boutique hotel that—fortunately or unfortunately—has been discovered by celebrities. Four large, architecturally fascinating suites with shady terraces—two of which are at beach level—are beautifully decorated in elegant neutral colors and furnished in minimalist style with enormous Bajan mahogany beds, chic Italian-designed upholstered furniture, and Phillipe Starck fixtures in the bathrooms. The Lincoln Bedroom is named for the car, not the American president. Other suites are appropriately dubbed Buick, Cord, and Studebaker. Each suite has its own communications and entertainment center, with a TV, stereo/CD player, and DVD. The Beach House, a separate coral-stone villa, can be rented in its entirety or as one- or two-bedroom private suites. Its Caribbean-style decor is quite different from the hotel rooms, with comfy furniture, antiques, and tasteful artwork from the owners' personal collection. The beach is at your door; golf, tennis, fishing, snorkeling, scuba diving, and horseback riding are available nearby. The restaurant is extraordinary—both in terms of cuisine and atmosphere. **Pros:** Rub shoulders and chill with celebs (perhaps), enjoy great cuisine, you'll love the decor. **Cons:** Rubbing shoulders and chilling with celebs can get very expensive. ✉*Hwy. 1, Holetown, St. James* ☎*246/419–0599* ⊕*www.thelonestar.com* ⋨*4 rooms, 2 suites* ⅙*In-room: refrigerator, DVD, ethernet. In-hotel: restaurant, room service, bar, beachfront, no elevator* ⊟*AE, MC, V* ⑩*BP.*

$$$$ ⓣ**Mango Bay.** Mango Bay has a whole new look and attitude. Reopened in 2006 after a $10 million upgrade, it now has a completely transformed entrance, grander accommodations, 10 new deluxe rooms and two 1,200-square-foot oceanfront penthouse suites, and a partially enclosed dining room that provides both alfresco and air-conditioned dining options. All-inclusive rates include accommodations, meals, brand-name beverages, and a host of water sports (including waterskiing), as well as off-property sightseeing experiences such as a glass-bottom boat trip, a shopping excursion to Bridgetown, and a catamaran day sail along the coast. Located in the heart of Holetown, this convenient boutique resort is also within walking distance of shops, restaurants, nightspots, historic sites, and the public bus to either Bridgetown or Speightstown. **Pros:** Nice rooms, great food, friendly staff, walk to Holetown shopping and entertainment. **Cons:** Although heroic measures continue to try to address the problem, a natural drainage stream on the north side of the property can sometimes become odoriferous. ✉*2nd St., Holetown, St. James* ☎*246/432–1384* 🖷*246/432–5297* ⊕*www.mangobaybarbados.com* ➷*64 rooms, 10 suites, 2 penthouse suites* ♿*In-room: safe, refrigerator (some), ethernet. In-hotel: restaurant, bar, pool, beachfront, water sports, public Internet, public Wi-Fi* ☰*AE, D, DC, MC, V* ⊙*AI.*

$$$$ 🖵 **The Sandpiper.** This little gem just north of Holetown is
★ every bit as elegant as its sister hotel, Coral Reef Club, yet the atmosphere is even more relaxed, more like a private hideaway. Guest rooms and suites are arranged in a loose "S" shape on 7 acres of gardens. All rooms have a toaster to ensure freshly made, warm toast with your room-service breakfast. One- and two-bedroom suites have a separate living room and full kitchen. Each unit has a CD player; those who can't live without TV can rent one by the week. Extensive renovations in 2005 added two beachfront Tree Top Suites that are luxuriously spacious—with bathrooms as big as some Manhattan apartments; each Tree Top Suite has a wraparound terrace with a wet bar and plunge pool. Water sports, including waterskiing, are complimentary. Scuba diving, children's programs, massage, and other personal services are available at the Coral Reef Club, which is nearby. **Pros:** Chic and sophisticated, the Tree Top Suites are fabulous, the bathrooms are amazing. **Cons:** Beach is small—typical of west-coast beaches, hotel is small and many guests return year after year, so reservations can be hard to get. ✉*Hwy. 1, Holetown, St. James* ☎*246/422–2251* 🖷*246/422–1776* ⊕*www.sandpiperbarbados.com* ➷*22 rooms, 25 suites* ♿*In-room: safe, kitchen (some), refrigerator, no TV, ethernet, Wi-Fi. In-hotel: restaurant, room service, bars, tennis courts, pool, gym, beachfront, water sports, public Internet, public Wi-Fi, no kids under 12 Jan. 15–Mar. 15* ☰*AE, MC, V* ⊙*Closed Sept.* ⊙*BP.*

$$ 🖵 **Discovery Bay.** This large plantation-style building just off the road has deluxe and club rooms that overlook the beach, while superior and garden-view rooms overlook the pool and gardens. The rooms are good-sized but rather basic in terms of style, but the price is right considering the beachfront location and convenience to the shopping, restaurants, and nightlife opportunities in Holetown—a five-minute walk from your room. The hotel offers accommodations-only rates, but most guests choose to pay about

$50 more per day for the all-inclusive meal plan, which includes three meals a day, afternoon tea, beverages, and some activities. The food is pretty good—buffet breakfast and lunch are served by the pool; dinner, often themed, in the restaurant. **Pros:** Great Holetown location, good beach, good value. **Cons:** Rooms are basic. ⊠*Hwy. 1, Holetown, St. James* ☎*246/432–1301* ⊕*www.rexresorts.com* ⤳*79 rooms, 9 suites* ⌂*In-room: safe, refrigerator, dial-up. In-hotel, 2 restaurants, room service, bars, tennis court, gym, pool, beachfront, diving, water sports, no elevator, laundry service, no-smoking rooms* ⊟*AE, MC, V* ⍻*EP.*

EAST COAST

Hotel locations on the east coast are plotted on the Central Barbados map.

HOTELS

$-$$ ▨**New Edgewater Hotel.** While not exactly beachfront, the New Edgewater Hotel overlooks a 9-mi stretch of the stunning east coast, including Bathsheba Beach and its famous Soup Bowl. As if that's not enough natural beauty, the western side of the hotel backs up against Joe's River and the 85-acre Joe's River Tropical Rainforest, complete with trails through the hills, gullies, and dense foliage. The hotel itself has been a cliffside retreat since the 1700s. A more recent owner made, by hand, all of the sturdy mahogany furniture in the hotel—and there's lots of it. You'll marvel at the parquet ceilings and magnificent leaded-glass windows throughout the hotel—and the pool that's shaped like Barbados. Today the hotel is comparatively rustic and attracts guests who are content with taking a walk or curling up with a good book, as well as surfers who like the location. All but two rooms have at least a partial ocean view, and many have balconies. The view from Room 222 is particularly amazing. **Pros:** Spectacular setting, surfers' paradise, quite and peaceful, nice pool area. **Cons:** Remote location, no nearby beach for swimming, don't expect luxury, public bathroom needs some attention. ⊠*Bathsheba Beach, Bathsheba, St. Joseph* ☎*246/433–9900* ⊕*www.newedgewater.com* ⤳*20 rooms, 4 suites* ⌂*In-room: refrigerator, ethernet. In-hotel: restaurant, bar, pool, no elevator* ⊟*AE, MC, V* ⍻*CP.*

$-$$ ▨**Round House Inn.** It's hard to tell which is more appealing: the view of the rugged coastline or the magnificent historic (1832) manse strategically perched on the cliff to take advantage of the view. This cozy little enclave is owned and operated by Robert and Gail Manley, who also oversee what has become one of the most popular dining establishments on the east coast. Guestrooms are tastefully decorated in subdued colors and furnished in a simple style—a clean, contemporary look without being "moderne." Each room has a great view of the ocean, and some rooms look out onto the pretty courtyard. Room No. 3 opens to a large sundeck with a small plunge pool. While few activities are offered on the property itself, snorkeling, diving, horseback riding, hiking, and, of course, surfing at nearby Bathsheba Soup Bowl can be arranged. **Pros:** Beautiful east-coast views, lovely accommodations, excellent restaurant, small and intimate. **Cons:** Remote location, no TV (if you care), quite a hike to the beach, where you can only surf or wade. ⊠, *Bathsheba, St. Joseph,* ☎*246/433–9678* ⊕*www. roundhousebarbados.com* ↳*6 rooms* ⌂*In-room: no a/c, no phone (some), safe, no TV (some). In-hotel: restaurant, bar, pools, beachfront, no elevator* ⊟*AE, D, MC, V* ⍩*EP.*

$–$$ 🖾**Sea-U Guest House.** Uschi Wetzels, a German travel writer in an earlier life, became smitten with the wild and woolly east coast of Barbados while on assignment and returned in 1999 to build this tiny guesthouse. The main house, where she also lives with her daughter, is built in the traditional wooden colonial style. Its four simple guest rooms, each with a kitchenette, are cooled by ceiling fans and sea breezes. A cottage next door has two air-conditioned studios, also with kitchenettes, that can be connected to become a large suite. The property, perched on a cliff overlooking the sea, is thick with palm trees and other tropical foliage. A casual restaurant offers a full breakfast each day and a three-course, fixed-price (inexpensive) dinner three nights a week prepared by Wetzels and her Bajan chef. The honor bar, which you settle upon checkout, is a gathering place for guests each evening—and sometimes in the afternoon. During the day, though, guests are more likely to while away their time in a hammock, wander down to Bathsheba Beach for a dip in the tidal pools, or walk over to nearby Andromeda Botanical Gardens. **Pros:** Peaceful and relaxing, couldn't be friendlier, and there's Wi-Fi. **Cons:** Simple accommodations, few amenities, remote location. ⊠*Tent Bay, Bathsheba, St. Joseph* ☎*246/433–9450* ⊕*www.seaubarbados.com* ↳*6 rooms* ⌂*In-room: no a/c (some), no phone, kitchen, no TV, Wi-Fi. In-hotel: restaurant, bar, no elevator, public Wi-Fi, no smoking rooms* ⊟*MC, V* ⍩*BP.*

WEST COAST

Hotel locations on the west coast are plotted on the Holetown & Vicinity and Northern Barbados maps.

HOTELS

$$$$ 🏨 **Almond Beach Club & Spa.** Among several similar beachfront resorts south of Holetown, Almond Beach Club distinguishes itself with its all-inclusive rates (only spa and salon services are extra), an adults-only environment, and reciprocal guest privileges (including shuttle service) at its enormous sister resort, Almond Beach Village. A horseshoe of rooms and suites decorated in a British-colonial theme faces the sea, although most units overlook the pools and gardens. Lavish breakfast buffets, four-course lunches, afternoon teas, and intimate dinners are served in the main dining room—or dine on seafood at Water's Edge or West Indian cuisine at Enid's, the colorful Bajan restaurant that also offers free cooking classes. The soundproof piano bar remains open until the last guest leaves. **Pros:** Adults only, intimate atmosphere, short walk to Holetown, next door to Sandy Lane Beach. **Cons:** Beach erodes to almost nothing at certain times of the year. ⊠*Hwy. 1, Vauxhall, St. James* ☎*246/432–7840* 🖷*246/432–2115* ⊕*www.almondresorts. com* ➪*133 rooms, 28 suites* &*In-room: safe, refrigerator. In-hotel: 3 restaurants, room service, bars, tennis court, pools, gym, spa, beachfront, water sports, no elevator, laundry service, public Internet, airport shuttle, no kids under 16* ⊟*AE, D, MC, V* ⊚*AI.*

$$$$ 🏨 **Almond Beach Village.** Barbados's premier family resort ☺ is massive enough to be a popular conference venue and ★ romantic enough to host intimate weddings. Situated on an 18th-century sugar plantation north of Speightstown, the Village's 32 acres front a mile-long, powdery beach. Rooms and pools at the north end of the property, near a historic sugar mill, are reserved for adults; at the south end, junior and one-bedroom suites targeted to families with children are close to special facilities for kids and teens. A plethora of activities—golf, sailing, waterskiing, shopping excursions to Bridgetown, an off-site Bajan picnic, and more—are all included. Not enough? Hop the shuttle to Almond Beach Club and enjoy the (adults-only) facilities there. **Pros:** Family resort with certain areas for adults only, lots to do and all included, complimentary Bajan cooking lessons, sugar mill is a picturesque wedding venue. **Cons:** It's huge, some liken it to a holiday camp, more emphasis should be placed

on room renovations and less on expansion. ✉*Hwy. 1B, Heywoods, St. Peter* ☎*246/422–4900* 🖷*246/422–0617* ⊕*www.almondresorts.com* ⇴*355 rooms, 40 suites* &*In-room: safe. In-hotel: 5 restaurants, room service, bars, golf course, tennis courts, pools, gym, spa, beachfront, water sports, no elevator, children's programs (ages infant–17), public Internet, airport shuttle* ▭*AE, D, MC, V* ⏍*AI.*

$$$$ 🖩**Cobblers Cove Hotel.** "English Country" best describes the
🕒 style of this pretty-in-pink resort, favored by British sophis-
★ ticates who return year after year. Flanked by tropical gardens on one side and the sea on the other, each elegant
suite has a comfy sitting room with a sofa bed and a wall
of louvered shutters that open onto a patio, a trouser press,
and a small library of books. The view of the gently splash-
ing surf or the starry evening sky is mesmerizing from the
four oceanfront suites. For all-out luxury, the sublime (and
enormous) Colleton and Camelot penthouse suites each
have a richly decorated sitting room, king-size four-poster
bed, dressing room, whirlpool bath, private sundeck, and
large plunge pool. Socializing occurs in the library, which
doubles as a TV lounge, and at the alfresco restaurant,
which receives well-deserved raves for superb dining. **Pros:**
Very classy establishment, lovely grounds, the penthouse
suites are amazing, very quiet. **Cons:** Very quiet, only bed-
rooms have air-conditioning. ✉*Road View, Speightstown, St. Peter* ☎*246/422–2291* 🖷*246/422–1460* ⊕*www. cobblerscove.com* ⇴*40 suites* &*In-room: safe, refrigerator, no TV, dial-up, Wi-Fi. In-hotel: restaurant, room service, bar, tennis court, pool, gym, spa, beachfront, water sports, no elevator, children's programs (ages 2–12), public Inter-net, public Wi-Fi, no kids under 12 Jan.–Mar.* ▭*AE, D, MC, V* ⏍*BP.*

$$$$ 🖩**Colony Club Hotel.** As the signature hotel of five Elegant
Hotel properties on Barbados, the Colony Club is certainly
elegant—but with a quiet, friendly, understated style. The
main building and grounds were once a private gentlemen's club. Today hotel guests experience a similar sense
of belonging. A lagoon pool meanders through the central
gardens, and 20 rooms have private access to the lagoon
directly from their patios. Relax on the beach, soak in one
of four pools, and enjoy an exquisite meal in the air-conditioned Orchids restaurant or a more informal repast at the
open-air Laguna Restaurant. Non-motorized water sports,
an in-pool scuba-diving lesson, and tennis are all included.
A free water taxi provides transportation to two sister hotels

located along the west coast. **Pros:** Clubby atmosphere, choose a room with direct lagoon pool access. **Cons:** Relatively pricey, beach comes and goes depending on storms. ⊠*Hwy. 1, Porters, St. James* ☎*246/422–2335* 📠*246/422–0667* ⊕*www.colonyclubhotel.com* ⇆*64 rooms, 32 junior suites* ♿*In-room: safe, refrigerator. In-hotel: 2 restaurants, room service, bars, tennis courts, pools, gym, spa, beachfront, water sports, no elevator, laundry service, public Internet* ⊟*AE, DC, MC, V* ⏏*EP.*

$$$$ ☒**Crystal Cove Hotel.** One of four Elegant Hotel properties on the island, Crystal Cove is a colony of attached duplex whitewashed cottages that are trimmed in the perky pastels typical of the Caribbean. Each room is bright and spacious with a balcony or patio. Most have hammocks and a water view; some are literally inches from the beach. Winding garden paths connect the units, which spill down a hillside to the beach where you can swim, sail, snorkel, water-ski, windsurf, or kayak to your heart's content—or play tennis, dip in the pool, or take advantage of preferred tee times at Royal Westmoreland Golf Course & Country Club. Meals are bountiful and delicious—buffets and snacks at Drifters Beach Bar and a table-d'hôte menu at Reflections Restaurant. Each night there's entertainment in the form of a steel band or other live music. For change of scene, a free water taxi travels all day long (weather permitting) between the three sister properties on the west coast. Crystal Cove guests can also participate in a dine-around program with those resorts. **Pros:** Rooms are large and comfortable, good food, nice beach, exchange dining program with sister resorts. **Cons:** Not much available immediately outside the resort, ⊠*Hwy. 1, Appleby, St. James* ☎*246/432–2683* ⊕*www.crystalcovehotelbarbados.com* ⇆*62 rooms, 26 suites* ♿*In-room: safe, refrigerator. In-hotel: 2 restaurants, room service, bars, tennis courts, pools, gym, beachfront, water sports, no elevator, children's programs (ages 3–11), laundry service, public Internet* ⊟*AE, DC, MC, V* ⏏*AI.*

$$$$ ☒**The Fairmont Royal Pavilion.** Unique among west-coast
★ hotels of the same upscale caliber, every suite in this adults-oriented resort has a view of the sea from its broad balcony or patio. From ground-floor patios, in fact, you can step directly onto the sand. In the style of a Barbadian plantation house, all rooms have rich mahogany furniture and sisal rugs on ceramic floor tiles; rooms are also equipped with 27-inch flat-screen TVs and DVD/CD players. The resort's traditional, personalized service continues on the

beach, where "Beach Butlers" cater to your every seaside whim—a fresh towel, sunscreen, mineral water, or perhaps an icy treat delivered to your beach chair. Breakfast and lunch are served alfresco near the beach; afternoon tea and dinner in the exquisite Palm Terrace. **Pros:** Beautiful resort, excellent service—everyone remembers your name, dining is excellent. **Cons:** Dining is expensive—in fact, everything is expensive. ⊠*Hwy. 1, Porters, St. James* ☎*246/422–5555* 🖷*246/422–3940* ⊕*www.fairmont.com/royalpavilion* 🛏*72 rooms, 1 3-bedroom villa* ⟷*In-room: safe, refrigerator, dial-up. In-hotel: 2 restaurants, room service, bars, tennis courts, pool, gym, beachfront, diving, water sports, no elevator, laundry service, concierge, public Internet, no kids under 12 Nov.–Apr., no-smoking rooms* ⊟*AE, D, DC, MC, V* ⦿*EP.*

$$$$ 🏠**The House.** Privacy, luxury, and service are hallmarks of this adult sanctuary next door to sister resort Tamarind Cove. The 34 junior and one-bedroom suites are simply but elegantly decorated in tranquil white, ivory, and cream with splashes of dark and azure blue to highlight the Caribbean Sea just beyond the terrace. Beds and pillows are big, soft, and fitted with luxurious Egyptian cotton linens. This may not be home, but guests are certainly made to feel welcome with the service, the personalized attention, and the privacy. A 24-hour "ambassador" service caters to your every whim. Daphne's Restaurant, the Caribbean branch of the renowned London establishment, is situated directly between The House and Tamarind Cove, the adjacent sister property where guests can enjoy the pools, restaurants, and water-sports opportunities—including complimentary windsurfing, boogie boarding, kayaking, waterskiing, tube rides, banana boats, and sailing on a Hobie Cat. Preferred tee times can be arranged at Royal Westmoreland Golf & Country Club, just a 10-minute ride away. Champagne breakfast, afternoon tea, and canapés at sundown make The House a home. But perhaps most appreciated, a complimentary "jet-lag massage" is yours upon arrival. **Pros:** Trendy, stylish, upscale, private, pure relaxation. **Cons:** If it begins to get a little stuffy, head next door to Tamarind Cove. ⊠*Hwy. 1, Paynes Bay, St. James* ☎*246/432–5525* ⊕*www.thehousebarbados.com* 🛏*34 suites* ⟷*In-room: safe, refrigerator, DVD (some), Wi-Fi. In-hotel: restaurant, gym, beachfront, water sports, no elevator, no kids under 18, public Wi-Fi* ⊟*AE, DC, MC, V* ⦿*BP.*

★ **Fodor's**Choice ☎**Sandy Lane Hotel & Golf Club.** Few places on
$$$$ earth can compare to Sandy Lane's luxurious facilities and
⏱ ultra-pampering service—or to its astronomical prices.
Taking "upscale" to an entirely new level, Sandy Lane is
by far the priciest and most exclusive resort in Barbados
and is among the most expensive in the world, but for
the few who can afford to stay here—royals, celebrities,
and business moguls among them—it's an unparalleled
experience. The main building of this exquisite resort is
a coral-stone, Palladian-style mansion facing a sweeping
stretch of beach shaded by mature trees. Guest accommodations, sumptuous in every detail, include three plasma
TVs with DVD players, a full in-room wet bar, a personal
butler, and remote-controlled everything—even the draper-
ies! The world-class spa, housed in a magnificent Roman-
esque building, is a vacation in itself. Add elegant dining,
the Caribbean's best golf courses, a tennis center, a full
complement of water sports, a special lounge for teenag-
ers, incomparable style—you get the picture. Sandy Lane is
extraordinary. **Pros:** Top of the line, cream of the crop, no
debate about it—and the spa is amazing. **Cons:** Over the
top for most mortals, and you feel like dressing up just to
walk through the lobby. ⊠*Hwy. 1, Paynes Bay, St. James*
☎*246/444–2000* ⊠*246/444–2222* ⊕*www.sandylane.com*
⮌*102 rooms, 10 suites, 1 5-bedroom villa* ⏱*In-room:
safe, refrigerator, dial-up. In-hotel: 3 restaurants, room
service, bars, golf courses, tennis courts, pool, spa, beachfront, water sports, children's programs (ages 3–12), laundry service, concierge, public Internet* ▤*AE, D, DC, MC,
V* ⏶*BP.*

$$$$ ☎**Tamarind Cove Hotel.** This Mediterranean-style resort
⏱ sprawls along 750 feet of prime west-coast beachfront and
is large enough to cater to sophisticated couples and active
families—while at the same time offering cozy privacy to
honeymooners. Most rooms provide a panoramic view of
the sea, which is gorgeous by day and spectacular at sunset.
Four-poster beds in the 10 luxury oceanfront suites add a
touch of romance. Junior suites are great for couples or
families with one or two small children; families with older
kids might prefer the space and privacy of a one-bedroom
suite. Tamarind offers an array of water sports, as well
as golf privileges at the Royal Westmoreland Golf Club.
Among its three restaurants, Daphne's Barbados is a fashionable oasis for grand wining and dining. A free water taxi
shuttles to two sister hotels. **Pros:** Nice location on Paynes

Bay Beach, lots of free water sports, Daphne's is great. **Cons:** Rooms could use a little loving care, service is a little slow. ⊠*Hwy. 1, Paynes Bay, St. James* ☎*246/432–1332* 🖷*246/432–6317* ⊕*www.tamarindcovehotel.com* ↘*58 rooms, 47 suites* ⚒*In-room: safe, refrigerator. In-hotel: 3 restaurants, room service, bars, tennis courts, pools, gym, beachfront, water sports, no elevator, laundry service, concierge, public Internet* ▤*AE, D, DC, MC, V* ⌖*EP.*

$$$$ 🏨**Treasure Beach.** Quiet, upscale, and friendly, this boutique all-suites hotel has a residential quality. Many guests—mostly British—are regulars, returning every year for two- or three-week stays. But the rates are relatively expensive when compared, say, to the posh and much larger (in terms of facilities and amenities) Coral Reef Club. Nevertheless, the hotel's high number of repeat guests suggests that the ambience here is well worth the price. Two floors of one-bedroom suites form a horseshoe around a small garden and pool. Most have a sea view, and all are just steps from the strip of sandy beach. The superdeluxe Hemmingway Suite blends antiques with modern luxury, an enormous terrace, and whirlpool tub. All suites have comfortable sitting rooms with ceiling fans, plasma TVs, shelves of books, and open-air fourth walls that can be shuttered at night for privacy. Only the bedrooms are air-conditioned. Suites easily accommodate three adults or two adults and two children. The resort's restaurant enjoys a well-deserved reputation among guests and locals alike for its fine cuisine and pleasant atmosphere. **Pros:** Quiet retreat, lots of repeat British guests, congenial crowd, swim with the turtles just offshore. **Cons:** Narrow beach, only bedrooms are air-conditioned, offshore turtles attract boatloads of tourists. ⊠*Hwy. 1, Paynes Bay, St. James* ☎*246/432–1346* 🖷*246/432–1094* ⊕*www.treasurebeachhotel.com* ↘*29 suites* ⚒*In-room: safe, refrigerator, dial-up. In-hotel: restaurant, room service, bar, pool, gym, beachfront, water sports, no elevator, laundry service, public Internet, no kids under 2 Nov.–May 15* ▤*AE, MC, V* ⊘*Closed Sept.* ⌖*EP.*

$$$–$$$$ 🏨**St. James Apartment Hotel.** Location, location, location—British families have discovered the St. James Apartment Hotel. And why not? It's perfectly situated right on Paynes Bay beach, one of the best on the west coast and, for golfers, just a half-mile north of Sandy Lane Country Club. It's also just a mile south of Holetown's shopping, restaurants, and entertainment. In fact, a half-dozen excellent restau-

rants are within walking distance of the St. James. Self-catering, however, is the appeal of staying in one of these elegant apartments—and they really are elegant. The hotel has three studios, two one-bedroom units, and six two-bedroom apartments. All have fully equipped, Italian-design, open-plan kitchens. Spacious sitting rooms have cushy seating and a large dining table, with French doors that open to a substantial patio or balcony—a perfect place to be for breakfast in the morning or cocktails at sunset. Each bedroom has its own private bath. Want to get to know your neighbors? Step through the lobby to a sundeck, available to all guests, and to the powdery sand and the sea. **Pros:** Great quarters for independent travelers and long stays, beach and sundeck are wonderful, convenient to shopping and restaurants. **Cons:** No pool, no organized activities. ⊠*Hwy. 1, Paynes Bay, St. James* 📞*246/432–0489* ⊕*www. the-stjames.com* 🛏*11 apartments* 🖒*In room: safe, kitchen, dial-up. In-hotel: beachfront, laundry service, no-smoking rooms* ⏸*EP.*

$$$ 🖈**Divi Heritage Beach Resort.** Divi Heritage is a small oceanfront enclave—a home away from home—for adults only. Intentionally quiet, on-site activities are limited to tennis, snorkeling, and the beach, although day passes are available to guests who wish to use the pools, gym, water sports, spa, and restaurants at Almond Beach Club right next door. All suites, whether studio-size or one bedroom, are airy and spacious, with fully equipped kitchens, king-size beds, sleeper sofas in the sitting area, clay-tile floors, and arched doorways opening onto a patio or balcony. Oceanfront studios each have a private hot tub on the patio. Sunset Crest shopping mall (with a supermarket) is directly across the street, and it's a short walk to the restaurants, shops, and sights in the center of Holetown. **Pros:** Great location, walk to shopping and restaurants, access to pool and activities next door. **Cons:** Tiny beach, rooms are due for an overhaul. ⊠*Hwy. 1, Sunset Crest, St. James* 📞*246/432–2968* 🖷*246/432–1527* ⊕*www.diviresorts.com* 🛏*22 suites* 🖒*In-room: kitchen. In-hotel: tennis court, beachfront, water sports, no elevator, no kids under 16* ⊟*AE, D, DC, MC, V* ⏸*EP.*

VILLA & CONDO COMPLEXES

$$$$ 🖈**Little Good Harbour.** This cluster of modern, spacious 🕭 self-catering cottages with one-, two-, and three-bedroom duplex suites overlooks a narrow strip of beach in the far north of Barbados—just below the picturesque fishing vil-

lage of Six Men's Bay. Built in updated chattel-house style, with gingerbread balconies, this little enclave is a world away from anything remotely touristy. It's a perfect choice for self-sufficient travelers who don't need the hand-holding that resorts provide and relish the chance to experience a delightful slice of Bajan village life nearly at the front door. Some suites are directly on Shermans Bay beach, sharing a building—an old stone fort with louvered shutters on the windows—with the excellent hotel restaurant, The Fish Pot. You can arrange for a personal cook from the restaurant, if you wish, and stocked groceries upon arrival. Most suites are across the road in a grouping of cottages surrounded by palms and facing a pair of pools. All but a few suites have ocean views. While you're mostly on your own in terms of entertainment, the hotel will arrange activities and tours. It also has snorkeling equipment that you can use at the beach. **Pros:** Laid-back atmosphere, good for families, individualized experience. **Cons:** Busy road, tiny beach, remote location. ⊠*Hwy. 1B, Shermans, St. Peter* ☎*246/439–3000* ⊕*www.littlegoodharbourbarbados.com* ↘*21 suites* ₺*In-room: safe, kitchen. In-hotel: restaurant, room service, pools, gym, beachfront, water sports, no elevator, laundry facilities* ⊟*MC, V* ⊗*Closed September* ☜*EP.*

$$$$ 🖼**Port St. Charles.** A luxury residential marina develop-
🕘 ment near historic Speightstown on the northwest tip of Barbados, Port St. Charles is a perfect choice for boating enthusiasts who either arrive on their own yacht or plan to charter one during their stay. Each villa is an intimate private home, decorated by its individual owners, and has its own mega yacht berth on the property's picturesque lagoon. Port St. Charles also serves as a customs and immigration port of entry for boaters. Villas, which have anywhere from one to three bedrooms, surround a man-made lagoon or face the beach. Many have their own private plunge pools. Complimentary water taxis ferry guests around the property during the day—including over to the pool and pool bar at Sunset Island in the middle of the lagoon. Cook for yourself, arrange a private chef, or head over to La Mer, overlooking the lagoon, for a fabulous dinner or Sunday brunch. **Pros:** A boater's dream, well-appointed units with beautiful views, friendly and safe, La Mer is a definite attribute. **Cons:** Not the best spot for little kids. ⊠*Hwy. 1B, Heywoods, St. Peter* ☎*246/419–1000* ⊕*www.portstcharles.com* ↘*31 villas* ₺*In-room: kitchen,*

DVD, dial-up. In-hotel: 2 restaurants, bars, tennis court, pools, gym, beachfront, water sports, no elevator, laundry facilities, public Internet, no-smoking rooms ⊟*AE, MC, V* ⊚*EP.*

$$$$ ⊠**Royal Westmoreland Villas.** Located on a ridge overlooking the sea, this villa community was the first of its kind in Barbados. The villas were built on a 500-acre estate in the mid-1990s in conjunction with the construction of Royal Westmoreland Golf Club's championship golf course. Owners and guests value privacy and exclusivity, so access is granted by appointment only. A Royal Westmoreland villa is, therefore, an ideal base for golfers. Villas have two, three, or four bedrooms and fully equipped kitchens and dining areas. Cassia Heights Resort Club villas are modern, two-bedroom town houses located in the center of the estate near the clubhouse; Forest Hills Resort Club villas are two-bedroom houses with a common pool for the exclusive use of Forest Hills guests. Royal villas, designed by noted architect Ian Morrison, have vaulted ceilings, three large bedrooms with ensuite bathrooms, and enormous sitting rooms with French doors that open to a terrace and—in some cases—a private swimming pool. When they're not golfing or playing tennis, villa guests can laze around the pool, chill at the spa, or head for the beach at the nearby Colony Club to swim in the sea, snorkel, kayak, sail, or simply sunbathe. Also, Folkestone Marine Park is nearby for diving and snorkeling excursions. And while there are dozens of units on the property, only a few are rented to vacationers through Royal Westmoreland. Some owners contract property management services with outside real-estate agencies such as Island Villas. **Pros:** Nirvana for golfers, huge accommodations with every possible convenience, lots of activities and amenities for families, private and safe. **Cons:** Very expensive, not on the beach. ⊠*Hwy. 2A, Westmoreland, St. James* ☎*246/422–4653* ⊕*www.royal-westmoreland.com* ⤳*5 villas* ⌂*In-room: kitchen. In-hotel: 3 restaurants, bars, golf course, tennis courts, pools, gym, spa, no elevators, children's program (ages 4–12), laundry facilities, concierge* ⊟*AE, MC, V* ⊚*EP.*

$$ ⊠**All Seasons Resort–Europa.** Just a few blocks inland from downtown Holetown, Sunset Crest is a cottage community that spreads over 130 acres and was originally developed as an inexpensive holiday village for Canadian vacationers. Many of the cottages are now privately owned. In the middle of the community, All Seasons Resort–Europa is

a grouping of duplex self-catering cottages that surround a large grassy lawn, a pool with three Jacuzzis, a recreation room, and a restaurant and bar. Accommodations are rather simple and priced accordingly. Shuttle service to the beach and shops is free. The resort boasts a huge number of repeat guests, some who have been coming back for 10 or 15 years and who stay for several weeks and even months at a time. They obviously like the friendly atmosphere. **Pros:** Inexpensive, good for long stays, congenial atmosphere, like a holiday camp. **Cons:** Must shuttle to beach and town, rooms are simple but have kitchens and sitting areas. ⊠ *Palm Ave., Sunset Crest, St. James* ☎ *246/432–5046* ⊕ *www.allseasonsresort.bb* ⤍ *48 rooms* ⌂ *In-room: safe, kitchen, Wi-Fi. In-hotel: restaurant, bar, tennis court, pool, no elevator, laundry service, public Internet, public Wi-Fi, no-smoking rooms* ⊟ *MC, V* ⦙◎⦙ *EP.*

PRIVATE VILLAS

$$$$ ▦ **Azzurro at Old Trees Bay.** The west coast of Barbados is alive with condo construction, and Old Trees Bay has a spot-on beachfront location just south of Sandy Lane Hotel. Azzurro is a spacious, two-bedroom Old Trees Bay residence with magnificent water views from the living room, dining room, and master bedroom terraces. The second bedroom has two double beds, so the apartment sleeps four very comfortably. It's fully equipped with all the comforts of home—plus a private plunge pool incorporated into the living room. In addition, the garden area has a communal swimming pool. The staff, which includes a cook and a maid/laundress, works mornings and evenings. **Pros:** Lovely location with beautiful water views, close to shopping and restaurants. **Cons:** Beach can be narrow at certain times of year. ⊠ *Hwy. 1, Paynes Bay, St. James (Altman Real Estate* ⊕ *www.aaaltman.com)* ⤍ *2 bedrooms, 2 baths* ⌂ *safe, dishwasher, VCR, daily maid service, cook, on-site security, pools, beachfront, laundry facilities* ⊟ *AE, MC, V* ⦙◎⦙ *EP.*

$$$$ ▦ **Crystal Springs.** Ideal for a large group or family reunion, ☾ Crystal Springs is a fabulous beachfront estate near Holetown that sleeps 16 people in the main house and several outbuildings. This is one of the few remaining properties that was redesigned by Britain's celebrated theatrical designer Oliver Messel in the 1960s. Elegant murals grace the ceiling of the dining terrace, which opens to the garden and is perfect for alfresco meals. This villa has a separate home theater and a game room with a mini gym.

A private beach cove is excellent for swimming and snorkeling. Rentals include the use of a speedboat equipped for waterskiing; a 32-foot Boston Whaler is available for an additional fee. The staff includes a butler, housekeeper, laundress, gardener, night watchman, cooks, maids, and even a boatman. Children are welcome if accompanied by a nanny. **Pros:** Big enough to host a large group without tripping over each other, every feature and amenity you could imagine, that speedboat—and a boatman, to boot. **Cons:** Nothing—unless you can't afford it. ⊠*The Garden, Holetown, St. James (Bajan Service ⊕www.bajanservices. com)* ⊅*8 bedrooms, 8 baths ⌂dishwasher, DVD, VCR, fully staffed, gym, beachfront, water toys, laundry facilities* ⊟*AE, MC. V* ⦿*EP.*

$$$$ 🔲**Jacaranda.** A family-friendly villa, Jacaranda is located in a residential area that's a short walk from lovely Gibbs Beach. The home is designed around a central atrium with a large and inviting plunge pool. A spacious living room opens to a partially covered sundeck filled with comfortable furniture and loungers, and an outdoor swimming pool. The surrounding gardens create a peaceful retreat and provide privacy. Villa staff includes a cook (who specializes in preparing vegetarian meals), a maid/laundress, and a night watchman. **Pros:** Big sundeck with comfy furniture, children are welcome, vegetarians will love the cook. **Cons:** Not on the beach, watch the kids around that plunge pool. ⊠*Gibbs Glade, Speightstown, St. Peter (Bajan Services ⊕www.bajanservices.com)* ⊅*3 bedrooms, 4 baths ⌂dishwasher, DVD, VCR, Wi-Fi, daily maid service, cook, on-site security, pools, laundry facilities* ⊟*AE, MC, V* ⦿*EP.*

$$$$ 🔲**Turtle Nest.** Location is the drawing card for Turtle Nest. Walk through your private tropical garden and step directly onto the south end of Mullins Beach, one of the best beaches on the west coast. In addition, it's a short walk to the popular Mannie's Suga Suga restaurant and beach bar and all the water toys that are for rent there. The Suga Suga spa, just across the street, is also very inviting. This tastefully furnished beachfront cottage is fully air-conditioned, with fans in each room as well. The living room opens onto a dining veranda with a sweeping view of Mullins Bay. Both bedrooms have sea views, too. The cottage is fully enclosed, and its entrance is controlled by electronic security gates. **Pros:** Right on the beach, lots of action nearby, safe and secure. **Cons:** If you need electronic toys other than a TV, bring your own. ✉*Mullins Beach, Speightstown, St. Peter (Island Villas* ⊕*www.island-villas. com)* ⤵*2 bedrooms, 2 baths* ⚬*dishwasher, ethernet, daily maid service, cook, on-site security, beachfront, laundry facilities* ▱*AE, MC, V* ⍩*EP.*

$$$–$$$$ ⌧**High Constantia Cottage.** Perched on a ridge overlooking Golden Mile Beach, High Constantia Cottage is a delightful Spanish-style villa with two air-conditioned double bedrooms, each with a private bath; and spectacular views of the sea from the living and dining rooms and patio. The hillside location catches every breeze, but each room has a ceiling fan just in case. You can also take a refreshing dip in the pool or soothe yourself in the Jacuzzi. The cook/housekeeper is available mornings through lunch and again in the evening. **Pros:** Private and secluded, lovely views. **Cons:** Not on the beach, only the bedrooms are air-conditioned. ✉*Coleridge Parry Rd., Heywood, St. Peter (Altman Real Estate* ⊕*www.aaaltman.com)* ⤵*2 bedrooms, 2 baths* ⚬*dishwasher, VCR, daily maid service, cook, pool, laundry facilities* ▱*AE, MC, V* ⍩*EP.*

NIGHTLIFE

When the sun goes down, the people come out to "lime" (which may be anything from a "chat-up" to a full-blown "jump-up"). Performances by world-renowned stars and regional groups are major events, and tickets can be hard to come by—but give it a try. Most resorts have nightly entertainment in season, and nightclubs often have live bands for listening and dancing. The busiest bars and dance clubs rage until 3 AM. On Saturday nights some clubs—especially those with live music—charge a cover of about $15.

☾ The **Oistins Fish Fry** is the place to be on weekend evenings,
★ when the south-coast fishing village becomes a convivial outdoor street fair. Barbecued chicken and flying fish are served right from the grill and consumed at roadside picnic tables; servings are huge, and prices are inexpensive—about $5. Drinks, music, and dancing add to the fun.

BAXTER'S ROAD IS SOMETIMES CALLED "THE STREET THAT NEVER SLEEPS." Night owls head for Baxter's Road, in Bridgetown, any night of the week for after-hours fun and food. The strip of rum shops begins to hit its stride at 11 PM, but locals usually show up around 3 AM. Street vendors sell freshly made "Baxter's Road" fried chicken and other snacks all night long, but Enid's is the place to see and be seen.

BARS

Barbados supports the rum industry with more than 1,600 "rum shops," simple bars where men (mostly) congregate to discuss the world (or life in general), drink rum, and eat a "cutter" (sandwich). In more sophisticated establishments you can find world-class rum drinks made with the island's renowned Mount Gay and Cockspur brands—and no shortage of Barbados's own Banks Beer.

The **Boatyard** (⊠*Bay St., Carlisle Bay, Bridgetown, St. Michael* ☎*246/436–2622*) is a popular pub with both a DJ and live bands; from happy hour until the wee hours, the patrons are mostly local and visiting professionals. **Waterfront Cafe** (⊠*The Careenage, Bridgetown, St. Michael* ☎*246/427–0093*) has live jazz in the evening, with a small dance floor for dancing. The picturesque location alongside the wharf is also a draw.

On the south coast, **Bubba's Sports Bar** (⊠*Main Rd., Rockley, Christ Church* ☎*246/435–8731*) offers merrymakers and sports lovers live sports on three 10-foot video screens and a dozen TVs, along with a Bajan à la carte menu and, of course, drinks at the bar. **Jumbie's** (⊠*St. Lawrence Gap, Christ Church* ☎*246/420–7615*) has an open-air party room with either a DJ or live music every night. Happy hours run from 5 PM to 7 PM and again from 10 PM to 1 AM every night and all day Sunday! Obviously, a very happy place to congregate in the evening. **McBride's Pub** (⊠*St. Lawrence Gap, Christ Church* ☎*246/436–6352*) is, as you night have guessed, an Irish pub with Irish beer on tap, pub grub from the kitchen, and Irish music, karaoke, reggae, rock, Latin, or techno music every night. Happy hour(s) run from 11 PM to 1 AM every night.

On the west coast, **Coach House** (⊠*Hwy. 1, Paynes Bay, St. James* ☎*246/432–1163*) has live entertainment nightly and international sports via satellite TV. **Lexy's Piano Bar** (⊠*2nd St., Holetown, St. James* ☎*246/432–5399*) is a cool, trendy club named for owner Alex Santoriello, a Broadway singer and actor who moved to Barbados in early 2007. A changing roster of singer/pianists play singalong standards, classic rock, R&B, and Broadway tunes. International guest artists are featured during the winter season. Most any night, you'll find Santoriello there—playing requests on the piano, singing along, or sitting at the bar having a chat. **Upstairs at Olives** (⊠*2nd St., Holetown, St. James* ☎*246/432–2112*) is a sophisticated watering hole. Enjoy cocktails and conversation seated amid potted palms and cooled by ceiling fans—either before or after dinner downstairs.

DANCE CLUBS

After Dark (⊠*St. Lawrence Gap, Dover, Christ Church* ☎*246/435–6547*) attracts mostly young people with live appearances of reggae, calypso, and *soca* (an upbeat, sexy variation of calypso) headliners such as Krosfyah. **Club Xtreme** (⊠*Main Rd., Worthing, Christ Church* ☎*246/228–2582*) attracts a young crowd on Wednesday, Friday, and Saturday nights for the latest DJ-spun alternative, dance, R&B, reggae, and other party music. The open-air, beach-front **Harbour Lights** (⊠*Upper Bay St., Bridgetown, St. Michael* ☎*246/436–7225*) claims to be the "home of the party animal" and has dancing under the stars most nights to live reggae and soca music. The **Ship Inn** (⊠*St. Lawrence Gap, Dover, Christ Church* ☎*246/435–6961*) is a large, friendly pub with local band music every night for dancing.

THEME NIGHTS

☼ On Wednesday and Friday evenings at the **Plantation Restau-**
★ **rant and Garden Theater** (⊠*St. Lawrence Main Rd., Dover, Christ Church* ☎*246/428–5048*) the Tropical Spectacular calypso cabaret presents "Bajan Roots & Rhythms," a delightful extravaganza that the whole family will enjoy. The show includes steel-band music, fire eating, limbo, and dancing to the reggae, soca, and pop music sounds of popular Barbadian singer John King and the Plantation House Band. The fun begins at 6:30 PM. A Barbadian buffet dinner, unlimited drinks, transportation, and the show cost $75; for the show and drinks only, it's $37.50.

CLOSE UP

Nightspots A-Plenty

St. Lawrence Gap, the narrow waterfront byway with restaurants, bars, and nightclubs one right after another, is where the action is on the south coast. In Holetown, on the west coast, the restaurants and clubs on First and Second streets are giving "the Gap" a run for its money. Along with a half-dozen or so restaurants that offer fare ranging from ribs or pizza to elegant cuisine, a handful of nightspots and night "experiences" have cropped up recently. After-dinner drinks at The Mews or at Lexy's Piano Bar are popular any evening, but on Sunday evenings locals and tourists alike descend on One Love Rum Shop for the karaoke and to Ragamuffin's restaurant, next door, for the after-dinner drag show.

BEACHES

Bajan beaches have fine white sand, and all are open to the public. Most are accessible from the road, so nonguest bathers don't have to pass through hotel properties. When the surf is too high and swimming is dangerous, a red flag will be hoisted on the beach. A yellow flag—or a red flag at half-mast—means swim with caution. Topless sunbathing—on the beach or at the pool—is not allowed anywhere in Barbados by government regulation.

BEACH MASSAGE, LADY? The latest trend among beach vendors is offering massage services—sometimes including what they call reflexology—to sunbathers. While a beach massage sounds refreshing and may even feel good, these people are certainly not trained therapists. At best, you'll get a soothing back or foot rub. Be advised, though, that they use raw aloe vera as their massage oil, which can permanently stain clothing, towels, and chair cushions.

EAST COAST

With long stretches of open beach, crashing ocean surf, rocky cliffs, and verdant hills, the Atlantic (windward) side of Barbados is where Barbadians spend their holidays. But be cautioned: swimming at east-coast beaches is treacherous, even for strong swimmers, and is *not* recommended.

Waves are high, the bottom tends to be rocky, the currents are unpredictable, and the undertow is dangerously strong.

Barclays Park. Serious swimming is unwise at this beach, which follows the coastline in St. Andrew, but you can take a dip, wade, and play in the tide pools. A lovely shaded area with picnic tables is directly across the road. ✉*Ermy Bourne Hwy., north of Bathsheba, St. Andrew.*

★ **Bathsheba/Cattlewash.** Although it's not safe for swimming, the miles of untouched, windswept sand along the East Coast Road in St. Joseph Parish are great for beachcombing and wading. As you approach Bathsheba Soup Bowl, the southernmost stretch just below Tent Bay, the enormous mushroom-like boulders and rolling surf are uniquely impressive. This is also where expert surfers from around the world converge each November for the Independence Classic Surfing Championship. ✉*East Coast Rd., Bathsheba, St. Joseph.*

SOUTH COAST

A young, energetic crowd favors the south-coast beaches, which are broad and breezy, blessed with powdery white sand, and dotted with tall palms. The reef-protected areas with crystal-clear water are safe for swimming and snorkeling. The surf is medium to high, and the waves get bigger and the winds stronger (windsurfers take note) the farther southeast you go.

Accra Beach. This popular beach, also known as Rockley Beach, is next to the Accra Hotel. Look forward to gentle surf and a lifeguard, plenty of nearby restaurants for refreshments, a children's playground, and beach stalls for renting chairs and equipment for snorkeling and other water sports. Parking is available at an on-site lot. ✉*Hwy. 7, Rockley, Christ Church.*

★ **Bottom Bay.** Popular for fashion and travel-industry photo shoots, Bottom Bay is the quintessential Caribbean beach. Surrounded by a coral cliff, studded with a stand of palms, and an endless ocean view, this dreamy enclave is near the southeasternmost tip of the island. Swimming is not recommended, as the waves can be very strong, but it's the picture-perfect place for sunbathing, having a picnic lunch, or simply enjoying the view. Park at the top of the cliff and follow the steps down to the beach. ✉*Dover, St. Philip.*

CLOSE UP

Turtle Time

1

Along Casuarina Beach, which stretches in front of both Almond Casuarina Resort and the aptly named Turtle Beach Resort, mother hawksbill turtles dig a pit in the sand, lay 100 or more eggs, cover the nest with sand, and then return to the sea. The eggs, which look just like Ping-Pong balls, are usually deposited between May and November and take about 60 days to hatch. If you happen to be strolling along the beach at the time they emerge, you'll see a mass of newborn turtles scrambling out of the sand and making a dash (at turtle speed, of course) for the sea. While the journey takes only a few minutes, this can be a very dangerous time for the tiny turtles. They are easy prey for gulls and large crabs. Meantime, the folks involved in the Barbados Sea Turtle Project (246/230–0142) at the University of the West Indies are working hard to protect and conserve the marine turtle populations in Barbados through educational workshops, tagging programs, and other research efforts.

Carlisle Bay. Adjacent to the Hilton Barbados and Grand Barbados hotels just south of Bridgetown, this broad half-circle of white sand is one of the island's best beaches—but it can become crowded on weekends and holidays. Park at Harbour Lights or at the Boatyard Bar and Bayshore Complex, both on Bay Street, where you can also rent umbrellas and beach chairs and buy refreshments. ⊠*Aquatic Gap, Needham's Point, St. Michael.*

Casuarina Beach. Stretched in front of the Almond Casuarina Resort, where St. Lawrence Gap meets the Maxwell Coast Road, this broad strand of powdery white sand is great for both sunbathing and strolling. The sea ranges from turquoise to azure; the surf from low to medium. Find public access and parking on Maxwell Coast Road, near the Bougainvillea Resort. ⊠*Maxwell Coast Rd., Dover, Christ Church.*

★ **Crane Beach.** An exquisite crescent of pink sand on the southeast coast, Crane Beach is protected by steep cliffs on the land side and a reef on the water side. As attractive as this location is now, it was named not for the elegant long-legged wading birds but for the crane used for hauling and loading cargo when this area was a busy port. Crane Beach usually has a steady breeze and lightly rolling surf that is great for bodysurfing. A lifeguard is on duty. Changing rooms are available at the Crane resort for a small fee (which you can apply toward drinks or a meal at the restaurant). Access is through the hotel and down to the beach via either a cliff-side elevator or 98 steps. ✉*Crane Bay, St. Philip.*

★ **Miami Beach.** Also called Enterprise Beach, this isolated spot on Enterprise Coast Road, just east of Oistins, is a picturesque slice of pure white sand with cliffs on either side and crystal-clear water. You can find a palm-shaded parking area, snack carts, and chair rentals. Bring a picnic or have lunch across the road at Café Luna in Little Arches Hotel. ✉*Enterprise Beach Rd., Enterprise, Christ Church.*

Sandy Beach. Next to the Sandy Bay Beach Resort, this beach has shallow, calm waters and a picturesque lagoon, making it an ideal location for families with small kids. Park right on the main road. You can rent beach chairs and umbrellas, and plenty of places nearby sell food and drinks. ✉*Hwy. 7, Worthing, Christ Church.*

Silver Sands–Silver Rock Beach. Nestled between South Point, the southernmost tip of the island, and Inch Marlowe Point, Silver Sands–Silver Rock is a beautiful strand of white sand that always has a stiff breeze. That makes this beach the best in Barbados for intermediate and advanced windsurfers and, more recently, kite surfers. ✉*Off Hwy. 7, Christ Church.*

WEST COAST

Gentle Caribbean waves lap the west coast, and its stunning coves and sandy beaches are shaded by leafy mahogany trees. The water is perfect for swimming and water sports. An almost unbroken chain of beaches runs between Bridgetown and Speightstown. Elegant homes and luxury hotels face much of the beachfront property in this area, dubbed Barbados's "Platinum Coast."

West-coast beaches are considerably smaller and narrower than those on the south coast. Also, prolonged stormy weather in September and October may cause sand erosion, temporarily making the beach even narrower. Even so, west-coast beaches are seldom crowded. Vendors stroll by, selling handmade baskets, hats, dolls, jewelry, even original watercolors; owners of private boats offer waterskiing, parasailing, and snorkeling excursions. There are no concession stands, but hotels and beachside restaurants welcome nonguests for terrace lunches (wear a cover-up), and you can buy picnic items at supermarkets in Holetown.

Brighton Beach. Calm as a lake, this is where you can find locals taking a quick dip on hot days. Just north of Bridgetown, Brighton Beach is also home to the Malibu Beach Club. ⊠*Spring Garden Hwy., Brighton, St. Michael.*

★ **Mullins Beach.** This lovely beach just south of Speightstown is a perfect place to spend the day. The water is safe for swimming and snorkeling, there's easy parking on the main road, and Mannie's Suga Suga Restaurant serves snacks, meals, and drinks—and rents chairs and umbrellas. ⊠*Hwy. 1, Mullins Bay, St. Peter.*

Paynes Bay. The stretch of beach just south of Sandy Lane is lined with luxury hotels. It's a very pretty area, with plenty of beach to go around and good snorkeling. Public access is available at several locations along Highway 1; parking is limited. Grab liquid refreshments and a bite to eat at Bomba's Beach Bar. ⊠*Hwy. 1, Paynes Bay, St. James.*

SPORTS & THE OUTDOORS

Cricket, football (soccer), polo, and rugby are extremely popular sports in Barbados among participants and spectators alike, with local, regional, and international matches held throughout the year. Contact the Barbados Tourism Authority or check local newspapers for information about schedules and tickets.

DIVING & SNORKELING

More than two dozen dive sites lie along the west coast between Maycocks Bay and Bridgetown and off the south coast as far as St. Lawrence Gap. Certified divers can explore flat coral reefs and see sea fans, huge barrel sponges, and more than 50 varieties of fish. Nine sunken wrecks are dived regularly, and at least 10 more are accessible to experts. Underwater visibility is generally 80 to 90 feet. The calm waters along the west coast are also ideal for snorkeling. The marine reserve, a stretch of protected reef

Beware the Dreaded Manchineel Tree

Large, leafy manchineel trees grow along many of the west-coast beaches. While they look like perfect shade trees, just touching a leaf or the bark can cause nasty blisters. And don't seek refuge under the tree during a rain shower, as even drips from its leaves can affect sensitive skin. The fruit of the tree, which looks like a tiny green apple, is toxic. Most of the manchineels are marked with signs or with red bands painted on the trunk. Why not just cut them all down? Their root systems are extremely important for preventing beach erosion.

between Sandy Lane and the Colony Club, contains beautiful coral formations accessible from the beach.

On the west coast, **Bell Buoy** is a large, dome-shaped reef where huge brown coral-tree forests and schools of fish delight all categories of divers at depths ranging from 20 to 60 feet. At **Dottins Reef,** off Holetown, you can see schooling fish, barracudas, and turtles at depths of 40 to 60 feet. **Maycocks Bay,** on the northwest coast, is a particularly enticing site; large coral reefs are separated by corridors of white sand, and visibility is often 100 feet or more. The 165-foot freighter *Pamir* lies in 60 feet of water off Six Men's Bay; it's still intact, and you can peer through its portholes and view dozens of varieties of tropical fish. **Silver Bank** is a healthy coral reef with beautiful fish and sea fans; you may get a glimpse of the *Atlantis* submarine at 60 to 80 feet. Not to be missed is the *Stavronikita,* a scuttled Greek freighter at about 135 feet; hundreds of butterfly fish hang out around its mast, and the thin rays of sunlight filtering down through the water make fully exploring the huge ship a wonderfully eerie experience.

Farther south, **Carlisle Bay** is a natural harbor and marine park just below Bridgetown. Here you can retrieve empty bottles thrown overboard by generations of sailors and see cannons and cannonballs, anchors, and six unique shipwrecks lying in 25 to 60 feet of water, all close enough to visit on the same dive (*Berwyn, Fox, CTrek, Eilon,* the barge *Cornwallis,* and the island's newest wreck, *Bajan Queen,* a cruise vessel that sank in 2002).

Dive shops provide a two-hour beginner's "resort" course ($70 to $75) followed by a shallow dive, or a weeklong certification course (about $350). Once you're certified, a one-tank dive runs about $50 to $55; a two-tank dive is $70 to $80. All equipment is supplied, and you can purchase multi-dive packages. Gear for snorkeling is available (free or for a small rental fee) from most hotels. Snorkelers can usually accompany dive trips for $20 for a one- or two-hour trip. Most dive shops have relationships with several hotels and offer special dive packages, including transportation, to hotel guests.

On the west coast, **Dive Barbados** (✉*Mount Standfast, St. James* ☎*246/422–3133* ⊕*www.divebarbados.net*), on the beach next to the Lone Star Hotel, offers all levels of PADI instruction, two or three reef and wreck dives daily for up to six divers each time, snorkeling with hawksbill turtles just offshore, as well as underwater camera rental and free transportation.

On the south coast, the **Dive Shop, Ltd.** (✉*Bay St., Aquatic Gap, St. Michael* ☎*246/426–9947, 888/898–3483 in U.S., 888/575–3483 in Canada* ⊕*www.divebds.com*), the island's oldest dive shop, offers daily reef and wreck dives, plus beginner classes, certification courses, and underwater photography instruction. Underwater cameras are available for rent.

Hightide Water Sports (✉*Coral Reef Club, Holetown, St. James* ☎*246/432–0931 or 800/513–5761* ⊕*www.dive hightide.com*) offers three dive trips—one- and two-tank dives and night reef/wreck/drift dives—daily for up to eight divers, along with PADI instruction, equipment rental, and free transportation.

FISHING

Fishing is a year-round activity in Barbados, but its prime time is January through April, when game fish are in season. Whether you're a serious deep-sea fisher looking for marlin, sailfish, tuna, and other billfish or you prefer angling in calm coastal waters where wahoo, barracuda, and other small fish reside, you can choose from a variety of half- or full-day charter trips departing from the Careenage in Bridgetown. Expect to pay $100 per person for a shared charter; for a private charter, expect to pay $400

Sports Legend: Sir Garfield Sobers

Cricket is more than a national pastime in Barbados. It's a passion. And no one is more revered than Sir Garfield Sobers, the greatest sportsman ever to come from Barbados and globally acknowledged as the greatest all-round cricketer the game has ever seen. Sobers played his first test match in 1953 at the age of 17 and continually set and broke records until his last test match in 1973. He was an equally accomplished batsman and bowler. He was knighted by Queen Elizabeth II in 1974 for his contributions to the sport and honored as a national hero of Barbados in 1999.

per boat for a four-hour half-day or $750 for an eight-hour full-day charter.

Billfisher II (☎246/431–0741), a 40-foot Pacemaker, accommodates up to six passengers with three fishing chairs and five rods. Captain Winston ("The Colonel") White has been fishing these waters since 1975. His full-day charters include a full lunch and guaranteed fish (or a 25% refund); all trips include drinks and transportation to and from the boat.

Blue Jay (☎246/429–2326 ⊕www.bluemarlinbarbados. com) is a spacious, fully equipped, 45-foot Sport Fisherman with a crew that knows the water's denizens—blue marlin, sailfish, barracuda, and kingfish. Four to six people can be accommodated—it's the only charter boat on the island with four chairs. Most fishing is done by trolling. Drinks, snacks, bait, tackle, and transfers are provided.

Cannon II (☎246/424–6107), a 42-foot Hatteras Sport Fisherman, has three chairs and five rods and accommodates six passengers; drinks and snacks are complimentary, and lunch is served on full-day charters.

GOLF

Barbadians love golf, and golfers love Barbados. In addition to the courses listed below, Almond Beach Village has a 9-hole, par-3 executive course open only to guests. **Barbados Golf Club** (⊠*Hwy. 7, Durants, Christ Church* ☎*246/428–8463* ⊕*www.barbadosgolfclub.com*), the first public golf course on Barbados, is an 18-hole championship course (6,805 yards, par 72) redesigned in 2000 by golf course architect Ron Kirby. Greens fees are $135 for 18 holes, plus a $20 per-person cart fee. Unlimited three-day and seven-day golf passes are available. Several hotels offer preferential tee-time reservations and reduced rates. Club and shoe rentals are available.

★ Fodor'sChoice At the prestigious **Country Club at Sandy Lane** (⊠*Hwy. 1, Paynes Bay, St. James* ☎*246/444–2500* ⊕*www. sandylane.com/golf*), golfers can play on the Old Nine or on either of two 18-hole championship courses: the Tom Fazio–designed Country Club Course or the spectacular Green Monkey Course, which opened in October 2004 and is reserved for hotel guests and club members only. Golfers have complimentary use of the club's driving range. The Country Club Restaurant and Bar, which overlooks the 18th hole, is open to the public. Greens fees in high season are $150 for 9 holes ($130 for hotel guests) or $235 for 18 holes ($200 for hotel guests). Golf carts, caddies, or trolleys are available for hire, as well as clubs and shoes. Carts are equipped with GPS, which alerts you to upcoming traps and hazards, provides tips on how to play the hole, and allows you to order refreshments!

Rockley Golf & Country Club (⊠*Golf Club Rd., Worthing, Christ Church* ☎*246/435–7873* ⊕*www.rockleygolfclub. com*), on the southeast coast, has a challenging 9-hole course (2,800 yards, par 35) that can be played as 18 from varying tee positions. Club and cart rentals are available. Greens fees are $96 for 18 holes and $74 for 9 holes.

★ The **Royal Westmoreland Golf Club** (⊠*Westmoreland, St. James* ☎*246/422–4653* ⊕*www.royal-westmoreland.com*) has a world-class Robert Trent Jones, Jr.–designed, 18-hole championship course (6,870 yards, par 72) that meanders through the 500-acre property, formerly the Westmoreland Sugar Estate. This challenging course is primarily for villa renters, with a few mid-morning tee times for visitors subject to availability; greens fees for villa renters are $200 for 18 holes, $100 for 9 holes; for visitors, $250 for 18 holes.

Greens fees include use of an electric cart (required); club rental is available.

HIKING

Hilly but not mountainous, the northern interior and the east coast are ideal for hiking. The **Arbib Heritage & Nature Trail** (✉*Speightstown, St. Peter* ☎246/426–2421), maintained by the Barbados National Trust, is actually two trails—one offers a rigorous hike through gullies and plantations to old ruins and remote north-country areas; the other is a shorter, easier walk through Speightstown's side streets, past chattel houses and an ancient church. Guided hikes take place on Wednesday, Thursday, and Saturday at 9 AM (book by 3 PM the day before) and cost $7.50.

The **Barbados National Trust** (✉*Wildey House, Wildey, St. Michael* ☎246/426–2421 ⊕*www.hikebarbados.com*) sponsors free walks, called **Hike Barbados,** year-round on Sunday from 6 AM to about 9 AM and from 3:30 PM to 6 PM; once a month, a moonlight hike substitutes for the afternoon hike and begins at 5:30 PM (bring a flashlight). Experienced guides group you with others of similar levels of ability. Stop & Stare hikes go 5 to 6 mi (8 to 10 km); Here & There, 8 to 10 mi (13 to 16 km); and Grin & Bear, 12 to 14 mi (19 to 23 km). Wear loose clothes, sensible shoes, sunscreen, and a hat, and bring your camera and a bottle of water. Routes and locations change, but each hike is a loop, finishing in the same spot where it began. Check local newspapers, call the Trust, or check online for the scheduled meeting place on a particular Sunday.

HORSE RACING

Horse racing is administered by the **Barbados Turf Club** (☎246/426–3980 ⊕*www.barbadosturfclub.com*) and races take place on alternate Saturdays throughout the year at the Garrison Savannah, a 6-furlong grass oval in Christ Church, about 3 mi (5 km) south of Bridgetown. The important races are the Sandy Lane Barbados Gold Cup, held in late February or early March, and the United Insurance Barbados Derby Day in August. Post time is 1:30 PM. General admission is $5 for grandstand seats and $10.00 for the Club House. (Prices are double on Gold Cup day.)

SEA EXCURSIONS

Mini-submarine voyages are enormously popular with families and those who enjoy watching fish but who don't wish to snorkel or dive. Party boats depart from Bridgetown's Deep Water Harbour for sightseeing and snorkeling or romantic sunset cruises. Prices are $60 to $80 per person for daytime cruises and $35 to $65 for three-hour sunset cruises, depending on the type of refreshments and entertainment included; transportation to and from the dock is provided. For an excursion that may be less splashy in terms of a party atmosphere—but definitely splashier in terms of the actual experience—turtle tours allow participants to feed and swim with a resident group of hawksbill and leatherback sea turtles.

The 48-passenger **Atlantis III** (⊠*Shallow Draught, Bridgetown* ☎*246/436–8929* ⊕*www.atlantisadventures. com*) turns the Caribbean into a giant aquarium. The 45-minute trip aboard the 50-foot submarine takes you to wrecks and reefs as deep as 150 feet.

Four- and five-hour daytime cruises along the west coast on the 100-foot MV **Harbour Master** (☎*246/430–0900* ⊕*www. tallshipscruises.com*) stop in Holetown and land at beaches along the way; evening cruises are shorter but add a buffet dinner and entertainment. Day or night you can view the briny deep from the ship's onboard 34-seat semisubmersible.

A daytime cruise on the 57-foot catamaran **Heatwave** (☎*246/429–9283*) includes stops along the coast for swimming and snorkeling and a barbecue lunch. The sunset cruise includes dinner.

The red-sail **Jolly Roger** (☎*246/228–8142*) "pirate" ship runs four-hour lunch-and-snorkeling sails along the south and west coasts. Be prepared for a rather raucous time, with rope swinging, plank walking, and other games—and plenty of calypso music and complimentary drinks. The sunset cruise, also four hours, includes a buffet dinner, drinks, and entertainment.

The 44-foot CSY sailing yacht **Limbo Lady** (☎*246/420–5418*) sails along the captivating west coast, stopping for a swim, snorkeling, and a Bajan buffet lunch on board. Sunset cruises are another option.

CLOSE UP

Sea Urchin Alert

Black spiny sea urchins lurk in the sand on the shallow sea bottom and near reefs. Should you step on one, its sharp venon-filled spines will cause a painful wound. They've even been known to pierce wet suits, so divers should be careful when brushing up against submerged rock walls. Getting several stings at once can cause muscle spasms and breathing difficulties for some people, so victims need to get help immediately. Clean the wound before carefully removing the stinger(s). Some say ammonia (aka, urine) is the best remedy. We say it's lime and alcohol. So should the worst happen, find the nearest bartender.

The 53-foot catamaran **Tiami** (☎246/430–0900 ⊕*www. tallshipscruises.com*) offers a luncheon cruise to a secluded bay or a romantic sunset and moonlight cruise with special catering and live music.

☽ **Just Breezing Water Sports** (☎246/262–7960 ⊕*www.just breezingwatersports.com*), based in Holetown, has a 32-foot glass-bottom boat from which guests can view, snorkel, and swim with the turtles. The cruise is particularly fun for families with young children. Two trips depart daily, at 10 AM and 2 PM. They cover about 6 mi of coastline along the west coast, cost $45 per adult, and last two hours each. Hotel transportation, cool drinks, snorkels, and masks are all included.

SURFING

The best surfing is on the east coast, at Bathsheba Soup Bowl, but the water on the windward side of the island is safe only for the most experienced swimmers. Surfers also congregate at Surfer's Point, at the southern tip of Barbados near Inch Marlow, where the Atlantic Ocean meets the Caribbean Sea. **Zed's Surfing Adventures** (⊠*Surfer's Point, Inch Marlow, Christ Church* ☎246/428–7873 ⊕*www. barbadossurf.com*) rents surfboards, offers lessons, and offers surf tours—which include equipment, a guide, and transportation to surf breaks appropriate for your experience.

Dread or Dead Surf Shop (⌂*Hastings Main Rd., Hastings, Christ Church* ☎*246/228–4785* ⊕*www.dreadordead.com*) promises to get beginners from "zero to standing up and surfing" in a single afternoon. The four-hour course—"or until you stand up or give up"—costs $75 per person and includes a board, wax, a rash guard (if necessary), a ride to and from the surf break, and an instructor. Intermediate or experienced surfers can get all the equipment and the instructor for a full day of surfing for $150.

The Independence Classic Surfing Championship (an international competition) is held at Bathsheba Soup Bowl every November—when the surf is at its peak. For information, contact the **Barbados Surfing Association** (☎*246/228–5117* ⊕*www.bsasurf.com*).

WINDSURFING

Barbados is on the World Cup Windsurfing Circuit and is one of the prime locations in the world for windsurfing. Winds are strongest November through April at the island's southern tip, at Silver Sand–Silver Rock Beach, which is where the Barbados Windsurfing Championships are held in mid-January. Use of boards and equipment is often among the amenities included at larger hotels; equipment can usually be rented by nonguests.

More experienced windsurfers congregate at **Silver Rock Windsurfing Club** (⌂*Silver Sands–Silver Rock Beach, Christ Church* ☎*246/428–2866*), where the surf ranges from 3 to 15 feet and provides an exhilarating windsurfing experience.

SHOPPING

Shoppers will find plenty of satisfaction in Barbados. There's something for everyone, whether you're interested in duty-free perfumes, china, and jewelry or are more enticed by handmade crafts made by local artisans—pottery, wood carvings, textiles, watercolors, sculptures, and more. And then there's rum. You'll definitely want to bring home a bottle. Maybe two.

AREAS & MALLS

Bridgetown's **Broad Street** is the primary downtown shopping area. **DaCostas Mall**, in the historic Colonnade Building on Broad Street, has more than 25 shops that sell everything from Piaget to postcards; across the street, **Mall 34** has 22 shops where you can buy duty-free goods, souvenirs, and snacks. At the **Cruise Ship Terminal** shopping arcade, passengers can buy both duty-free goods and Barbadian-made crafts at more than 30 boutiques and a dozen vendor carts and stalls. **Pelican Craft Centre** is a cluster of workshops halfway between the Cruise Ship Terminal and downtown Bridgetown, where craftspeople create and sell locally made items.

BRIDGETOWN SHOPPING SHUTTLE. A free Bridgetown shuttle serves hotels on the south and west coasts, so guests can visit downtown shops, see the sites, and perhaps have lunch. The shuttle operates Monday through Saturday, departing from the hotels at 9:30 and 11 AM and returning from Bridgetown at 1:30 and 3 PM. Reserve your seat with your hotel concierge a day ahead.

Holetown and St. Lawrence Gap each have a **Chattel House Village**, a cluster of brightly colored shops selling local products, fashions, beachwear, and souvenirs. Also in Holetown, **Sunset Crest Mall** has two branches of the Cave Shepherd department store, a bank, a pharmacy, and several small shops; at **West Coast Mall** you can buy duty-free goods, island wear, and groceries. In Rockley, Christ Church, **Quayside Shopping Center** houses a small group of boutiques, restaurants, and services.

DEPARTMENT STORES

Cave Shepherd (⊠*Broad St., Bridgetown, St. Michael* ☎*246/431–2121*) offers a wide selection of clothing and luxury goods; branch stores are in Holetown, at the airport, and at the Cruise Ship Terminal.

Harrison's (⊠*Broad St., Bridgetown, St. Michael* ☎*246/431–5500*) has 11 locations—including its two large stores on Broad Street and one each at the airport and the Cruise Ship Terminal—offering luxury name-brand goods from the fashion corners of the world.

SPECIALTY STORES

ANTIQUES

Although many of the private homes, great houses, and museums in Barbados are filled with priceless antiques, you'll find few for sale—mainly British antiques and some local pieces, particularly mahogany furniture. Look especially for planters' chairs and the classic Barbadian rocking chair, as well as old prints and paintings. **Greenwich House Antiques** (⊠*Greenwich Village, Trents Hill, St. James* ☎*246/432–1169*) fills an entire plantation house with vintage Barbadian mahogany furniture, Art Deco pieces, crystal, silver, china, books, and pictures; it's open daily from 10:30 to 5:30.

ART

Perhaps one of the most long-lasting souvenirs to bring home from Barbados is a piece of authentic Caribbean art. The colorful flowers, quaint villages, mesmerizing seascapes, and fascinating cultural experiences and activities that are endemic to the region and familiar to visitors have been translated by local artists onto canvas and into photographs, sculpture, and other media. Gift shops and even some restaurants display local artwork for sale, but the broadest array of artwork will be found in an art gallery. **Gallery of Caribbean Art** (⊠*Northern Business Centre, Queen St., Speightstown, St. Peter* ☎*246/419–0585*) is committed to promoting Caribbean art from Cuba to Curaçao, including a number of pieces by Barbadian artists. A branch gallery is located at the Hilton Barbados Hotel, Needham's Point.

On the Wall Art Gallery (⊠*#2, Edgehill Heights, St. Thomas* ☎*246/425–0223*), next door to Earthworks Pottery, has an array of original paintings by Barbadian artists, along with arts and crafts products. Additional galleries are located in dedicated space at The Tides restaurant on the west coast and Champers restaurant on the south coast.

CLOTHING

Dingolay (⊠*Bay St., Bridgetown, St. Michael* ☎*246/436–2157* ⊠*Hwy. 1, Holetown, St. James* ☎*246/432–8709*) sells tropical clothing designed and made in Barbados for ladies and girls as well as shoes, handbags, and accessories from around the world.

At **Kosmic Vibes Designs** (⊠*Spirit Bond Mall #5, Bridgetown, St. Michael* ☎246/268–9732) designer Karen Brathwaite creates linen dresses, pants, and shirts (for women and men) that are made on-site and hand-painted with tropical motifs, tie-dyed in subtle colorations (definitely not your Grateful Dead look), or simply constructed in high style. Hand-beaded jewelry, macramé belts and bags, and other accessories are also designed by Brathwaite and produced in the shop. Custom orders are welcome and will be fulfilled in two weeks or less.

Check out the colorful T-shirts from **Irie Blue** (⊠*Lower Broad St., Bridgetown, St. Michael* ☎246/426–8464)

DUTY-FREE GOODS

Duty-free luxury goods—china, crystal, cameras, porcelain, leather items, electronics, jewelry, perfume, and clothing—are found in Bridgetown's Broad Street department stores and their branches, at the Cruise Ship Terminal shops (for passengers only), and in the departure lounge shops at Grantley Adams International Airport. Prices are often 30% to 40% less than at home. To buy goods at duty-free prices, you must produce your passport, immigration form, or driver's license, along with departure information (e.g., flight number and date) at the time of purchase—or you can have your purchases delivered free to the airport or harbor for pickup. Duty-free alcohol, tobacco products, and some electronic equipment *must* be delivered to you at the airport or harbor.

Little Switzerland (⊠*DaCostas Mall, Broad St., Bridgetown, St. Michael* ☎246/431–0030) is the anchor shop at DaCostas Mall and has branches at the Cruise Ship Terminal and at West Coast Mall, Sunset Crest, in Holetown. Here you can find perfume, jewelry, cameras, audio equipment, Swarovski and Waterford crystal, and Wedgwood china.

The **Royal Shop** (⊠*32 Broad St., Bridgetown* ☎246/429–7072) carries fine watches and jewelry fashioned in Italian gold, Caribbean silver, diamonds, and other gems.

HANDICRAFTS

Typical crafts include pottery, shell and glass art, wood carvings, handmade dolls, watercolors, and other artwork (both originals and prints). **Best of Barbados** (⊠*Worthing, Christ Church* ☎246/421–6900), was the brainchild of architect Jimmy Walker as a place to showcase the works of his artist wife. Now with seven locations, the shops offer products that range from Jill Walker framable prints and Jill Walker-designed housewares and textiles to arts and crafts in both "native" style and modern designs. Everything is made or designed on Barbados.

★ Fodor'sChoice **Earthworks Pottery** (✉*No. 2, Edgehill Heights, St. Thomas* ☎*246/425–0223*) is a family-owned and -operated pottery where you can purchase anything from a dish or knickknack to a complete dinner service or one-of-a-kind art piece. You can find the characteristically blue or green pottery decorating hotel rooms for sale in gift shops throughout the island, but the biggest selection (including some "seconds") is at Earthworks, where you also can watch the potters work.

Island Crafts (✉*5 Pelican Craft Centre, Bridgetown, St. Michael* ☎*246/426–4391*) offers locally made pottery, wood carvings, straw items, glass art, batik, and wire sculptures. Additional shops are at Harrison's Cave, the airport courtyard, and the airport departure lounge.

Pelican Craft Centre (✉*Princess Alice Hwy., Bridgetown, St. Michael* ☎*246/427–5350*) is a cluster of workshops halfway between the Cruise Ship Terminal and downtown Bridgetown where craftspeople create and sell locally made leather goods, batik, basketry, carvings, jewelry, glass art, paintings, pottery, and other items. It's open weekdays 9 AM to 5 PM and Saturday 9AM to 2 PM, with extended hours during holidays or cruise-ship arrivals.

Port O Trade (✉*Broad St., Bridgetown, St. Michael* ☎*246/429–2285*), next to Cave Shepherd, is full of colorful jewelry, linens, pottery, dinnerware, beadwork, carvings, clothing, and other handcrafted products—both practical and whimsical—that were all made in South Africa. You're bound to find something here that catches your eye.

☺ **Red Clay Pottery and Fairfield Gallery** (✉*Fairfield House, Fairfield Cross Rd., Fairfield, St. Michael* ☎*246/424–3800*) has been operated by potter Denis Bell all his life, "save a little time spent doing some engineering and raising a family." Visitors are welcome to watch the potters at work in the studio, which is in an old sugar-boiling house; and, in the adjacent shop, purchase plates, platters, bowls, place settings, and fine decorative items designed by Bell's daughter Maggie.

In the chattel houses at **Tyrol Cot Heritage Village** (✉*Co-drington Hill, St. Michael* ☎*246/424–2074*) you can watch local artisans make hand-painted figurines, straw baskets, clothing, paintings, and pottery—and, of course, buy their wares.

St. Lucia

By Jane E.
Zarem

ALL EYES FOCUS ON ST. LUCIA FOR 10 DAYS EACH MAY, when the St. Lucia Jazz Festival welcomes renowned international musicians who perform for enthusiastic fans at Pigeon Island National Park and other island venues. St. Lucians themselves love jazz—and, of course, the beat of Caribbean music resonates through their very souls. The irony is that if you randomly ask 10 St. Lucians to name their favorite kind of music, most would say "country." One possible explanation is that many young St. Lucian men take short-term jobs overseas, cutting sugarcane in Florida and working on farms elsewhere in the South, where they inevitably hear country music. And while the work experience isn't something most remember fondly, the music apparently is.

The pirate François Le Clerc, nicknamed Jambe de Bois (Wooden Leg) for obvious reasons, was the first European "settler" in St. Lucia (pronounced *loo*-sha). In the late 16th century, Le Clerc holed up on Pigeon Island, just off the island's northernmost point, and used it as a staging ground for attacking passing ships. Now Pigeon Island is a national park, a playground for locals and visitors alike, and, as mentioned, the most popular performance venue for the annual St. Lucia Jazz Festival. Several years ago a man-made causeway attached Pigeon Island to the mainland; today Sandals Grande St. Lucian Spa and Beach Resort, one of the largest resorts in St. Lucia, and The Landings, a luxury villa community that opened in 2008, are sprawled along that causeway.

St. Lucia has evolved over the years into one of the most popular vacation destinations in the Caribbean—particularly for honeymooners and other romantics, who are enticed by the island's natural beauty, its many splendid resorts and friendly inns, and its welcoming atmosphere. And the evolution continues. Renewed emphasis from both the public and private sectors is being placed on enhancing the island's tourism industry and supporting new and revamped lodgings, activities, and attractions. That's great news for visitors, who already appear delighted with St. Lucia.

Located between Martinique and St. Vincent, and 100 mi (160 km) due west of Barbados, the 27-mi by 14-mi (43½-km by 22½-km) island of St. Lucia occupies a prime position in the Caribbean. Its striking natural beauty easily earns it the moniker "Helen of the West Indies." The capi-

ST. LUCIA TOP 5

■ Magnificent, lush scenery, particularly in the South and around Soufrière, makes St. Lucia one of the Caribbean's most beautiful islands.

■ A popular honeymoon spot, St. Lucia is filled with romantic retreats.

■ Sybaritic lodging options include an all-inclusive spa resort with daily pampering on the menu, a posh dive resort sandwiched between a mountain and the beach, and two picturesque resorts optimally positioned right between the Pitons.

■ The St. Lucia Jazz Festival draws performers and listeners from all over the world.

■ The friendly St. Lucians love sharing their island and their cultural heritage with visitors.

tal city of Castries and nearby villages in the northwest are home to 40% of the population and, along with Rodney Bay farther north and Marigot Bay just south of the capital, are the destinations of most vacationers. In the central and southern parts of the island, dense rain forest, jungle-covered mountains, and vast banana plantations dominate the landscape. A torturously winding road follows most of the coastline, bisecting small villages, cutting through mountains and thick forests, and passing through fertile valleys. On the southwest coast, Petit Piton and Gros Piton, the island's unusual twin peaks that rise out of the sea to more than 2,600 feet, are familiar navigational landmarks for sailors and aviators alike. Divers are attracted to the reefs found just north of Soufrière, the quaint city that was the capital during French colonial times. Most of the natural tourist attractions are in this area. "If you haven't been to Soufrière," St. Lucians will tell you, "you haven't been to St. Lucia."

Like most of its Caribbean neighbors, St. Lucia was first inhabited by the Arawaks and then the Carib Indians. British settlers attempted to colonize the island twice in the early 1600s, but it wasn't until 1651, after the French West India Company secured the island from the Caribs, that Europeans gained a foothold. For 150 years the French and the British frequently battled for possession of the island, with a dizzying 14 changes in power before the British finally took possession in 1814. The Europeans established sugar plantations, using slaves from West Africa to work the fields. By 1838, when the slaves were emancipated, more than 90% of the population was of African descent—which is also the approximate proportion of today's 170,000 St. Lucians. Indentured East Indian laborers were brought over in 1882 to help bail out the sugar industry, which collapsed when slavery was abolished and all but died in the 1960s, when bananas became the major crop.

On February 22, 1979, St. Lucia became an independent state within the British Commonwealth of Nations, with a resident governor-general appointed by the Queen. Still, the island appears to have retained more relics of French influence—notably the patois, cuisine, village names, and surnames—than that of the British. Most likely, that's because the British contribution primarily involved the English language, the educational and legal systems, and the political structure, while the French culture historically had more impact on the arts—music, dance, and all that jazz!

EXPLORING ST. LUCIA

Except for a small area in the extreme northeast, one main route circles all of St. Lucia. The road snakes along the coast, cuts across mountains, makes hairpin turns and sheer drops, and reaches dizzying heights. It takes at least four hours to drive the whole loop. Even at a leisurely pace with frequent sightseeing stops, the curvy roads make it a tiring drive in a single outing.

The West Coast Road between Castries and Soufrière (a 1½- to 2-hour journey) has steep hills and sharp turns, but it's well marked and incredibly scenic. South of Castries, the road tunnels through Morne Fortune, skirts the island's largest banana plantation (more than 127 varieties of bananas, called "figs" in this part of the Caribbean, are grown on the island), and passes through tiny fishing villages. Just north of Soufrière is the island's fruit basket, where most of the mangoes, breadfruit, tomatoes, limes, and oranges are grown. In the mountainous region that forms a backdrop for Soufrière, you will notice 3,118-foot Mount Gimie (pronounced Jimmy), St. Lucia's highest peak. As you approach Soufrière, you'll also have spectacular views of the Pitons.

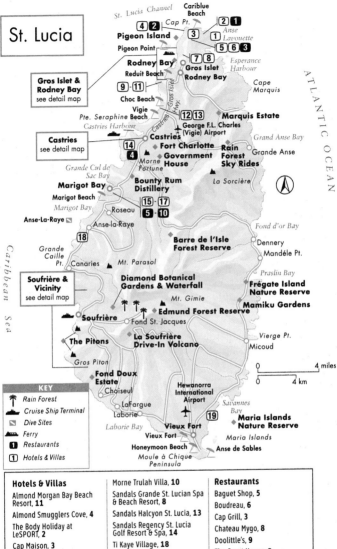

St. Lucia

St. Lucia Channel

Cariblue Beach

Cap Pt.

② ①
④ ②
Pigeon Island
③
Anse Lavouette
① ⑤ ⑥ ③

Pigeon Point

Gros Islet & Rodney Bay
see detail map

Rodney Bay
Reduit Beach
⑦ ⑧
Esperance Harbour

Gros Islet Rodney Bay

⑨ ⑪

Cape Marquis

Choc Beach

Vigie
Pte. Seraphine Beach
⑫ ⑬
Marquis Estate

Castries Harbour

Castries
see detail map

George F.L. Charles (Vigie) Airport

⑭
④

✝ **Castries**
Fort Charlotte
Government House
Morne Fortune

Rain Forest Sky Rides

Grand Anse Bay

Grande Anse

Grande Cul de Sac Bay

Marigot Bay
Marigot Beach
Marigot Bay

Bounty Rum Distillery

⑮ ⑰
⑤ ⑩

La Sorcière

Anse-La-Raye ◰

Roseau

Anse-la-Raye

Fond d'or Bay

⑱

Grande Caille Pt.

Canaries
Mt. Parasol

Barre de l'Isle Forest Reserve

Dennery
Mandéle Pt.

Praslin Bay

Soufrière & Vicinity
see detail map

Diamond Botanical Gardens & Waterfall

Mt. Gimie

Frégate Island Nature Reserve

Edmund Forest Reserve

Mamiku Gardens

Soufrière
Fond St. Jacques

Vierge Pt.

The Pitons

La Soufrière Drive-In Volcano

Micoud

Gros Piton

Fond Doux Estate
Choiseul

Hewanorra International Airport

Savannes Bay

LaFargue
Laborie

⑲

Maria Islands Nature Reserve

Caribbean Sea

ATLANTIC OCEAN

Laborie Bay

Vieux Fort
Vieux Fort ⚓
Honeymoon Beach
Moule à Chique Peninsula

Maria Islands

Anse de Sables

0   4 miles
0   4 km

KEY

✱ Rain Forest
⚓ Cruise Ship Terminal
◰ Dive Sites
⛴ Ferry
■ Restaurants
① Hotels & Villas

Hotels & Villas

Almond Morgan Bay Beach Resort, **11**
Almond Smugglers Cove, **4**
The Body Holiday at LeSPORT, **2**
Cap Maison, **3**
Coconut Bay, **19**
Cotton Bay Village, **1**
Discovery at Marigot Bay, **15**
Inn on the Bay, **17**
The Landings, **7**
Marigot Beach Club & Dive Resort, **16**

Morne Trulah Villa, **10**
Sandals Grande St. Lucian Spa & Beach Resort, **8**
Sandals Halcyon St. Lucia, **13**
Sandals Regency St. Lucia Golf Resort & Spa, **14**
Ti Kaye Village, **18**
Tree Tops Villa, **5**
Villa Beach Cottages, **12**
Villa Tranquility, **6**
Windjammer Landing Villa Beach Resort, **9**

Restaurants

Baguet Shop, **5**
Boudreau, **6**
Cap Grill, **3**
Chateau Mygo, **8**
Doolittle's, **9**
The Great House, **2**
Green Parrot, **4**
Rainforest Hideaway, **7**
Restaurant de Palétuvier, **10**
Tao, **1**

The landscape changes dramatically between the Pitons and Vieux Fort on the island's southeastern tip. Along the South Coast Road, the terrain starts as steep mountainside with dense vegetation, progresses to undulating hills, and finally becomes rather flat and comparatively arid. Anyone arriving at Hewanorra International Airport, which is located in Vieux Fort, and staying at a resort near Soufrière will travel along this route, a journey of about 30 minutes.

From Vieux Fort north to Castries, a 1¼-hour drive, the East Coast Road twists through Micoud, Dennery, and other coastal villages. It then winds up, down, and around mountains, crosses Barre de l'Isle Ridge, and slices through the rain forest. The scenery is breathtaking. The Atlantic Ocean pounds against rocky cliffs, and acres and acres of bananas and coconut palms blanket the hillsides. If you arrive at Hewanorra and stay at a resort near Castries, you'll travel along the East Coast Road.

ABOUT THE HOTELS

Nearly all of St. Lucia's villas, hotels, resorts, and inns are concentrated in three locations along the calm Caribbean coast. They're located in the greater Castries area between Marigot Bay, a few miles south of the capital, and Choc Bay in the north; in and around Rodney Bay and north to Cap Estate; and around Soufrière in the southwestern coast near the Pitons. Currently, only one resort is in Vieux Fort, near Hewanorra International Airport, although the area along the southern and southeastern coasts is ripe for development. Resorts and small inns are tucked into lush surroundings on secluded coves, unspoiled beaches, or forested hillsides. The advantage of being in the north is easier access to a wider range of restaurants and nightlife; in the south, you're limited to your own resort's dining offerings, nearby resort dining rooms, and a handful of local restaurants in Soufrière. On the other hand, many of the island's natural attractions are in and around Soufrière.

Prices in St. Lucia can be twice as high in-season (December 15–April 15) as during the quieter months. Most hotels don't include meals in their rates, but some will offer breakfast or a meal plan. Others require you to purchase a meal plan in the high season, and a few offer all-inclusive packages.

Assume that all hotels operate on the European Plan (**EP**—with no meals) unless we specify that they use the Continental Plan (**CP**—with a continental breakfast), Breakfast Plan (**BP**—with full breakfast), or the Modified American Plan (**MAP**—with breakfast and dinner). Other hotels may offer the Full American Plan (**FAP**—including all meals but no drinks) or may be All-Inclusive (**AI**—with all meals, drinks, and most activities.)

ABOUT THE RESTAURANTS

Bananas, mangoes, passion fruit, plantains, breadfruit, okra, avocados, limes, pumpkins, cucumbers, papaya, yams, christophenes (also called chayote), and coconuts are among the fresh local fruits and vegetables that grace St. Lucian menus. The French influence is strong, and most chefs cook with a Creole flair. Resort buffets and restaurant fare run the gamut from steaks and chops to pasta and pizza. Every menu lists fresh fish along with the ever-popular lobster. Caribbean standards include callaloo, stuffed crab back, pepperpot stew, curried chicken or goat, and *lambi* (conch). The national dish of salt fish and green fig—a stew of dried, salted codfish and boiled green banana—is, let's say, an acquired taste. Soups and stews are traditionally prepared in a coal pot, a rustic clay casserole on a matching clay stand that holds the hot coals. Chicken and pork dishes and barbecues are also popular here. Fresh lobster is available in season, which lasts from August through March each year. As they do throughout the Caribbean, local vendors who set up barbecues along the roadside, at street fairs, and at Friday-night "jump-ups" do a land-office business selling grilled fish or chicken legs, bakes (fried biscuits), and beer—you can get a full meal for about $5. Most other meats are imported—beef from Argentina and Iowa, lamb from New Zealand. Piton is the local brew; Bounty, the local rum.

Dress on St. Lucia is casual but conservative. Shorts are usually fine during the day, but bathing suits and immodest clothing are frowned upon anywhere but at the beach. In the evening the mood is casually elegant, but even the fanciest places generally expect only a collared shirt and long pants for men and a sundress or slacks for women. And any form of camouflage—even a baby's T-shirt—may not be worn anywhere in St. Lucia and will be confiscated by the police.

WHAT IT COSTS IN U.S. DOLLARS				
$$$$	$$$	$$	$	¢
RESTAURANTS				
over $30	$20–$30	$12–$20	$8–$12	under $8
HOTELS*				
over $350	$250–$350	$150–$250	$80–$150	under $80
HOTELS*				
over $450	$350–$450	$250–$350	$125–$250	under $125

*EP, BP, CP **AI, FAP, MAP Restaurant prices are for a main course at dinner and do not include 8% tax or customary 10% service charge. Hotel prices are per night for a double room in high season, excluding 8% tax and meal plans (except at all-inclusives)

TIMING

St. Lucia is busiest in the high season, which runs from mid-December to mid-April; outside of that period, hotel rates can be significantly cheaper.

In April the **St. Lucia Golf Open** is an amateur tournament held at the St. Lucia Golf & Country Club in Cap Estate.

In early May the weeklong **St. Lucia Jazz Festival** is one of the premier events of its kind in the Caribbean. International jazz greats perform at outdoor venues on Pigeon Island and at various hotels, restaurants, and nightspots throughout the island; free concerts are also held at Derek Walcott Square in downtown Castries. Despite the fact that it's the beginning of the off-season, you may have trouble finding a hotel room at any price during Jazz Festival week.

St. Lucia's summer **Carnival** is a monthlong festival, with musical shows, road marches (parades), calypso, soca, and panorama (steel drum) competitions, king and queen pageants, jump-ups (street dancing), and other events held in and around Castries from late June through early July. It is the island's biggest and most inclusive event—or, more appropriately, series of events.

The **St. Lucia Billfishing Tournament** is a three-day competition held in late September or early October, which attracts anglers from throughout the Caribbean who hope to catch the biggest fish. Marlin weighing less than 250 pounds are tagged and returned to the sea, so you can imagine the size of the winner—and even the runners-up. You can take a look at each day's catch at the weighing station at Rodney Bay Marina.

October is **Creole Heritage Month.** The monthlong series of cultural events, which are held in communities throughout the island, culminates on the last Sunday of the month with Jounen Kweyol Etenasyonnal (International Creole Day), a celebration that includes food, crafts, song, and dance.

In late November or early December, the finish of the **Atlantic Rally for Cruisers,** the world's largest ocean-crossing race, is marked by a week of concerts and other festivities at Rodney Bay. More than 200 yachts usually make the crossing each year.

NORTH OF VIGIE TO POINTE DU CAP

After you pass northern St. Lucia's Vigie airport, going north from Castries toward Rodney Bay, Gros Islet, and Cap Estate, the roads are straight, mostly flat, and easy to navigate. Many of the island's resorts, restaurants, and nightspots are in this area. The beaches are also some of the island's best. Pigeon Island, one of the important historical sites, is at the island's northwestern tip.

RENT A CAR? Driving yourself is a fine idea if you want to do some exploring and try lots of restaurants during your stay. If you're staying at an all-inclusive beach resort and plan limited excursions off the property, taxis would be a better choice. The drive from Castries to Soufrière is magnificent, but the winding, mountainous coastal roads can be exhausting for the uninitiated; local drivers are accustomed to the trek.

WHAT TO SEE

Pigeon Island National Park. Jutting out from the northwest coast, Pigeon Island is connected to the mainland by a causeway. Tales are told of the pirate Jambe de Bois (Wooden Leg), who once hid out on this 44-acre hilltop islet—a strategic point during the French and British struggles for control of St. Lucia. Now it's a national park and a venue for concerts, festivals, and family gatherings. There are two small beaches with calm waters for swimming and snorkeling, a restaurant, and picnic areas. Scattered around the grounds are ruins of barracks, batteries, and garrisons that date from 18th-century French and English battles. In the Museum and Interpretative Centre, housed in the restored British officers' mess, a multimedia display explains the island's ecological and historical significance. ⊠*Pigeon Island, St. Lucia National Trust, Rodney Bay* ☎*758/452–5005* ⊕*www.slunatrust.org* ☜*$4* ☺*Daily 9–5.*

Marquis Estate. If you want a close-up view of a working plantation and are willing to get a little wet and muddy in the process, you can tour the island's largest one. The 600-acre Marquis Estate, situated on the northern Atlantic coast, began as a sugar plantation. Now it produces bananas and copra (dried coconut processed for oil) for export, as well as a number of other tropical fruits and vegetables for local consumption. St. Lucia Representative Services Ltd. conducts the tour and will pick you up at your hotel in an air-conditioned bus. You can see the estate by bus or on horseback; a river ride to the coast and lunch at the plantation house are both included. Self-drive tours and private taxi tours aren't permitted. Wear casual clothes. ⊠*Marquis Bay* ☎*758/452–3762.*

☺ ★ **Rain Forest Sky Rides.** Ever wish you could get a bird's-eye view of the rain forest or experience it without hiking up and down miles of mountain trails? Here's your chance. Depending on your athleticism, choose the 75-minute aerial tram ride, the zip-line experience, or both. Either ride guarantees a magnificent view of nature—from up close and personal to as far as the eye can see—as you peacefully slip or actively zip through and sometimes above the canopy of the 3,442-acre Castries Waterworks Rain Forest in Babonneau, just 30 minutes east of Rodney Bay. On the tram ride, eight-passenger gondolas glide slowly among the giant trees, twisting vines, and dense thickets of vegetation accented by colorful flowers as a tour guide explains and shares anecdotes about the various trees, plants, birds, and other wonders of nature found in the area. You'll learn, for example, that 80% of the species living in the forest never come down to the ground. And of the 300 species of birds found in St. Lucia, five of the seven endemic species are found in this forest—including the sometimes elusive St. Lucia parrot, *Amazona versicolor.* Five species of snakes are also found in St. Lucia and in this forest—perhaps the best reason to be sitting in a gondola traveling 60 to 120 meters above the ground! The zip line, on the other hand, is a thrilling experience in which you're rigged with a harness, helmet, and clamps that attach to cables strategically strung through the forest. Short trails connect the 10 lines, so riders come down to earth briefly and hike to the next station before speeding through the forest canopy to the next stop. Bring binoculars and a camera. ⊠*Chassin, Babonneau* ☎*758/458–5151* ⊕*www.rfat.cm* ☎*$72, tram; $60, zip line; $85, combo* ⊙*Daily, 9-4.*

RODNEY BAY, THEN AND NOW. A mosquito-infested swamp near beautiful Reduit Beach was drained and opened up to the sea in the 1970s, creating a beautiful lagoon and ensuring the value of the surrounding real estate for tourism development. Today Rodney Bay Village is a hive of tourist activity, with hotels, restaurants, much of the island's nightlife, and, of course, Rodney Bay Marina.

Rodney Bay. About 15 minutes north of Castries, the natural bay and an 80-acre man-made lagoon—surrounded by hotels and many popular restaurants—are named for British admiral George Rodney, who sailed the English Navy out of Gros Islet Bay in 1780 to attack and ultimately decimate the French fleet. Rodney Bay Marina is one of the Caribbean's premier yachting centers—an official port of entry for visitors arriving by private yacht, and the destination of the Atlantic Rally for Cruisers (transatlantic yacht crossing) each December. Yacht charters and sightseeing day trips can be arranged at the marina. The Rodney Bay Ferry makes hourly crossings between the marina and the shopping complex, as well as daily excursions to Pigeon Island.

GREATER CASTRIES

Castries, the capital city, and the area north and just south of it are the island's most developed areas. About 15 minutes south of Castries, lovely Marigot Bay is both a yacht haven and a picture-pretty destination for landlubbers.

The capital, a busy commercial city of about 65,000 people, wraps around a sheltered bay. Morne Fortune rises sharply to the south of town, creating a dramatic green backdrop. The charm of Castries lies almost entirely in its liveliness, since most of the colonial buildings were destroyed by four fires that occurred between 1796 and 1948. Freighters (exporting bananas, coconut, cocoa, mace, nutmeg, and

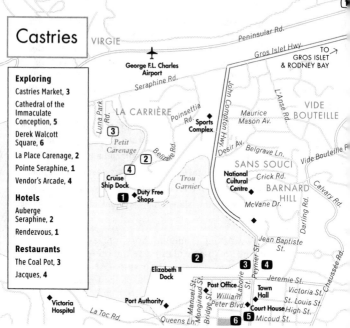

Castries

VIRGIE

Exploring

Castries Market, **3**

Cathedral of the Immaculate Conception, **5**

Derek Walcott Square, **6**

La Place Carenage, **2**

Pointe Seraphine, **1**

Vendor's Arcade, **4**

Hotels

Auberge Seraphine, **2**

Rendezvous, **1**

Restaurants

The Coal Pot, **3**

Jacques, **4**

Peninsular Rd.

Gros Islet Hwy.

TO
GROS ISLET
& RODNEY BAY

George F.L. Charles Airport

Seraphine Rd.

Poinsettia Rd.

John Compton Hwy.

L'Anse Rd.

VIDE BOUTEILLE

LA CARRIÈRE

Luna Park Rd.

Maurice Mason Av.

Belaire Rd.

Sports Complex

Desir Av.

Belgrave Ln.

Vide Bouteille P.

Petit Carenage

SANS SOUCI

Trou Garnier

National Cultural Centre

Crick Rd.

BARNARD HILL

Calvary Rd.

Cruise Ship Dock

Duty Free Shops

McVane Dr.

Darling Rd.

Jean Baptiste St.

Elizabeth II Dock

St. Permer St.

Jeremie St.

Victoria St.

Chaussee Rd.

Port Authority

Manuel St.

Mongiraud St.

Bridge St.

Laborie

Post Office

William Peter Blvd.

Town Hall

St. Louis St.

High St.

Victoria Hospital

La Toc Rd.

Queens Ln.

Court House

Micoud St.

citrus fruits) and cruise ships come and go daily, making Castries Harbour one of the Caribbean's busiest ports.

Numbers in the margin correspond to points of interest on the Castries map.

WHAT TO SEE

Bounty Rum Distillery. St. Lucia Distillers, which produces the island's own Bounty Rum, offers 90-minute "Rhythm and Rum" tours of its distillery, including information on the history of sugar, the background of rum, a detailed description of the distillation process, colorful displays of local architecture, a glimpse at a typical rum shop, Caribbean music, and, of course, a chance to sample the company's rums and liqueurs. The distillery is at the Roseau Sugar Factory in the Roseau Valley, on the island's largest banana plantation, a few miles south of Castries and not far from Marigot. Reservations for the tour are essential. ⊠ *Roseau Sugar Factory, West Coast Rd., Roseau* ☎ 758/451–4315 ☎ *$5* ⊙ *Weekdays 9–3.*

Basilica of the Immaculate Conception. Directly across Laborie Street from Derek Walcott Square stands Castries's Roman Catholic church, which was built in 1897. Though it's

CLOSE UP

Dunstan St. Omer

The murals of Dunstan St. Omer, one of St. Lucia's leading artists—if not *the* leading artist—adorn many walls and churches throughout the island, and his paintings and portraits are prized both locally and internationally. St. Omer is best known locally for frescoing the walls of the ❺ **Cathedral of the Immaculate Conception**, in Castries, with the images of black saints just prior to a visit by Pope John Paul II in 1985. He also designed St. Lucia's national flag. A 2004 recipient of the St. Lucia Cross, the nation's highest award, he inspired generations of youngsters for more than 30 years as an art instructor in the public schools. St. Omer is also the father of nine children, two of whom—Luigi and Julio—inherited their father's talent and have followed in his footsteps.

rather somber on the outside, the interior walls are decorated with colorful murals reworked by St. Lucian artist Dunstan St. Omer in 1985, just prior to Pope John Paul II's visit. This church has an active parish and is open daily for both public viewing and religious services. ⊠*Laborie St., Castries* ⊙*Daily.*

❸ **Castries Market.** At the corner of Jeremie and Peynier streets, spreading beyond its brilliant orange roof and full of excitement and bustle, the market is open every day except Sunday. It's liveliest on Saturday morning, when farmers bring their fresh produce and spices to town, as they have for more than a century. Adjacent to the produce market is the **Craft Market,** where you can buy pottery, wood carvings, and handwoven straw articles.

❹ Across Peynier Street from the Craft Market, at the **Vendor's Arcade** you'll find a maze of many more handicraft and souvenir vendors. ⊠*Corner of Jeremie and Peynier Sts., Castries* ⊙*Mon.–Sat. 6–5.*

❻ **Derek Walcott Square.** The city's green oasis is bordered by Brazil, Laborie, Micoud, and Bourbon streets. Formerly Columbus Square, it was renamed to honor the hometown poet who won the 1992 Nobel prize for literature—one of two Nobel laureates from St. Lucia (the late Sir W. Arthur Lewis won the 1979 Nobel prize in economics). Some of the 19th-century buildings that have survived fire, wind, and rain can be seen on Brazil Street, the square's southern border. On the Laborie Street side there's a huge, 400-year-old samaan tree with leafy branches that shades a good portion of the square. ⊠*Bordered by Brazil, Laborie, Micoud, and Bourbon streets, Castries.*

Fort Charlotte. Begun in 1764 by the French as the Citadelle du Morne Fortune, Fort Charlotte was completed after 20 years of battling and changing hands. Its old barracks and batteries are now government buildings and local educational facilities, but you can drive around and look at the remains, including redoubts, a guardroom, stables, and cells. You can also walk up to the Inniskilling Monument, a tribute to the 1796 battle in which the 27th Foot Royal Inniskilling Fusiliers wrested the Morne from the French. At the military cemetery, which was first used in 1782, faint inscriptions on the tombstones tell the tales of French and English soldiers who died here. Six former governors of the island are buried here as well. From this point atop Morne Fortune you can view Martinique to the north and the twin peaks of the Pitons to the south.

Government House. The official residence of the governor-general of St. Lucia, one of the island's few remaining examples of Victorian architecture, is perched high above Castries, halfway up Morne Fortune—the "Hill of Good Fortune"—which forms a backdrop for the capital city. Morne Fortune has also overlooked more than its share of *bad* luck over the years, including devastating hurricanes and four fires that leveled Castries. Within Government House itself is **Le Pavillon Royal Museum,** which houses important historical photographs and documents, artifacts, crockery, silverware, medals, and awards; original architectural drawings of Government House are displayed on the walls. However, you must make an appointment to visit. ⊠*Morne Fortune, Castries* ☎*758/452–2481* ⛁*Free* ☉*Tues. and Thurs. 10–noon and 2–4, by appointment only.*

Marigot Bay. This is one of the prettiest natural harbors in the Caribbean. In 1778 British admiral Samuel Barrington sailed into this secluded bay-within-a-bay and covered his ships with palm fronds to hide them from the French. Today this picturesque community—where parts of the original *Doctor Dolittle* movie were filmed in the late 1960s—is a favorite anchorage. A 24-hour ferry ($2 round-trip) connects the bay's two shores—a voyage that takes about a minute each way. Marigot Bay has undergone a radical yet environmentally friendly transformation.

Discovery at Marigot Bay—a luxury resort, marina, and marina village with restaurants, bars, grocery store, bakery, boutiques, and other services and activities—has totally revitalized the area without damaging either the beauty or the ecology of Marigot Bay in the least.

2 La Place Carenage. On the south side of the harbor near the pier and markets is another duty-free shopping complex with a dozen or shops and a café. ⊠*Jeremie St., Castries* ☎758/453–2451 ☉ *Weekdays 9–4, Sat. 9–1.*

1 Pointe Seraphine. This duty-free shopping complex is on the north side of the harbor, about a 20-minute walk or two-minute cab ride from the city center; a launch ferries passengers across the harbor when ships are in port. Pointe Seraphine's attractive Spanish-style architecture houses more than 20 upscale duty-free shops, a tourist information kiosk, a taxi stand, and car-rental agencies. The shopping center is adjacent to the cruise-ship pier. ⊠*Castries Harbour, Castries* ☎758/452–3036 ☉ *Weekdays 9–4, Sat. 9–1.*

SOUFRIÈRE & THE SOUTH

Most sightseeing trips from the big hotels in the Rodney Bay area head south toward Soufrière. This is where you can view the landmark Pitons and explore the French-colonial capital of St. Lucia, with its drive-in volcano, botanical gardens, working plantations, and countless other examples of the natural beauty for which St. Lucia is deservedly famous.

WAS THAT A SNAKE? Driving along the West Coast Road just north of Canaries, don't be surprised if you see a man selling coconuts on the northbound side of the road with a boa constrictor wrapped around his neck. The "snake man" has been a fixture here for years—usually from mid-morning to mid-afternoon—and we're sure the startled looks on tourists' faces give him a kick. Taxi drivers will stop if you want some coconut water or just a closer look. For a small tip, the "snake man" let you take his picture—wearing his boa, of course.

WHAT TO SEE

★ Fodor'sChoice **Diamond Botanical Gardens & Waterfall.** These splendid gardens are part of Soufrière Estate, a 2,000-acre land grant made in 1713 by Louis XIV to the three Devaux

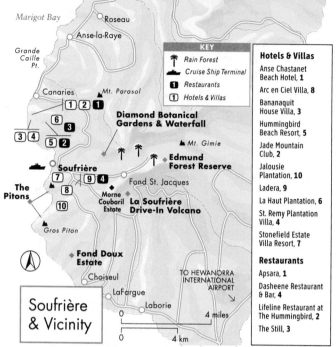

TO HEWANORRA
INTERNATIONAL
AIRPORT

Soufrière
& Vicinity

KEY

🌴	Rain Forest
⚓	Cruise Ship Terminal
1	Restaurants
⓵	Hotels & Villas

Hotels & Villas

Anse Chastanet
Beach Hotel, **1**

Arc en Ciel Villa, **8**

Bananaquit
House Villa, **3**

Hummingbird
Beach Resort, **5**

Jade Mountain
Club, **2**

Jalousie
Plantation, **10**

Ladera, **9**

La Haut Plantation, **6**

St. Remy Plantation
Villa, **4**

Stonefield Estate
Villa Resort, **7**

Restaurants

Apsara, **1**

Dasheene Restaurant
& Bar, **4**

Lifeline Restaurant at
The Hummingbird, **2**

The Still, **3**

brothers from Normandy in recognition of their services to France. The estate is still owned by their descendants; Joan Du Bouley Devaux maintains the gardens. Bushes and shrubs bursting with brilliant flowers grow beneath towering trees and line pathways that lead to a natural gorge. Water bubbling to the surface from underground sulfur springs streams downhill in rivulets to become Diamond Waterfall, deep within the botanical gardens. Through the centuries, the rocks over which the cascade spills have become encrusted with minerals and tinted yellow, green, and purple. Near the falls, curative mineral baths are fed by the underground springs. For a small fee you can slip into your swimsuit and bathe for 30 minutes in one of the outside pools; a private bath costs slightly more. King Louis XVI of France provided funds in 1784 for the construction of a building with a dozen large stone baths to fortify his troops against the St. Lucian climate. It's claimed that Joséphine Bonaparte bathed here as a young girl while visiting her father's plantation nearby. During the Brigand's War, just after the French Revolution, the bathhouse was destroyed. In 1930 the site was excavated by André Du Boulay, and two of the original stone baths were restored for his use. The outside baths were added later. In recent years, Diamond Botanical Gardens was a location shot for two blockbuster movies: *Superman II* (when Christopher Reeve flew in and picked a flower for Lois Lane) and *Romancing the Stone*. ⊠*Soufrière Estate, Diamond Rd., Soufrière* ☎*758/452–4759 or 758/454–7565* ☖*$2.75, outside bath $2.50, private bath $3.75* ☉*Mon.–Sat. 10–5, Sun. 10–3.*

Edmund Forest Reserve. Dense tropical rain forest stretches from one side of the island to the other, sprawling over 19,000 acres of mountains and valleys. It's home to a multitude of exotic flowers and plants, as well as rare birds—including the brightly feathered Jacquot parrot. The Edmund Forest Reserve, on the island's western side, is most easily accessible from just east of Soufrière, on the road to Fond St. Jacques. A trek through the pristine landscape, with its lush foliage and spectacular views of mountains, valleys, and the sea beyond, can take three or more hours. It takes an hour or more just to reach the reserve by car from the northern end of the island. It's a strenuous hike, so you need plenty of stamina and sturdy hiking shoes. Permission from the Forest & Lands Department is required to access reserve trails; the department also requires that a naturalist or forest officer guide you because the vegetation is so dense. ⊠*East of Fond St. Jacques* ☎*758/450–2231, 758/450–2078 for Forest & Lands Department* ☖*Guide $10; guided tours that include round-trip transportation from your hotel $55–$85* ☉*Daily by appointment only.*

☙ **Fond Doux Estate.** One of the earliest French estates established by land grant (1745 and 1763), 135 hilly acres of this old plantation still produce cocoa, citrus, bananas, coconut, and vegetables; the restored 1864 plantation house is still in use as well. A 30-minute walking tour begins at the cocoa fermentary, where you can see the drying process under way. You then follow a trail through the lush cultivated area, where a guide points out the various fruit- or spice-bearing trees and tropical flowers. Additional trails lead to old military ruins, a religious shrine, and another vantage point for the spectacular Pitons. Cool drinks—including rum punch, local fruit juices, and coconut water—and a Creole buffet lunch are available at the restaurant. Souvenirs, including just-made chocolate balls, are sold at the boutique. ⊠*Chateaubelair, Soufrière* ☎*758/459–7545* ⊕*www.fonddouxestate.com* ☖*$6, buffet lunch $14* ☉*Daily 9–4.*

☺ **La Soufrière Drive-In Volcano.** As you approach, your nose will
★ pick up the strong scent of the sulfur springs—more than
20 belching pools of muddy water and multicolor deposits
of sulfur and other assorted minerals baking and steaming
on the surface. Actually, you don't drive in. You drive up to
within a few hundred feet of the gurgling, steaming mass,
then walk behind your guide—whose service is included
in the admission price—around a fault in the substratum
rock. It's a fascinating, educational half hour, though it
can also be pretty stinky on a hot day. ⊠*Bay St., Soufrière*
☎*758/459–5500* ⊑*$1.25* ☉*Daily 9–5.*

☺ **Morne Coubaril.** On the site of an 18th-century estate, a
250-acre land grant by Louis XIV of France in 1713, the
original plantation house has been renovated and a farm
worker's village has been recreated to show visitors what
life was like for both the owners (a single family that owned
the land until 1960) and those who did all the hard labor
over the centuries producing cotton, coffee, sugarcane, and
cocoa. Cocoa, coconuts, and manioc are still grown on the
estate using traditional agricultural methods. Guides show
how coconuts are opened and roasted for use as oil and
animal feed and how cocoa is fermented, dried, crushed by
a man dancing on the beans, and finally formed into chocolate sticks. Manioc roots are grated, squeezed of excess
water, dried, and turned into farina and cassava used in
baking. The grounds are lovely for walking or hiking, and
the view of mountain and sea are spellbinding. The Pitt, a
large, open-air restaurant, serves a Creole buffet at lunchtime by reservation only. ⊠*Soufrière* ☎*758/459–7340*
⊑*$5.50; $10 including lunch* ☉*Daily, 9–4:30.*

★ **Fodor's**Choice **The Pitons.** These two unusual mountains,
named a UNESCO World Heritage Site in 2004, rise pre-
cipitously from the cobalt-blue Caribbean Sea just south
of Soufrière. The Pitons are, in fact, the symbol of St.
Lucia. Covered with thick tropical vegetation, the massive outcroppings were formed by lava from a volcanic
eruption 30 to 40 million years ago. They are not iden-
tical twins since—confusingly—2,619-foot Petit Piton is
taller than 2,461-foot Gros Piton, though Gros Piton is
broader. Gros Piton is the easier climb, though the trail up
even this shorter Piton is one very tough trek and requires
the permission of the Forest & Lands Department and a
knowledgeable guide. ☎*758/450–2231, 758/450–2078*
for St. Lucia Forest & Lands Department, 758/459–9748

Plas Kassav

As you're traveling south to Soufrière, watch for Plas Kassav Bread Bakery in Anse La Verdure, a blink-and-you'll-miss-it spot on the West Coast Road between Anse la Raye and Canaries. If you're there early enough, you can see the cassava roots being grated and processed into flour using traditional methods, and the cassava bread dough being mixed in huge copper caldrons. Cinnamon, cherries and raisins, coconut, and other flavorings are added, then the dough—13 varieties in all—is formed into small buns, placed on banana leaves, and baked over hot coals. Plas Kassav (Creole for Cassava Place) began as a small family bakery in 1998 and has grown into a popular local enterprise simply by word of mouth. There is a large sign, but taxi drivers all know where it is and will not hesitate to stop so you can try a warm, mouthwatering treat that is a staple of St. Lucia's traditional cuisine.

for Pitons Tour Guide Association ✉*Guide services $45* ☉*Daily by appointment only.*

Soufrière. The oldest town in St. Lucia and the former French-colonial capital, Soufrière was founded by the French in 1746 and named for its proximity to the volcano. The wharf is the center of activity in this sleepy town (which currently has a population of about 9,000), particularly when a cruise ship is moored in pretty Soufrière Bay. French-colonial influences can be noticed in the architecture of the wooden buildings, with second-story verandas and gingerbread trim that surround the market square. The market building itself is decorated with colorful murals. The **Soufrière Tourist Information Centre** (✉*Bay St., Soufrière* ☎*758/459–7200*) provides information about area attractions. Note that outside some of the popular attractions in and around Soufrière, souvenir vendors can be persistent. Be polite but firm if you're not interested in their wares.

VIEUX FORT & THE EAST COAST

Vieux Fort is on the southeast tip of St. Lucia and is the location of Hewanorra International Airport, which serves all jet aircraft arriving at and departing from St. Lucia. While less developed for tourism than the island's north and west (although that is expected to change dramatically

St. Lucia's Two Nobel Laureates

Sir W. Arthur Lewis won the Nobel Price in Economics in 1979. Born in St. Lucia in 1915, Lewis graduated with distinction from the London School of Economics and went on to earn a Ph.D. in industrial economics. His life interest—and his influence—was in economic development and the transformation and expansion of university education in the Caribbean. Lewis died in 1991 and was buried on the grounds of Sir Arthur Lewis Community College in St. Lucia.

Sir Derek Walcott was born in Castries in 1930. *Omeros*—an epic poem about his journey around the Caribbean, the American West, and London—contributed to his winning the Nobel Prize for Literature in 1992. Walcott is also a writer, playwright, and painter of watercolors. Today, in addition to spending time at his home in St. Lucia, he teaches poetry and drama at Boston University and lectures and gives readings throughout the world.

in coming years), the area around Vieux Fort and along the east coast is home to some of St. Lucia's unique ecosystems and interesting natural attractions.

WHAT TO SEE

Barre de l'Isle Forest Reserve. St. Lucia is divided into eastern and western halves by Barre de L'isle ridge. A mile-long (1½-km-long) trail cuts through the reserve, and four lookout points provide panoramic views. Visible in the distance are Mount Gimie, immense green valleys, both the Caribbean Sea and the Atlantic Ocean, and coastal communities. The reserve is about a half-hour drive from Castries; it takes about an hour to walk the trail—an easy hike—and another hour to climb Mount La Combe Ridge. Permission from the St. Lucia Forest & Lands Department is required to access the trail in Barre de L'isle; a naturalist or forest officer guide will accompany you. ⊠ *Trailhead on East Coast Rd., near Ravine Poisson, midway between Castries and Dennery* ☎ *758/450–2231 or 758/450–2078* 🖃 *$10 for guide services* ⊙ *Daily by appointment only.*

Frégate Island Nature Reserve. A mile-long (1½-km) trail encircles the nature reserve, which you reach from the East Coast Road near the fishing village of Praslin. In this area boat builders still fashion traditional fishing canoes, called *gommiers* after the trees from which the hulls are made. The ancient design was used by the original Amerindian

people who populated the Caribbean. A natural prom-
ontory at Praslin provides a lookout from which you can
view the two small islets Frégate Major and Frégate Minor
and—with luck—the frigate birds that nest here from May
to July. The only way to visit is on a guided tour, which
includes a ride in a gommier to Frégate Minor for a picnic
lunch and a swim; all trips are by reservation only and
require a minimum of two people. Arrange visits through
your hotel, a tour operator, or the St. Lucia National
Trust; many tours include round-trip transportation from
your hotel as well as the tour cost. ✉ *Praslin* ☎ *758/452–
5005, 758/453–7656, 758/454–5014 for tour reservations*
⊕ *www.slunatrust.org* 🖃 *$18* ⊗ *Daily by appointment.*

Mamiku Gardens. One of St. Lucia's largest and loveli-
est botanical gardens surrounds the hilltop ruins of the
Micoud Estate. Baron Micoud, an 18th-century colonel in
the French Army and governor general of St. Lucia, deeded
the land to his wife, Madame de Micoud, to avoid confis-
cation by the British during one of the many times when
St. Lucia changed hands. Locals abbreviated her name to
"Ma Micoud," which, over time, became "Mamiku." Nevertheless, the estate did become a British military outpost in
1796 but, shortly thereafter, was burned to the ground by
slaves during the Brigand's War. The estate is now primarily
a banana plantation, but the gardens themselves—including several secluded or "secret" gardens—are filled with
tropical flowers and plants, including delicate orchids and
fragrant herbs. Admission includes a guided tour. ✉ *Vieux
Fort Hwy., Praslin* ☎ *758/455–3729* 🖃 *$6* ⊗ *Daily, 9–5.*

Maria Islands Nature Reserve. Two tiny islands in the Atlantic Ocean, off St. Lucia's southeast coast, compose the
reserve, which has its own interpretive center. The 25-acre
Maria Major and the 4-acre Maria Minor, its little sister,
are inhabited by two rare species of reptiles (the colorful
Zandoli terre ground lizard and the harmless Kouwes grass
snake) that share their home with frigate birds, terns, doves,
and other wildlife. There's a small beach for swimming and
snorkeling, as well as an undisturbed forest, a vertical cliff
covered with cacti, and a coral reef for snorkeling or diving. Tours, including the boat trip to the islands, are offered
by the St. Lucia National Trust by appointment only; you
should bring your own picnic lunch, because there are no
facilities. ✉ *St. Lucia National Trust Regional Office, Vieux
Fort* ☎ *758/452–5005, 758/453–7656, 758/454–5014 for*

tour reservations ⊕*www.slunatrust.org* ✉*$35* ⊗*Aug.–mid-May, Wed.–Sun. 9:30–5, by appointment only.*

Vieux Fort. St. Lucia's second-largest port is where you'll find Hewanorra International Airport. From the Moule à Chique Peninsula, the island's southernmost tip, you can see all of St. Lucia to the north and the island of St. Vincent 21 mi (34 km) south. This is where the waters of the clear Caribbean Sea blend with those of the deeper blue Atlantic Ocean.

WHERE TO EAT

With so many popular all-inclusive resorts, guests take most meals at hotel restaurants—which are generally quite good, and in some cases exceptional. It's fun when vacationing, however, to try some of the local restaurants, as well—for lunch when sightseeing or for a special night out.

NORTH OF VIGIE TO POINTE DU CAP

Restaurant locations can be found on the Gros Islet & Rodney Bay and St. Lucia maps.

ASIAN

$$$–$$$$ ✕**Tao.** For exquisite dining, head for Tao at the Body Holi-
★ day at LeSPORT. It welcomes nonguests, but the place is small and folks tend to linger—so reserve early. Perched on a second-floor balcony at the edge of Cariblue Beach, you're guaranteed a pleasant breeze and a starry sky while you enjoy fusion cuisine—a marriage of Asian tastes with a Caribbean touch. Choose from appetizers such as seafood dumplings, sashimi salad, or miso eggplant timbale, followed by tender slices of pork loin teriyaki, twice-cooked duck, wok-seared calves' liver, or tandoori chicken—the results are mouthwatering. Fine wines accompany the meal, desserts are extravagant, and service is superb. Seating is limited; hotel guests have priority. ⊠*The Body Holiday at LeSPORT, Cap Estate* ☎*758/450–8551* ⚞*Reservations essential* ⊟*AE, MC, V* ⊗*No lunch.*

CARIBBEAN

$$–$$$ ✕**Ti Bananne.** Poolside at the Coco Palm hotel in Rodney
★ Bay, Ti Bananne is an airy Caribbean-style bistro and bar that serves breakfast, lunch, and dinner daily. Breakfast attracts mostly hotel guests, but the elegant yet casual restaurant has been positioned as an independent restaurant

CLOSE UP

Embracing Kwéyòl

English is St. Lucia's official language, but most St. Lucians speak and often use Kwéyòl—a French-based Creole language—for informal conversations among themselves. Primarily a spoken language, Kwéyòl in its written version doesn't look at all like French; pronounce the words phonetically, though—*entenasyonnal* (international), for example, or the word *Kwéyòl* (Creole) itself—and you indeed sound as if you're speaking French.

Pretty much the same version of the Creole language, or patois, is spoken in the nearby island of Dominica. Otherwise, the St. Lucian Kwéyòl is quite different from that spoken in other Caribbean islands with a French and African heritage such as Haiti, Guadeloupe, and Martinique—or elsewhere, such as Louisiana, Mauritius, and Madagascar. Interestingly, the Kwéyòl spoken in St. Lucia and Dominica is mostly unintelligible to people from those other locations—and vice versa.

St. Lucia embraces its Creole heritage by devoting the month of October each year to celebrations that preserve and promote Creole culture, language, and traditions. In selected communities throughout the island, events and performances highlight Creole music, food, dance, theater, native costumes, church services, traditional games, folklore, native medicine—a little bit of everything, or *"tout bagay"* as you say in Kwéyòl.

Creole Heritage Month culminates at the end of October with all-day events and activities on Jounen Kwéyòl Entenasyonnal, or International Creole Day, which is recognized by all countries that speak a version of the Creole language.

2

to attract both guests and nonguests for lunch and dinner. Lunch is a good bet if you're poking around Rodney Bay, need a break from Reduit Beach, or are just looking for a good meal in a friendly spot. On Wednesday there's a special Creole lunch buffet; for Sunday brunch, a barbecue buffet. In the evening, stop first at the bar for a fruity rum drink, cold Piton beer, or something stronger—but the open-to-the-breeze dining room is where the magic really comes through. Executive chef Richard Skinner and head chef Giancarlo Crumps, both natives of Trinidad & Tobago with extensive experience throughout the Caribbean, conjure up exquisite French-inspired, Creole-influenced dishes such as panfried snapper with orange and butter sauce and green fig lyonnaise. Leave room for dessert—the trio of

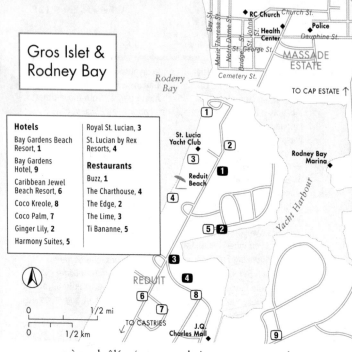

Gros Islet &
Rodney Bay

RC Church · Church St.
Police · Dauphine St.
Health Center
RC Church
St. George St.
MASSADE ESTATE
Rodeny Bay
Cemetery St.
TO CAP ESTATE ↑

Hotels
Bay Gardens Beach Resort, **1**
Bay Gardens Hotel, **9**
Caribbean Jewel Beach Resort, **6**
Coco Kreole, **8**
Coco Palm, **7**
Ginger Lily, **2**
Harmony Suites, **5**

Royal St. Lucian, **3**
St. Lucian by Rex Resorts, **4**

Restaurants
Buzz, **1**
The Charthouse, **4**
The Edge, **2**
The Lime, **3**
Ti Bananne, **5**

St. Lucia Yacht Club
Rodney Bay Marina
Reduit Beach
Yacht Harbour
REDUIT
TO CASTRIES
J.Q. Charles Mall

0 ___ 1/2 mi
0 ___ 1/2 km

crèmes brûlées (mango and ginger, coconut, and seamoss and cinnamon) is the showstopper. And speaking of the show, a live band entertains every evening. ⊠*Coco Palm, Rodney Bay, Gros Islet* ☎*758/456–2828* ⌖*Reservations essential* ⊟*AE, MC, V.*

ECLECTIC

$$$–$$$$ ✕ **The Edge.** Innovative Swedish chef Bobo Bergstrom, for-
★ merly the award-winning culinary director at Windjammer Landing and, even earlier, chef de cuisine at the famed Oper-akallaren in Stockholm, brought his "Eurobbean fusion" cuisine to his own fine-dining establishment, overlooking the harbor at Harmony Suites Hotel, in November 2005. Ever since, St. Lucian locals and visitors alike have been raving about Chef Bobo's culinary feats, the excellent wine list, and the island's first sushi bar. "Eurobbean" cuisine is a contemporary fusion style that combines the chef's European heritage with Caribbean traditions and ingredients and a touch of Asian influence. Among the dozen starters is a dreamy lobster bisque scented with saffron and paprika. Then try snapper braised in fennel bouillon, jerk-marinated and grilled beef tenderloin, spice-glazed rabbit roulade, or perhaps the five-course tasting menu. There's certain to be

a dish on the extensive menu (or at the sushi bar) that suits everyone in your party, and be sure to leave room for a fabulous dessert. ⊠*Harmony Suites Hotel, Rodney Bay* ☎*758/450–3343* ⊜*Reservations essential* ⊟*AE, MC, V.*

$–$$ ✕**The Lime.** A casual bistro with lime-green gingham curtains, straw hats decorating the ceiling, and hanging plants, the Lime specializes in local dishes such as spicy jerk chicken or pork and breadfruit salad—as well as char-grilled steak and fresh-caught fish. The meals are well prepared, the portions are plentiful, and the prices are reasonable, which is perhaps why you often see St. Lucians and visitors alike "liming" (an island term that means something akin to hanging around and relaxing) all day and most of the night at this popular restaurant. The Late Lime, a club where the crowd gathers as night turns to morning, is next door. ⊠*Rodney Bay* ☎*758/452–0761* ⊟*D, MC, V* ⊙*Closed Tues.*

FRENCH

$$$ ✕**The Great House.** Elegant, gracious, and romantic, The Great House was reconstructed on the foundation of an original Cap Estate plantation house adjacent to Almond Smugglers Cove Resort. The grandeur of those early days has been revived as well. The waitstaff wears traditional St. Lucian costumes. The chef adds a piquant Creole touch to traditional French cuisine—with excellent results. The menu, which changes nightly, might include pumpkin-and-potato soup, local crab back with lime vinaigrette, sautéed Antillean shrimp in a Creole sauce, and broiled sirloin with thyme butter and sweet-potato chips. Cocktails at the open-air bar are especially enjoyable at sunset. The Derek Walcott Theatre is next door. ⊠*Cap Estate* ☎*758/450–0450 or 758/450–0211* ⊜*Reservations essential* ⊟*AE, D, DC, MC, V* ⊙*No lunch.*

SEAFOOD

$$–$$$ ✕**Buzz.** Longtime St. Lucian restaurateur Pat Bowden opened Buzz in 2005 in "restaurant central"—busy Rodney Bay—opposite the Rex St. Lucian Hotel and Reduit Beach. Starting with cool drinks (maybe a Buzz cooler) and warm appetizers (perhaps lobster and crab cakes, crispy calamari, or tempura shrimp) at the friendly bar, diners make their way to the dining room or the garden for some serious seafood—or a good steak, baby back ribs, West Indian pepperpot stew, or spicy lamb shanks. The seared yellow-fin tuna, potato-crusted red snapper, and seafood Creole are big hits, though. Fresh lobster is available in season (August–March) ✉*Reduit Beach, Rodney Bay, Gros Islet* ☎*758/458–0450* ⚑*Reservations essential* ▭*AE, MC, V* ⊘*No lunch; Closed Monday, Apr.–Nov.*

STEAK

$$$–$$$$ ✕**Cap Grill.** If you're in the mood for a perfectly cooked steak—or seafood or pasta—head for the golf course. Cap Grill, in the impressive clubhouse of the St. Lucia Golf Club, serves breakfast and lunch daily, dinner Thursday–Saturday, and Sunday brunch in air-conditioned comfort or alfresco on the dining porch. In either case, your table will overlook the golf course, which is floodlit at night. Golfers come for an early breakfast or after-the-round lunch of Black Angus burgers, baguette sandwiches, fresh salads, or pasta specials. The Sports Bar is busy all afternoon. And you don't have to be a golfer to come for dinner. Start with fillet of beef, fish carpaccio, or Caribbean ceviche, followed perhaps by garlic soup or shrimp and corn chowder, and then on to the steak: perfectly grilled 12- or 16-ounce New York strip or beautifully tender 8-ounce filet mignon. Or opt for roast duck breast, blackened mahimahi, rack of lamb, coconut shrimp, roasted pork tenderloin, or stuffed chicken breast. It's like home away from home! ✉*St. Lucia Golf Club, Cap Estate* ☎*758/450–8523* ⚑*Reservations essential* ▭*AE, MC, V* ⊘*No dinner Sun.–Wed.*

$$$–$$$$ ✕**The Charthouse.** Since 1985 The Charthouse, part of the international chain, has been charcoal broiling U.S. Prime beefsteak and serving it up to hungry St. Lucians and vacationers in an open-air, waterfront location on Rodney Bay. Some prefer the hickory-smoked baby back ribs or the roast prime rib of beef—or even grilled seafood. In any case, it's all prepared and served by a friendly staff—most of whom have been with the restaurant for two decades. Fresh lobster is delivered daily in season. After dinner, gentlemen (and audacious ladies) can choose from a wide variety of Cuban cigars, if they wish. ✉*Rodney Bay Marina, Gros Islet* ☎*758/459–8115* ⚑*Reservations essential* ▭*AE, MC, V* ⊘*No lunch.*

GREATER CASTRIES

Restaurant locations can be found on the Castries and St. Lucia maps.

CAFÉS

¢–$ ✕**Baguet Shop.** Join the yachties and Discovery at Marigot Bay villa guests for breakfast, lunch, afternoon tea, an evening snack, or just dessert at this cute French bakery and patisserie in the Marina Village on Marigot Bay. Open every day from 7 AM to 7 PM, it offers freshly baked French bread, crusty croissants, and dreamy French pastries that are delivered to the shop daily from Martinique. Sandwiches are prepared on a baguette, croissant, or focaccia—your choice. Pair your favorite with a cup of cappuccino, mocha, or latte. Or hold the coffee until dessert, and pair your fruit tart, pain au chocolat, coconut flan, or another delicious pastry selection with a steaming cup of rich espresso. Eat in (well, outside on the dock) or take it out. Even if you eat in, you'll probably want a baguette—or a bagful—to take out, as well. ✉*Marina Village, Marigot Bay* ☎*758/451–4275* ⚓*No reservations accepted* ▭*AE, MC, V.*

CARIBBEAN

$$$–$$$$ ✕**Green Parrot.** One reason to dine in this English colonial–style hotel atop the Morne is the romantic view overlooking Castries Harbor and the twinkling lights of the city after dark. The food is good, too! Acclaimed Chef Harry Edwards, who trained years ago at Claridge's Hotel in London, prepares a menu of St. Lucian specialties and international dishes—and you can count on a good steak. There's also lively entertainment—a floor show with a belly dancer on Wednesday night and limbo dancing on Saturday. On Monday night the tradition is that a lady who wears a flower in her hair and is accompanied by a "well-dressed" gentleman might receive a free dinner. ✉*Morne Fortune, Castries* ☎*758/452–3399* ⚓*Reservations essential. Jacket required* ▭*AE, MC, V.*

CARIBBEAN/SEAFOOD

$$–$$$ ✕**Restaurant de Palétuvier.** The view from the waterfront restaurant at J.J.'s Paradise, overlooking pretty Marigot Bay, is enchanting, and the seafood prepared by owner-chef Gerard (J.J.) Felix is among the best on the island. Superbly grilled fish with fresh vegetables gets top honors, but you might also enjoy shellfish (lobster, prawns, or lambi), grilled T-bone steak, chicken (roasted, grilled, cur-

ried, or Creole), pork chops, a vegetarian platter, or something truly exotic such as curried octopus. The welcome is friendly; the atmosphere casual. Music and entertainment are on the menu most nights, as well. ⊠*Marigot Bay Rd., Marigot* ☎*758/451–4076* ⚓*Reservations essential* ▭*D, MC, V.*

$–$$$ ╳Chateau Mygo. Walk down a garden path to Chateau
Ⓢ Mygo (a corruption of the word "Marigot"), pick out a table on the dockside dining deck, pull up a chair, and soak up the waterfront atmosphere of what is arguably the prettiest bay in the Caribbean. The tableau is mesmerizing—and that's at lunch, when you can order a sandwich, burger, fish or chicken and chips, salads, or grilled fish or chicken with peas and rice and vegetables. At dinner, chef-owner Doreen Rambally—whose family has owned and operated this place since the mid-1970s—draws on three generations of East Indian and Creole family recipes. Beautifully grilled fresh tuna, red snapper, kingfish, mahimahi, and local lobster are embellished with flavors such as ginger, mango, papaya, or passion fruit, and then dished up with regional vegetables—perhaps callaloo, okra, dasheen, breadfruit, christophene, or yams. Of course, you can also have roast pork, beef, a chicken dish, or even pizza, if you wish. This is a very casual restaurant where locals, yachties, and frequent visitors know they'll get a delicious, reasonably priced meal right on the waterfront. And oh, that view! ⊠*Marigot Bay* ☎*758/451–4772* ▭*MC, V.*

CONTINENTAL/CARIBBEAN

$$ ╳Doolittle's. Named for the protagonist in the original (1967) *Dr. Doolittle* movie starring Rex Harrison, which was filmed right here in Marigot Bay, Doolittle's is the inside/outside waterfront restaurant at the Marigot Beach Club & Dive Center on the north side of the bay. You can watch yachts quietly slip by as you enjoy your meal. The menu offers a broad range of choices—light meals such as sandwiches, burgers, grilled chicken, and salads at lunchtime and, in the evening, seafood, steak, chicken, and Caribbean specials such as curries and stews. Take the little ferry across the bay to reach Doolittle's. During the day, bring your bathing suit. The beach is just outside the restaurant's door. ⊠*Marigot Beach Club, Marigot Bay* ☎*758/451–4974* ▭*MC, V.*

2

CONTINENTAL/SEAFOOD

$$$–$$$$ ×**Boudreau.** Simple and satisfying are words that come to
★ mind when dining at Boudreau, Discovery at Marigot Bay's
main dining room. In fact, that's the objective of Executive
Chef Frederic Wagnon, who heads the Discovery culinary
team. His passion for incorporating St. Lucian ingredients
into the menu brings him to market regularly to choose the
best fruits, roots, and greens to blend with fresh seafood
and prime meats—or to create a vegetarian dish that's both
filling and full of flavor. Seafood lovers may enjoy pan-
roasted kingfish with tempura vegetables, mashed sweet
potatoes, and maple mango sauce. Boudreau—which is
rather casual at breakfast and lunch but becomes rather
elegant at dinner—welcomes villa guests, yachties, and day-
trippers alike. The open-air restaurant is named for Walter
Boudreau, a schooner captain who sailed into Marigot Bay
50 years ago and built the original hotel where Discovery is
now located. Clearly, he would be impressed. ⊠*Discovery
at Marigot Bay, Marigot Bay* ☎*758/458–5300* ⚓*Reserva-
tions essential* ▭*AE, MC, V.*

ECLECTIC

★ Fodor'sChoice ×**Rainforest Hideaway.** British chef Jim Verity,
$$$–$$$$ whose parents own the new Discovery at Marigot Bay
resort, masters and beautifully presents fusion fare—in
this case, the exotic tastes and flavors influencing classical
French cuisine—at this romantic fine-dining hideaway on
the north shore of pretty Marigot Bay. It's definitely worth
the 20-minute-or-so drive from Castries. A little ferry whisks
you to the alfresco restaurant, perched on a dock, where
you're greeted with complimentary champagne. You'll be
duly impressed by entrées such as balsamic-glazed roast
quail, five-spice roast fillet of beef, or citrus-marinated wild
salmon, accompanied by rich sauces, exotic vegetables, and
excellent wines—not to mention the blanket of stars in the
sky overhead and the live jazz several times a week. Sun-
day brunch is a special treat in this picturesque setting on
the bay. ⊠*Marigot Bay* ☎*758/286–0511* ⚓*Reservations
essential* ▭*AE, D, MC, V* ⊗*No lunch.*

FRENCH

★ Fodor'sChoice ×**The Coal Pot.** Popular since the early 1960s,
$$ this tiny (only 10 tables) waterfront restaurant overlooking pretty Vigie Cove is managed by Michelle Elliott,
noted artist and daughter of the original owner, and her
French husband, chef Xavier Ribot. For a light lunch, opt
for Greek or shrimp salad or, perhaps, broiled fresh fish

with Creole sauce. Dinner might start with divine lobster bisque, followed by fresh seafood accompanied by one (or more) of the chef's fabulous sauces—ginger, coconut-curry, lemon-garlic butter, or wild mushroom. Hearty eaters may prefer duck, lamb, beef, or chicken laced with peppercorns, red wine, and onion or Roquefort sauce. ✉ *Vigie Marina, Castries* ☎758/452–5566 ♢*Reservations essential* ▭*AE, D, MC, V* ⊗*Closed Sun. No lunch Sat.*

$$ ╳**Jacques.** Chef-owner Jacky Rioux creates magical dishes
★ in his open-air garden restaurant (known for years as Froggie Jack's) overlooking Vigie Cove. The cooking style is decidedly French, as is Rioux, but fresh produce and local spices create a fusion cuisine that's memorable at lunch or dinner. You might start with a bowl of creamy tomato-basil or pumpkin soup, a grilled portobello mushroom, or octopus and conch in curried coconut sauce. Main courses include fresh seafood, such as oven-baked kingfish with a white wine and sweet pepper sauce, or breast of chicken stuffed with smoked salmon in a citrus butter sauce. The wine list is also impressive. ✉ *Vigie Marina, Castries* ☎758/458–1900 ♢*Reservations essential* ▭*AE, MC, V* ⊗*Closed Sun.*

SOUFRIÈRE & VICINITY

Restaurant locations can be found on the Soufrière & Vicinity map.

CARIBBEAN

$$$ ╳**Dasheene Restaurant & Bar.** The terrace restaurant at
★ Ladera Resort has breathtakingly close-up views of the Pitons and the sea between them, especially beautiful at sunset. Casual by day and magical at night, Dasheene offers a creative menu that executive chef Orlando Satchell likes to describe as "sexy Caribbean." Satchell, who has orchestrated Dasheene's cuisine since 1998, has earned praise and awards for his fresh, innovative—and, we will agree, "sexy"—approach to West Indian cuisine. He adds lightness and brightness to every dish by marinating and seasoning his raw materials—fresh fish, quality meats, and abundant local fruits and vegetables—with the delicate, savory, and/or piquant herbs and spices native to St. Lucia. Appetizers may include grilled crab claws with a choice of dips or silky pumpkin soup with ginger. Typical entrées are trigger fish seasoned and soaked in lime and fish stock and cooked in banana leaves, shrimp Dasheene (panfried with

local herbs), seared duck breast with passion-fruit jus, or baron fillet of beef with sweet-potato and green-banana mash. Callaloo and heart of palm quiche served in a bell pepper would appeal to any vegetarian. Light dishes, fresh salads, and sandwiches are served at lunchtime. ✉ *Ladera Resort, 2 mi (3 km) south of Soufrière* ☎758/459–7323 ☐*AE, D, DC, MC, V.*

$–$$ ✕**Lifeline Restaurant at the Hummingbird.** The chef at this cheerful restaurant-bar in the Hummingbird Beach Resort specializes in French Creole cuisine, starting with fresh seafood or chicken seasoned with local herbs and accompanied by a medley of vegetables just picked from the Hummingbird's garden. Sandwiches and salads are also available. If you stop for lunch, sit outside by the pool for a magnificent view of the Pitons (you can also take a dip), and be sure to visit the batik studio and art gallery of proprietor Joan Alexander and her son, adjacent to the dining room. ✉ *Hummingbird Beach Resort, Anse Chastanet Rd., Soufrière* ☎758/459–7232 ☐*AE, D, MC, V.*

$–$$ ✕**The Still.** If you're visiting Diamond Waterfall, this is a great lunch spot. The two dining rooms seat up to 400 people, so it's a popular stop for tour groups and cruise passengers. The emphasis is on local cuisine using vegetables such as christophenes, breadfruits, yams, and callaloo along with grilled fish or chicken, but there are also pork and beef dishes. All fruits and vegetables used in the restaurant are organically grown on the estate. ✉ *The Still Plantation, Sir Arthur Lewis St., Soufrière* ☎758/459–7261 ☐*MC, V.*

INDIAN

$$$–$$$$ ✕**Apsara.** India has had an important historical impact on many islands in the Caribbean, from the heritage of its people—descendents of both indentured servants and wealthy businessmen—to the colorful Madras plaids that adorn national costumes and the curry flavoring that is a staple of Caribbean cuisine. At night, Anse Chastanet's Trou au Diable restaurant transforms itself into Apsara, an upscale dining experience where modern Indian cuisine is served in an extraordinarily romantic, candlelit, beachfront setting. Chef Hemant Dadlani, who hails from Bombay, has created an innovative menu that fuses East Indian and Caribbean cooking. That translates to food that's full of flavor but not too spicy, although you can opt for some dishes that are hotter than others. You might start with mulligatawny soup with cumin yogurt or vegetable samosas, followed by coconut-chili king prawns, pork vindaloo, or tandoori-roasted salmon, lamb chops, chicken, or lobster. Definitely order the naan bread, either plain or flavored with almond, coconut, or raisin. And for dessert, depending on your appetite, choose the mango, saffron, or *seamoss kulfi* (Indian-style ice cream) or go all the way with Apsara's Temptation (tandoori-baked pineapple with honey, saffron, and passion-fruit syrup, Indian ice cream, and sun-blushed chili). ⊠*Anse Chastanet, Soufrière* ☎*758/459–7354* ⚑*Reservations essential.* ☐*AE, D, DC, MC, V* ⊘*No lunch, closed Tuesday.*

WHERE TO STAY

Most people—particularly honeymooning couples—choose to stay in one of St. Lucia's many beach resorts, the majority of which are upscale and fairly pricey. Several are all-inclusive, including the three Sandals resorts, two Almond resorts, and three resorts owned and/or managed by Sunswept (The Body Holiday at LeSport, Rendezvous, and Jalousie Plantation).

If you're looking for lodgings that are more intimate and less expensive, St. Lucia has dozens of small inns and hotels that are often locally owned, always charming, and usually less expensive—but that may or may not be directly on the beach. A group of these small inns and hotels market themselves through the St. Lucia Tourist Board as **INNtimate St. Lucia** (☎*758/452–4094* ⊕*www.inntimatestlucia*.org). Accommodations range in size from three to 75 rooms.

Luxury villa communities and independent private villas are another alternative in St. Lucia. Virtually all of the villa communities—which, as elsewhere in the Caribbean, continue to emerge in St. Lucia—are located in the north near Cap Estate, as well as south of Castries in Marigot Bay.

The lodgings listed below all have air-conditioning, telephones, and TVs in guest rooms unless otherwise noted.

VILLA COMMUNITIES & CONDOMINIUM COMPLEXES

Luxury villa communities are an important part of the accommodations mix in St. Lucia, as they can be an economical option for families, groups, or couples vacationing together. Several villa communities have opened in recent years, and more are on the way. The villas themselves are privately owned, but nonowners can rent individual units directly from the property managers for a vacation or short-term stay, the same as reserving hotel accommodations. Units with fully equipped kitchens, up to three bedrooms, and as many baths run $200 to $2,500 per night, depending on the size and the season.

PRIVATE VILLAS AND CONDOS

Local real-estate agencies will arrange vacation rentals of privately owned villas and condos that are fully furnished and equipped. Most private villas are located in the hills of Cap Estate in the very north of the island, in Rodney Bay or Bois d'Orange amid all the tourist activity, or in Soufrière among all the natural treasures of St. Lucia. Some are within walking distance of a beach. All rental villas are staffed with a housekeeper and a cook who specializes in local cuisine; in some cases, a caretaker lives on the property and a gardener and/or night watchman are on staff. All properties have telephones, and some have Internet access and/or fax machines. Telephones may be barred against outgoing overseas calls; plan to use a phone card or calling card. Most villas have TVs, DVDs and/or VCRs, and CD players. All private villas have a swimming pool; condos share a community pool. Vehicles are generally not included in the rates, but rental cars can be arranged and delivered to the villa upon request. Linens and basic supplies (e.g., bath soap, toilet tissue, dishwashing detergent) are included. Pre-arrival grocery stocking can be arranged.

Units with one to nine bedrooms and as many baths run $200 to $2,000 per night, depending on the size of the villa, the amenities, the number of guests, and the season. Rates include utilities and government taxes. Your only additional cost will be for groceries and staff gratuities. A security deposit is required upon booking and refunded after departure less any damages or unpaid miscellaneous charges.

RENTAL AGENCIES

Island Villas St. Lucia (⊠ *Rodney Bay, Gros Islet* ☎ *Box CP6384, Castries* ☎ *758/458–4903* ⊕ *www.island-villas. com/stlucia*). **Tropical Villas** (⊠ *Cap Estate, Gros Islet* ☎ *Box 189, Castries* ☎ *758/452–8240* ⊕ *www.tropicalvillas.net*).

NORTH OF VIGIE TO POINTE DU CAP

Hotel locations can be found on the Gros Islet & Rodney Bay and St. Lucia maps.

HOTELS

$$$$ ⛱**Almond Morgan Bay Beach Resort.** Almond Resorts com-
♻ pletely refurbished this venerable property in 2005, when
it purchased and repositioned it as an all-inclusive resort
appropriate for singles, couples, and families alike. Almond
Morgan Bay offers quiet seclusion on 22 acres surrounding a stretch of white-sand beach on a pretty cove—or an
action-packed vacation with more free sports and activities
than you'll probably be able to fit into your holiday. Rooms,
each with a private balcony or terrace, are in several buildings set among tropical gardens or facing the beachfront.
For your dining pleasure, choose among four restaurants.
The Palm is the main restaurant, serving three meals daily.
Le Jardin is an air-conditioned garden restaurant serving
French Creole cuisine at dinner. Bambou is right on the
waterfront and serves a mouthwatering fusion of Caribbean and Asian cuisines for three meals daily. At Morgan's
Pier, which stretches dramatically into the bay, seafood is
the obvious specialty at dinnertime. Four swimming pools
(two designated for adults only), and all manner of activities are available day and night—including simply relaxing under a palm tree with a frosty drink. **Pros:** Family
friendly, lots to do, the atmosphere at Morgan's Pier. **Cons:**
It's very large. ✉*Choc Bay, Gros Islet* 🏠*Box 2167, Castries* ☎*758/450–2511* 🖷*758/450–1050* ⊕*www.almond
resorts.com* ⚓*340 rooms* ⚙*In-room: safe. In-hotel: 4 restaurants, bars, tennis courts, pools, gym, spa, beachfront,
water sports, no elevator, children's programs (ages newborn–16), laundry service, concierge, public Internet* ☰*AE,
D, MC, V* ⦿*AI.*

$$$$ ⛱**Almond Smugglers Cove.** After investing $20 million in
♻ renovations, a few million more in landscaping, renaming
the (former Club St. Lucia) property, and "Almond-izing"
it with more food, fun, and features than you'll probably
have time to tap into during a week's vacation, Almond
Smugglers Cove opened in 2007. Set on 60 acres and overlooking a pretty bay at the island's northernmost point,
this all-inclusive family resort has amenities and activities for guests from newborn to 90. The 90-year-olds will
want to be somewhat fit, however, because guest rooms are
spread out over a broad hillside—a gentle slope, but still a

2

hill—although golf-cart transportation is available, if you wish. Rooms are rather basic but comfortable. There's a sandy beach, five swimming pools, and a laundry list of water sports to enjoy. The world-class St. Lucia Racquet Club, with seven tennis courts and a squash court, is on-site. Guests are entitled to free greens fees for three 18-hole rounds of golf at the nearby St. Lucia Golf Course. Four dining rooms offer as many cuisines, and libations flow freely from four bars. And there's live entertainment nightly. The plethora of planned entertainment gives the resort somewhat of a holiday camp atmosphere, but families love it—British families, in particular. **Pros:** Excellent children's program, excellent tennis facilities. **Cons:** Busy, busy, busy—not the place for a quiet getaway ⊠*Smugglers Cove, Cap Estate, Gros Islet* ☎*758/450–0551* ⊕*www. almondresorts.com* ⌐*258 rooms, 100 suites* ⌂*In-room: safe. In-hotel: 4 restaurants, room service, bars, tennis courts, pools, gym, spa, beachfront, water sports, no elevator, children's program (age newborn–16), laundry service, concierge, public Internet, Wi-Fi* ⏹*AI.*

$$$$ ▦**The Body Holiday at LeSPORT.** Even before you leave home,
★ you can customize your own "body holiday" online—from robe size to tee time—at this truly unique resort for adults seeking to refresh body, mind, and spirit in luxurious tropical surroundings. Indulge yourself with aromatherapy, a dozen different massages, Ayurvedic treatments, wraps, yoga, personal-trainer services, and more at the splendid Oasis spa; daily treatments are included in the all-inclusive rates. Otherwise, enjoy the beach, scuba diving, golf (greens fees are free at St. Lucia Golf Club, next door), and other sports—with free instruction, if needed. The concept is to combine an active beach vacation with revitalization for both body and mind. Rooms have marble floors and king-size four-poster or twin beds. The food is excellent at Cariblue (the main dining room), the Club House casual buffet restaurant, the Deli, or the top-of-the-line Tao. Enjoy nightly entertainment at the beachside lounge; the piano bar remains open until the last person says "good night." Special rates are offered for single guests. **Pros:** Daily spa treatments included, excellent dining, unusual activities such as archery, nice beach. **Cons:** Unremarkable rooms with small bathrooms and skimpy towels. ⊠*Cariblue Beach, Cap Estate Gros Islet* ⌂*Box 437, Castries* ☎*758/450–8551* ⊟*758/450–0368* ⊕*www. thebodyholiday.com* ⌐*152 rooms, 2 suites* ⌂*In-room:*

safe, refrigerator, no TV. In-hotel: 3 restaurants, bars, tennis courts, pools, gym, spa, beachfront, diving, water sports, concierge, public Internet, airport shuttle, no kids under 16 ⊟*AE, MC, V* ⊺⊙⊺*AI.*

$$$$ ⊠**Royal St. Lucian.** This classy, all-suites resort on Reduit ☾ Beach—St. Lucia's best beach—caters to your every whim. The reception area has a vaulted atrium, marble walls, a fountain, and a sweeping grand staircase. Just beyond, the free-form pool has Japanese-style bridges, a waterfall, and a swim-up bar. Guest suites all have sitting areas with soothing color schemes and large patios or balconies. Eight beachfront suites are huge, with special amenities such as a wide-screen TV, DVD, and stereo equipment. Massages, hydrotherapy, and other treatments can be arranged at the Royal Spa. Dine at the elegant Chic!, the sea-view L'Epicure, or lunch at the casual Beach Tent. Alternatively, you're within walking distance of a dozen or so Rodney Bay restaurants, nightclubs, and shopping areas. Tennis, water-sports facilities, and the children's club are shared with the adjacent Rex St. Lucian Hotel. **Pros:** Great beachfront, roomy accommodations, convenient to Rodney Bay Village. **Cons:** Sprucing up the guest rooms and dated baths is overdue. ⊠*Reduit Beach, Rodney Bay, Gros Islet* ✆*Box 977, Castries* ☎*758/452–9999* 📠*758/452–9639* ⊕*www. rexcaribbean.com* ♫*96 suites* ㊟*In-room: safe, refrigerator. In-hotel: 3 restaurants, room service, bars, tennis courts, pool, gym, spa, beachfront, diving, water sports, concierge, children's programs (ages 4–12), laundry service, public Internet* ⊟*AE, DC, MC, V* ⊺⊙⊺*EP.*

★ **Fodor's**Choice ⊠**Sandals Grande St. Lucian Spa & Beach Resort.**
$$$$ Grand, indeed! And busy, busy, busy. Couples—particularly young honeymooners and couples getting married here—love this place, the biggest and splashiest of the three Sandals resorts on St. Lucia. Several weddings take place here each day, in fact. Perched on the narrow Pigeon Island Causeway at St. Lucia's northern tip, Sandals Grande offers panoramic views of Rodney Bay on one side and the Atlantic Ocean on the other. Luxurious rooms, decorated with colorful fabrics and mahogany furniture, all have king-size beds; 24 lagoon-side rooms have swim-up verandas. With a plethora of land and water sports, a European-style full-service spa, five excellent restaurants, nightly entertainment, and romance in the air, there's never a dull moment. A complimentary shuttle connects all three Sandals properties for additional fun with full exchange privileges. **Pros:**

Beautiful white-sand beach, lots of water sports, brides and grooms love it, nice spa. **Cons:** The long ride to/from Hewanorra, buffet meals are uninspired ⊠*Pigeon Island Causeway, Gros Islet* ⬦*Box 2247, Castries* ☎*758/455–2000* ⬦*758/455–2001* ⬦*www.sandals.com* ⬦*271 rooms, 11 suites* ⬦*In-room: safe, dial-up. In-hotel: 5 restaurants, room service, bars, tennis courts, pools, gym, spa, beachfront, diving, water sports, laundry service, executive floor, public Internet, airport shuttle, no kids under 18* ☐*AE, D, DC, MC, V* ⬦*AI.*

$$$$ ⬚**Sandals Halcyon St. Lucia.** While not really small, this is the smallest—and, therefore, the most intimate and most low-key—of the three Sandals resorts on St. Lucia. Like the others, it's beachfront, all-inclusive, couples only, and loaded with amenities and activities. And just 10 minutes north of downtown Castries, it's also convenient to public transportation. Learn something new—perhaps sailing, windsurfing, or waterskiing—or just enjoy the sea and any of the three pools. Take a break and play a game of croquet, table tennis, or billiards. There are four restaurants: Bayside serves three meals daily, inside or outside. Beach Bistro serves grilled specials and snacks all day long. Mario's specializes in northern Italian cuisine. And The Pier, which is perched on a 150-foot pier on the waterfront, is the place to go for seafood. Then, of course, there are the five bars, which are always good places to meet and greet new friends. Still looking for something to do? An hourly shuttle connects the sister properties, so you can stay at one—but play (and eat) at three. **Pros:** All the Sandals amenities in an intimate setting, lots of dining and activity choices, easy access to public transportation. **Cons:** It's Sandals, so it's a theme property, after all. ⊠*Choc Bay, Castries* ☎*758/453–0222 or 800/223–6510* ⬦*www.sandals.com* ⬦*170 rooms* ⬦*In-room: safe, refrigerator, dial-up. In-hotel: 4 restaurants, room service, bars, tennis courts, pools, gym, spa, beachfront, diving, water sports, no elevator, laundry service, concierge, public Internet, airport shuttle, no kids under 18* ☐*AE, D, DC, MC, V* ⬦*AI.*

$$$$ ⬚**Sandals Regency St. Lucia Golf Resort & Spa.** One of three
★ Sandals resorts on St. Lucia, this is the second-largest and distinguishes itself with its own 9-hole golf course (for guests only). Like the others, it's for couples only and is all-inclusive. The resort covers 200 acres on a hillside overlooking the sea on the southern shore of Castries Bay. If you're flying into Castries and are sitting on the right-hand

side of the plane, you'll get a bird's-eye view of the resort just before you come in for a landing. Guest rooms are lavishly decorated with rich mahogany furniture and king-size four-poster beds. Many rooms have private plunge pools. The main pool, with its waterfall and bridges, and a long crescent beach are focal points for socializing and enjoying water sports. Massages (single or duet), scrubs, and wraps are available at the full-service spa (for an additional charge). Six restaurants serve Asian, continental, French, Mediterranean, Southwestern, or Caribbean cuisine. An hourly shuttle connects all three Sandals properties. **Pros:** A huge resort with lots to do, picturesque location, onsite golf, great spa. **Cons:** Somewhat isolated location. ⊠*La Toc Rd., Box 399, Castries* ☎*758/452–3081* 🖷*758/453– 7089* ⊕*www.sandals.com* 🛏*212 rooms, 116 suites* ⚷*In-room: safe. In-hotel: 6 restaurants, room service, bars, golf course, tennis courts, pools, gym, spa, beachfront, diving, water sports, laundry service, executive floor, public Internet, airport shuttle, no kids under 18* ⊟*AE, D, DC, MC, V* ⭗*AI.*

$$–$$$$ 🖵**St. Lucian by Rex Resorts.** In January 2008 the St. Lucian ⏾ by Rex incorporated the former Papillon by Rex property, next door, into a single resort. The resulting 260-room resort is on a long stretch of Reduit beachfront and is surrounded by gardens. Deluxe rooms face the beach; superior rooms have a sea or garden view. Standard Papillon rooms have no TVs, and the bathrooms have showers only. A TV lounge is available for those who don't have a room TV but must watch. Caribbean cuisine and international dishes are served at Mariners restaurant; Asian cuisine is served à la carte in the Oriental restaurant, and buffet-style meals are served in the Monarch restaurant. Admirals Lounge is the place to go for after-dinner drinks and nightly entertainment—steel bands and limbo dancing, for example. A covered walkway leads to the Royal St. Lucian, a sister resort, where guests can also dine, shop at its boutiques and vendors market, or visit the Royal Spa. **Pros:** Great beach and lots of water sports, excellent Rodney Bay Village location, easy access to Royal sister hotel. **Cons:** Basic Papillon rooms are pretty basic. ⊠*Reduit Beach, Rodney Bay, Gros Islet* ⏏*Box 512, Castries* ☎*758/452–8351* ⊕*www. rexresorts.com* 🛏*260 rooms* ⚷*In-room: safe, refrigerator (some), no TV (some), dial-up, Wi-Fi. In-hotel: 3 restaurants, room service, bars, tennis courts, pool, gym, beach-*

front, diving, water sports, no elevator, children's program (ages 4–12), laundry service, concierge, public Internet, public Wi-Fi, no-smoking rooms ⊟*AC, MC, V* ⑩*EP.*

$$ 🖻**Bay Gardens Beach Resort.** Opened in 2007, this newest of three Bay Gardens properties in Rodney Bay Village has a prime location directly on beautiful Reduit Beach. The resort has 36 one-bedroom and 36 two-bedroom suites, all with living and dining areas, full kitchens, and modern baths. Accommodations are in six three-story buildings that wrap around a lagoon-style pool; most suites have views of the sea from the balcony or terrace. All sorts of water sports and diving are available on the beach. Massages are available in poolside cabanas. Guests may dine at Pimento's, a fine-dining restaurant serving Mediterranean specialties; at Hi Tide, a casual beachside restaurant; at the Lo Tide deli; or at any of a dozen or more excellent restaurants in the Rodney Bay neighborhood. The Bay Gardens properties are well known for their friendly hospitality and exceptional service; in fact, the hotel clientele is 75 percent repeat guests. Add a beautiful beach to the equation, and this new addition is sure to be a winner. **Pros:** Idyllic beachfront location, excellent service, Wi-Fi even on the beach. **Cons:** When Phase II is underway, construction noise may be an issue. ⊠*Reduit Beach, Rodney Bay, Gros Islet* ⓓ*Box 1892, Gros Islet* ☎*758/452–8060* ⊕*www.bay gardensbeachresort.com* ⬗*72 suites* ⬧*In-room: safe, kitchen, DVD, ethernet. In-hotel: 2 restaurants, bar, pool, gym, beachfront, diving, water sports, no elevator, children's club (ages 4–12), laundry service, concierge, public Internet, public Wi-Fi, airport shuttle* ⊟*AE, D, MC, V* ⑩*EP.*

$$ 🖻**Caribbean Jewel Beach Resort.** Truly a bargain, considering the convenient location and generous size of the rooms and suites, Caribbean Jewel Beach Resort boutique resort sits on 60 hilltop acres at the southern end of Reduit Beach. Accommodations are in several pink villa-style buildings strategically positioned so that the enormous private balcony of each unit has a magnificent bird's-eye view of Rodney Bay, Pigeon Island, and the Caribbean Sea. Each room or suite is modern and comfortable. Suites have sitting rooms, dining areas, and full kitchens. Second-floor rooms have vaulted ceilings. Hang around two pools, dine on contemporary Caribbean cuisine at the restaurant, or walk down the hillside to the beach and all the action at Rodney Bay. The view, however, is the crowning jewel. **Pros:** 360-

degree view of Rodney Bay area, family friendly, excellent value, request a corner room for the most expansive view. **Cons:** Few on-site activities, the uphill walk back from the beach or the village ⊠*Rodney Bay, Gros Islet* ☎*Box GM503, Castries* ☎*758/452–9199* ⊕*www.caribbean jewelresort.com* ⌂*15 rooms, 15 suites* &*In-room: refrigerator (some), kitchen (some), Wi-Fi. In-hotel: restaurant, room service, bar, pools, beachfront, no elevator, concierge, public Internet* ⊟*AE, MC, V* ⓇEP.

$$ 🏨**Ginger Lily.** A small, modern enclave with its own restaurant and a swimming pool, the Ginger Lily is across the street from Reduit Beach and smack in the middle of Rodney Bay Village. It's so comfortable, so well located, and such a good deal that wedding parties or family reunions sometimes book the entire hotel. All rooms have a queen-size bed and a sofa bed in the sitting area. A pair of executive suites each have a separate bedroom and full kitchen. Ground-floor rooms have a terrace; upper-level rooms have a balcony. This is a good place to hang your hat if you don't need or want the amenities of a big resort, yet everything you might need or want—the beach, dining options, shopping, nightlife—is virtually at the front door. For anything else—such as diving, horseback riding, or tours—management will gladly make arrangements for you. **Pros:** Friendly service, good value, excellent location. **Cons:** Few on-site activities. ⊠*Rodney Bay, Gros Islet* ☎*Box CP6013, Rodney Bay Village* ☎*758/458–0300* ⊕*www.thegingerlily hotel.com* ⌂*9 rooms, 2 suites* &*In-room: safe, kitchen (some) Wi-Fi. In-hotel: restaurant, room service, bar, pool, Wi-Fi* ⊟*AE, MC, V* ⓇEP.

$-$$ 🏨**Coco Palm.** St. Lucia native Allen Chastanet opened this
★ stylish boutique hotel in Rodney Bay Village in 2005, adjacent to his Coco Kreole bed-and-breakfast inn. Guests check in and out in the comfort of their rooms, and personal hosts attend to any need or request. Guest rooms—including six swim-up rooms adjacent to the pool—and a dozen spacious suites are beautifully decorated in French Caribbean plantation style, with rich mahogany furniture and elegant upholstered chairs and loveseats; yet every modern convenience is also at hand. Cordless phones, CD and DVD players, free Wi-Fi and Internet access, flat-screen TVs (in suites), and ultramodern baths with walk-in showers and claw-foot tubs (in suites) are amenities you'd expect at much pricier resorts. Coco Palm combines a high-end atmosphere with extremely affordable rates, making it one

2

of St. Lucia's best deals. The excellent Ti Bananne restaurant and bar overlook the pool and bandstand, and all the action of Rodney Bay Village and beautiful Reduit Beach are within walking distance. **Pros:** Excellent value, fabulous rooms—especially the swim-up ones, fantastic dining. **Cons:** Not directly on the beach—but not far away. ☒*Reduit Beach Ave., Rodney Bay, Gros Islet* ☎*758/456–2800* ☎*758/452–0774* ⊕*www.coco-resorts.com* ⤶*60 rooms, 12 suites* ⚴*In-room: safe, refrigerator, VCRs (some), Wi-Fi. In-hotel: restaurant, bar, pool, no elevator, public Internet, public Wi-Fi* ═*AE, D, MC, V* ⦿*EP.*

$–$$ ▦**Harmony Suites.** Harmony Suites guests (adults only) are scuba divers, boaters, or others who don't need luxury but appreciate comfort and just like being close to Rodney Bay Marina. Of the 30 large, one-bedroom suites cloistered around the swimming pool, the eight waterfront suites, at a whopping 700 square feet each with a private sundeck, are the best choice. The Edge restaurant, where chef Bobo Bergstrom creates his self-described "Eurobbean" fusion cuisine, is on-site, and is one of the best restaurants in Rodney Bay. Reduit Beach is just across the road. **Pros:** Marina location, excellent on-site restaurant, waterfront suites. **Cons:** Rooms are fairly basic and could use a little TLC ☒*Rodney Bay, Gros Islet* ⎙*Box 155, Castries* ☎*758/452–8756* ⊕*www.harmonysuites.com* ⤶*30 suites* ⚴*In-room: refrigerator. In-hotel: restaurant, bar, pool, diving, no elevator, public Internet, laundry service, no kids under 13* ═*AE, MC, V* ⦿*EP.*

$ ▦**Bay Gardens Hotel.** Independent travelers and regional businesspeople swear by this cheerful, well-run boutique hotel at Rodney Bay Village. In fact, it's often booked. Never fear, however, as Bay Gardens Inn, a sister property, is next door and the Bay Gardens Beachfront Resort, opened in 2007, is minutes away on Reduit Beach. Modern, colorful, and surrounded by pretty flower gardens, the hotel is a short walk from beautiful Reduit Beach (shuttle transportation is also provided), several popular restaurants, and shops. Some rooms surround the serpentine pool and Jacuzzi and are close to the restaurant and lobby; more secluded rooms near the back of the property have easy access to a second pool that's smaller and quieter. The 16 Croton suites added in 2007 have full kitchens and interconnect to become two-bedroom suites. Spices restaurant offers a fairly extensive menu, along with lobster and shrimp specials, a weekly barbecue, and a Caribbean buffet night. **Pros:** Excellent service, excellent value, new Croton suites are a good bet. **Cons:** Not beachfront, heavy focus on business travelers ⊠*Rodney Bay, Gros Islet* ⊕*Box 1892, Castries* ☎*758/452–8060* 🖷*758/452–8059* ⊕*www.baygardenshotel.com* ⟿*59 rooms, 28 suites* ⟨*In-room: safe, kitchen (some), refrigerator, dial-up. In-hotel: restaurant, room service, bar, pools, no elevator, laundry service, public Internet* ⊟*AE, D, MC, V* ⦾*BP.*

$ ⊠**Coco Kreole.** More a guesthouse than a hotel, Coco Kreole is a stylish, inexpensive, 20-room treasure with an ambience reminiscent of the home of a good friend. There's no check-in at a main desk; rather, you enter what appears to be a living room or salon, decorated with the paintings of local artists, and are shown to your room. Complete the paperwork at your leisure. Located in the center of the action at Rodney Bay Village and adjacent to sister hotel Coco Palm, just behind, Coco Kreole is within walking distance of more than a dozen restaurants, several nightspots, a shopping mall, and beautiful Reduit Beach. Yet walk out the back door to peace and quiet in a pretty garden with a small pool, terrace, and bar. Owner Allan Chastanet has said that his aim at Coco Kreole was to combine the style of South Beach with a little European chic and a lot of Caribbean color and warmth. Looks like he hit the mark. **Pros:** Excellent value, friendly service, convenient location. **Cons:** Street noise can be distracting in front rooms at night, ⊠*Rodney Bay, Gros Islet* ⊕*Box GM605, Castries* ☎*758/452–0712* ⊕*www.cocokreole.com* ⟿*20 rooms* ⟨*In-room: safe, refrigerator, VCR, Wi-Fi. In-hotel: bar, pool, no elevator, laundry service, public Internet, no-smoking rooms* ⊟*AE, D, MC, V* ⦾*EP.*

VILLA COMPLEXES

$$$$ ⊠**Cap Maison.** Opened in spring 2008, Cap Maison is a boutique villa community with just 22 units that can be reconfigured as up to 50 rooms, junior suites, and oversized one-, two-, or three-bedroom villa suites. The Ocean View Grand Villa suites, for example, measure 3,000 square feet. Built on a seaside bluff, the elegant Spanish Caribbean architecture has wooden jalousie doors and windows, terra-cotta roof tiles, large private balconies, and large roof terraces with a plunge pool. A large infinity pool at the edge of the bluff and a hot tub are available to everyone. Truly luxurious service includes no formal check-in required, an unpacking service upon request, an honor bar, and a personal butler for any little needs and requests that may come

2

up—including arranging a romantic dinner, prepared and served in your suite by one of the resort's chefs. French Caribbean cuisine at the resort's cliff-top Cap Maison restaurant is another option. For extra pampering, there's a full-service spa and a calming Zen garden. The resort is on a seaside cliff, so getting down to Smugglers Cove Beach, a secluded crescent of sand, requires hiking down (and back up) several steps. The resort also has a 46-foot, 15-passenger power boat to take guests on day trips to Soufrière or nearby Martinique, or on honeymoon cruises. **Pros:** Near the golf course, private and elegant, those rooftop plunge pools. **Cons:** Beach access is difficult or impossible for anyone with physical disabilities. ⊠*Smugglers Cove, Cap Estate, Gros Islet* ☎*Box 2188, Gros Islet* ☎*758/285– 1274* ⊕*www.capmaison.co.uk* ⤳*11 rooms, 39 suites* ⌂*In-room: kitchen (some), refrigerator, DVD, Wi-Fi. In-hotel: restaurant, room service, bars, pool, gym, spa, beachfront, watersports, no elevator, laundry facilities, public Internet, public Wi-Fi, airport shuttle* ⊟*AE, MC, V* ⎖◎*EP.*

$$$$ ▣**The Landings.** Managed by RockResorts, the Landings is
★ set on 19 acres along the Pigeon Point Causeway, on the northern side of Rodney Bay. Phase I of the condo development—the first 62 units—opened in December 2007. Ultimately, the community will have 231 waterfront residences, ranging in size from 900 to 2,300 square feet (half with plunge pools), constructed in three phases, and completed by 2010. Each unit has a beautifully appointed living room, dining room, and kitchen; one, two, or three bedrooms with ensuite baths; and an enormous balcony or terrace with a private plunge pool. Buildings surround the 80-slip marina, making the atmosphere particularly conducive to yachting and boating. Nevertheless, landlubbers will love the 7,000-square-foot RockResorts Spa™, socializing at the lobby bar in the Grand Pavilion, and soaking up the sun at the beach club or at one of the (eventual) seven pools. Besides preparing your own meals, grab a snack at the gourmet deli, have a light meal on the pier at the Beach Bar, or enjoy the latest cuisine concepts in the Trend Room restaurant, where the type of food changes depending on what's "hot" at the time. Guests are also entitled to preferred tee times at the nearby St. Lucia Golf Club. The pampering begins with a personalized greeting upon arrival at the airport. **Pros:** Very spacious units with modern furnishings, good place for yachties to come ashore, the personal chef service. **Cons:** Construction through 2010 may

create noise and disruption. ⊠*Pigeon Island Causeway, Gros Islet* ☎*758/458–7300* ⊕*www.landings.rockresorts. com* ↪*62 units* ♿*In-room: kitchen, ethernet. In-hotel: 3 restaurants, room service, bars, tennis courts, pools, gym, spa, beachfront, water sports, no elevator, concierge, laundry facilities, no-smoking rooms, airport shuttle* ⊟*AE, D, DC, MC, V* ⊠*EP.*

$$$–$$$$ 🖫 **Cotton Bay Village.** Opened in 2007, Cotton Bay Village
♺ is a villa community on 9 idyllic acres at the northern tip of the island. Adjacent to The Body Holiday at LeSPORT, a sister operation, it's wedged between a quiet ocean beach and the St. Lucia Golf Club. Luxurious, individually designed and decorated colonial-style town houses and chateau-style villas surround a free-form lagoon pool. Units have spacious sitting rooms, dining terraces, fully equipped kitchens, and anywhere from one to four bedrooms. All are beautifully furnished in an eclectic style—painted French furniture, modern metal designs, traditional plantation mahogany. Accommodations also include dedicated service from a personal butler, who helps with special requests and the little chores associated with independent living. Guests may patronize the spa, two bars, a deli, coffee shop, and two restaurants—The Beach Club 14'61" (its latitude and longitude) and a second fine-dining restaurant. Cotton Bay beach, with its golden sand, is so secluded it's virtually private. Take lessons in windsurfing or kiteboarding, arrange a horseback trek along the beach, or charter a yacht for a day. You're living like royalty here, so you might as well go whole hog. Of course, greens fees at the next-door golf club are free. **Pros:** Truly luxurious accommodations, privacy, family-friendly. **Cons:** Isolated, rental car advised if you plan to leave the property. ⊠*Cotton Bay, Cap Estate, Gros Islet* ☎*758/456–5700* ⊕*www.cottonbayvillage.com* ↪*74 villas* ♿*In-room: kitchen, DVD. In-hotel: 2 restaurants, bars, pool, gym, spa, beachfront, water sports, no elevator, children's programs (3–7)* ⊟*AE, MC, V* ⊠*EP.*

$$$–$$$$ 🖫 **Windjammer Landing Villa Beach Resort.** Windjammer's
♺ Mediterranean-style villas, connected by brick paths, climb the sun-kissed hillside on one of St. Lucia's prettiest bays. As perfect for families as for a romantic getaway, the resort offers lots to do yet plenty of privacy. Windjammer's stylishly decorated villas can easily be closed off or opened up to become one-, two-, three-, or four-bedroom villa suites. Some have private plunge pools. The resort's reception area opens onto shops, restaurants, and two pools. Eat excel-

lently prepared cuisine in the restaurants, make your own meals, or have dinner prepared and served in your villa. Shuttles whoosh you between villas and activity areas—including two hillside pools connected by a waterfall. **Pros:** Lovely, spacious villas, beautiful sunset views, family-friendly. **Cons:** Rent a car if you plan to leave the property, as it's far from the main road. ⊠*Labrelotte Bay ✍Box 1504, Castries* ☎*758/452–0913* ⊟*758/452–9454* ⊕*www. windjammer-landing.com* ⚓*219 rooms* ⌂*In-room: safe, kitchen (some), refrigerator, DVD. In-hotel: 5 restaurants, room service, bars, tennis courts, pools, gym, spa, beach-front, diving, water sports, no elevator, children's pro-grams (ages 4–12), laundry service, concierge* ⊟*AE, MC, V* ⫶*EP.*

PRIVATE VILLAS

$$$$ ⌨**Morne Trulah.** On a clear day you can see as far as Mar-tinique; otherwise, you merely get a long-range view of Pigeon Island, Rodney Bay, and the Caribbean Sea from Morne Trulah villa, which was built on the site of an old French fort. The four bedrooms are of equal size, mak-ing this a good choice for couples traveling together, and each bedroom has its own bathroom, sitting area, and pri-vate patio area. The pool and sundeck are in a pretty gar-den with a beautiful view; Bois d'Orange beach is within walking distance; and water sports are available at nearby Windjammer Landing Resort. You'll want to rent a Jeep, though, to explore the island or to get to Rodney Bay to do errands, have dinner, or enjoy the nightlife. The cook and the maid work six days a week, from 8 AM to 4 PM. **Pros:** Four equal-size bedrooms, fully air-conditioned, family friendly. **Cons:** You'll need that Jeep to get around. ⊠*Bois d'Orange, Gros Islet (Tropical Villas* ☎*758/450–8240* ⊕*www.tropicalvillas.net)* ⚓*4 bedrooms, 4 bathrooms* ⌂*DVD, daily maid service, cook, pool, laundry facilities* ⊟*AE, MC, V.*

$$$$ ⌨**Villa Tranquility.** Overlooking Anse Galet Bay, all the rooms in Villa Tranquility—and the terrace that runs the length of the home—have a view of the sea. The three bed-rooms are air-conditioned, while ceiling fans and natural sea breezes cool all the other rooms. The villa has a large pool with a 45-foot lap lane and a big deck for poolside dining. Three beaches are five minutes away by car. Villa guests also enjoy a complimentary membership (for two people) at the nearby St. Lucia Golf Club, where the only cost will be $15 for cart rental. Besides daily maid service, the property has a gardener and pool boy; a chef can be provided upon request. **Pros:** A good choice for golfers, couples traveling together, or families with grown children. **Cons:** No a/c in the kitchen and living areas ⊠*Cap Estate, Gros Islet (Island Villas St. Lucia* ☎*758/458–4903* ⊕*www. island-villas.com/stlucia)* ⮫*3 bedrooms, 3 bathrooms* ⚠*no a/c (some rooms), safes, DVD, Wi-Fi, daily maid service, on-site security, pool, laundry facilities, no kids under 12, no-smoking* ⊟*AE, MC, V.*

$$–$$$ ⊞ **Tree Tops.** If you're looking for something rustic, unique, and inexpensive—yet comfortable, interesting, and well located, consider a tree house. A Canadian architect, who came to St. Lucia in the 1960s to "upgrade the architecture," designed Tree Tops, one of the oldest homes in Cap Estate. His masterpiece is this one-of-a-kind villa, with hardwood floors, cathedral ceilings, walls that slide to capture every breeze, and broad decks that connect one room to another. It's, well, very much like living in a tree house. A great room has a sitting area, dining and games tables, and a desk. The kitchen is large and bright. The two bedrooms have ceiling fans and mosquito netting on the beds. A kidney-shaped pool has lap lanes at one end and a sundeck for relaxing. Built on a hilltop, the Tree Tops has expansive views. You can see spectacular sunsets to the west, the sea to the north and east, and as far away as Mt. Gimie to the south. **Pros:** Rather exotic, yet convenient. **Cons:** No air-conditioning, perhaps an issue in humid periods during October and early November. ⊠*Saddleback, Cap Estate, Gros Islet (Tropical Villas* ☎*758/450–8240* ⊕*www.tropi calvillas.net)* ⮫*2 bedrooms, 2 bathrooms* ⚠*no a/c, daily maid service, pool, laundry facilities* ⊟*AE, MC, V.*

GREATER CASTRIES

Hotel locations can be found on the Castries and St. Lucia maps.

HOTELS

$$$$ ⊞ **Rendezvous.** Romance is alive and well at this easygoing, all-inclusive couples resort (male-female couples only), which stretches along the dreamy white sand of Malabar Beach opposite the George F. L. Charles Airport runway. The occasional distraction of prop aircraft taking off and landing is completely overshadowed by the beautiful gardens on this former coconut plantation and by the convenient access to town. Accommodations are in cheerful

2

gingerbread cottages, elegant oceanfront rooms with sunset-facing terraces (some with hammocks), or cozy poolside suites. Lounge on the beach or participate in a host of activities and sports—your choice and all included. Buffet-style meals are served at the beachfront terrace restaurant, with fine dining by reservation at the Trysting Place. **Pros:** Convenient to Castries and Vigie Airport, great beach, romance in the air. **Cons:** No room TV, occasional flyover noise (that you really don't notice after awhile) ⊠*Malabar Beach, Vigie* ⏏*Box 190, Castries* ☎*758/457–7900* ⊕*www.theromanticholiday.com* ⤢*81 rooms, 11 suites, 8 cottages* ♿*In-room: safe, refrigerator (some), no TV. In-hotel: 2 restaurants, bars, tennis courts, pools, gym, spa, beachfront, diving, bicycles, no elevator, concierge, laundry service, public Internet, airport shuttle, no kids under 18* ⊟*AE, MC, V* ⧖*AI.*

★ **Fodor's**Choice ⊺**Discovery at Marigot Bay.** Five miles (8 km)
$$$ south of Castries, on the mid-west coast of St. Lucia, Discovery at Marigot Bay climbs the hillside at the east end of what author James Michener rightly called "the most beautiful bay in the Caribbean." Each unit in this new resort (opened in October 2006) is exquisitely decorated with dark Balinese furniture accented by comfy earth-tone cushions, a four-poster bed with a pillow-top mattress, and dark hardwood flooring. Oversized bathrooms have walk-in "drench" showers and double basins set in slate vanities. Each suite has a full kitchen equipped with modern Euro-designer appliances (including an espresso machine), a spacious living room with sofa bed and dining area, flat-screen TVs in each room, a Bose music system with MP3 input capability, balcony or deck, and washer and dryer; half the suites have private plunge pools. At the water's edge, charter sailboats and privately owned yachts and mega-yachts tie up at the resort's dock—a pretty view (especially at sunset) from each guest room, the Boudreau fine dining restaurant, or the Hurricane Hole open-air bar. A solar-powered ferry, called *Sunshine Express*, transports guests back and forth across the bay to the beach or to the Rainforest Hideaway restaurant. The Marina Village, adjacent to the resort, has shops and services that appeal to guests who "discover" Marigot Bay—whether by land or by sea. **Pros:** The pretty view of Marigot Bay, excellent service, oversize accommodations, the village atmosphere. **Cons:** You'll need a rental car to explore beyond Marigot Bay. ⊠*Marigot Bay, Box MG7227, Marigot* ☎*758/458–*

5300 🖷*758/458–5299* ⊕*www.discoverystlucia.com* ⬎*67 rooms, 57 suites* ♿*In-room: safe, kitchen (some), DVD, VCR, ethernet, Wi-Fi. In-hotel: restaurant, room service, bars, pools, gym, spa, water sports, no elevator, laundry facilities, concierge, public Internet, public Wi-Fi* ▭*AE, MC, V* ⍟*EP.*

$$ ▨**Marigot Beach Club & Dive Resort.** Divers love this place, and everyone loves the location facing the little palm-studded beach at Marigot Bay. Owners poured some needed resources into the property in 2006—adding two guest rooms with plunge pools and redecorating existing units in pleasing light colors—perhaps because of the upgrading of the entire neighborhood by Discovery at Marigot Bay, their classy new neighbor across the bay. Some accommodations are right on the beachfront; others are on the hillside with a sweeping view of the bay. All units have either a kitchen or kitchenette. Villa accommodations, suitable for families and large groups, have two, three, or five bedrooms; the largest has two kitchens. Scuba courses and dive trips are available from the onsite PADI dive center; special dive packages include accommodations, meals, daily two-tank boat dives, and all equipment. Doolittle's, the waterfront restaurant, is popular for guests who want to escape their kitchenettes, as well as nonguests and yachties who like the food and the live entertainment. The Marina Village, Discovery's wonderful restaurants and bars, and Chateau Mygo are a one-minute ferry ride away. All guests get a ferry pass to come and go at will. **Pros:** Great value for divers, beautiful views of Marigot Bay, good casual dining, easy access to Marina Village. **Cons:** Beach is tiny (but picturesque) ⬚*Marigot Bay* 🖷*758/451–4974* ⊕*www. marigotdiveresort.com* ⬎*24 rooms, 3 villas* ♿*In room: safe, kitchen, dial-up, Wi-Fi. In hotel: restaurant, bar, pool, tennis court, gym, beachfront, diving, water sports, no elevator, laundry service, public Internet, public Wi-Fi* ▭*MC, V* ⍟*BP.*

$ ▨**Auberge Seraphine.** This is a good choice for independent vacationers who don't require a beachfront location or the breadth of activities found at a resort. Accommodations are spacious, cheerful, and bright. All but six rooms have a water view, and Room 307 has an amazing view from its balcony. What look like huge snow-white flowers are really cattle egrets nesting in the almond tree right outside the window; beautiful flowers bloom twice monthly in the lily pond down below. A broad, tiled sundeck, the center of activity, surrounds a small pool. Reserve ahead, as business travelers appreciate the Auberge's convenience to downtown Castries, the airport, and great eateries—including the inn's excellent restaurant, which has fine Caribbean, French, and continental cuisine in addition to a well-stocked wine cellar. **Pros:** Nice pool, good restaurant, Room 307. **Cons:** Somewhat basic accommodations, no beach, no resort activities ⌂*Vigie Cove, Castries* ⌂*Box 390, Castries* ☎*758/453–2073* ⌂*758/451–7001* ⊕*www.aubergeseraphine.com* ⌂*28 rooms* ⌂*In-room: refrigerator, dial-up. In-hotel: restaurant, bar, pool, no elevator, public Internet* ⊟*AE, MC, V* ⌂⊙*EP.*

$ ⌂ **Inn on the Bay.** With just five rooms, Normand Viau and Louise Boucher, the owners of this delightful aerie on the southern hillside at the entrance of Marigot Bay, treat you as their personal guests (adults only). The million-dollar view of the bay, the sea, and the constant comings and goings of beautiful yachts is sensational from guest-room balconies and the pool. Cool sea breezes truly obviate the need for air-conditioning. You won't mind the absence of televisions here. Breakfast is prepared by Louise and served in their kitchen whenever you're ready. Walk down a hillside path, through thick jungle, to a small white-sand beach. And if you need a lift to the village, a short but very steep walk, Normand is happy to comply. **Pros:** The view, the value, the pleasant hosts, and the personalized service. **Cons:** Few, if any, amenities besides peace, quiet, and nature. ⌂*Marigot Bay* ☎*758/451–4260* ⊕*www.saint-lucia.com* ⌂*5 rooms* ⌂*In room: no a/c, no phone. In hotel: pool, no elevator, public Internet, no kids under 16* ⊟*MC, V* ⌂⊙*BP.*

VILLA COMPLEXES

$$ ⌂ **Villa Beach Cottages.** Tidy housekeeping cottages with gingerbread-laced facades are steps from the beach at this family-run establishment three miles north of the airport in Castries. The self-contained units have either one or two bedrooms and fully equipped kitchens and are decorated with handcrafted wooden furniture. A pair of cottages date back to World War II. Dismantled and moved here in 1958 from Beanfield Air Base in Vieux Fort, one of those cottages was subsequently occupied several times by one of St. Lucia's two Nobel Laureates, Sir Derek Walcott, during holiday visits. Now dubbed "Nobel Cottage," it is decorated with some of his watercolors. Another, called the "Honeymoon Cottage," is a duplex; the sitting/dining

CLOSE UP

Bananas

More than 10,000 St. Lucian banana farmers produced 134,000 tons of the familiar fruit in the early 1990s, most of which was exported to Europe. By 2005, when the Caribbean nations had lost their preferential treatment in the European market, fewer than 2,000 banana farmers were producing about 30,000 tons. Nevertheless, you'll still see bananas growing throughout St. Lucia, especially in the rural areas around Babonneau in the northeast and south of Castries near Marigot. As you pass by the banana fields, you'll notice that the fruit is wrapped in blue plastic. That's to protect it from birds and insects—because there's no market for an imperfect banana.

room and kitchen are on the ground floor, and a spiral staircase leads to the upstairs bedroom and bath. Units are cozy and fairly close together, but each has a large balcony (with a hammock) facing the water, guaranteeing glorious sunset viewing every evening. Coconuts, a small open-air restaurant, serves meals only on request. There's a mini-mart on site for the convenience of guests, and a supermarket, bank, post office, and other shops are nearby. **Pros:** Directly on the beach, beautiful sunsets, peaceful and quiet. **Cons:** Close quarters ⊠*Choc Bay, Castries* ⌂*Box 129, Castries* ☎*758/450–2884* ⊕*www.villabeachcottages.com* ↰*14 units* ⚲*In room: safe, kitchen, dial-up. In-hotel: restaurant, pool, beachfront, water sports, no elevator, laundry service, airport shuttle* ▤*AE, D, MC, V* ⟦◯⟧*EP.*

SOUFRIÈRE & VICINITY

Hotel locations can be found on the Soufrière & Vicinity map.

HOTELS

$$$$ ▦**Anse Chastanet Beach Hotel.** Anse Chastanet is magical,
★ if you don't mind the two miles of bad road you must travel to get there, a bone-crushing dirt road between the town and the resort, and the steep climb to most rooms. Of course, there's the water taxi alternative to get where you're going, or you can just soak in the gorgeous isolation. And a shuttle service is available to get from the beach to the hillside rooms instead of climbing the 100 steps. Spectacular rooms and suites, some with fourth walls open

to stunning Piton vistas, peek through the thick rain forest that cascades down to the sea. Deluxe hillside rooms have a balcony, tile floors, madras fabrics, handmade wooden furniture, and impressive artwork. Octagonal gazebos and beachfront cottages have similar interiors but slightly less dramatic views. But you won't find any communication devices, technology, or interruption. It's delightfully peaceful. Diving, jungle biking through the estate's 600 acres, and ocean kayaking are premier activities here when you're not luxuriating in your room with a view or rejuvenating at the Kai Belte Spa. **Pros:** Great for divers, honeymooners love it, Room 14B with the tree growing through the bathroom, the Piton views, local artwork in the guest rooms. **Cons:** The entrance road is a nuisance but that's unlikely to change—management thinks it keeps out the merely nosey. ⊠*Anse Chastanet Rd., Soufrière* 🖅*Box 7000, Soufrière* 🕾*758/459–7000* 🖷*758/459–7700* ⊕*www.ansechastanet. com* ⏎*49 rooms* 🖴*In-room: no a/c, no phone, safe, refrigerator, no TV. In-hotel: 2 restaurants, room service, bars, tennis court, spa, beachfront, diving, watersports, bicycles, no elevator, laundry service, public Internet, airport shuttle, no kids under 10* ▤*AE, MC, V* ⋈*EP.*

★ Fodor'sChoice ⛱**Jade Mountain Club.** Is it a resort, a corporate
$$$$ headquarters, the mother ship? Arriving at the ground level concierge, you wonder. Owned by and adjacent to Anse Chastanet resort, this premium-level and premium-priced club is owner Nick Troubetzkoy's phantasmagorical engineering project, a five-level behemoth that looms out of the jungle about 1,000 feet up. Some 300 local men spent more than three years cutting into Morne Chastanet and building Jade Mountain Club without using any heavy equipment, save a couple of small concrete mixers. Once at eye level, the inside view is a mass of concrete sky-bridges, each one accessing a private "sanctuary." Indeed, you conclude, this is indeed the mother ship. Once inside, you're immediately transported to a different world—but it's not *Star Trek.* Your private sanctuary exudes style, luxury, privacy, and comfort. While no two sanctuaries are alike, the common themes are the sense of space, the screen saver–worthy view of the Pitons through the missing fourth wall, an en-suite bathroom that is truly en suite (no wall), substantial furniture made locally from more than 20 different species of hardwood, cutting edge Euro-style bathroom fixtures (including chroma-therapy whirlpool and shower massage), and—drumroll, please—an enormous infinity-edge

plunge pool in each room. The pools, which range in size from 400 to more than 900 square feet, are masterpieces in and of themselves, lined with iridescent tiles made of recycled glass that reflect the sunshine or submerged lights in individually controlled colors. Jade Mountain guests have access to a private restaurant, bar, and sky-top terrace and can also use Anse Chastanet's facilities—the beach, water sports, restaurants, and bars. Given the luxury, privacy, and amenities of the sanctuaries, room service is extremely popular. And like Anse Chastanet, Jade Mountain's sanctuaries are techno-free in terms of communication with the outside world. **Pros:** The amazing rooms, the huge in-room pools, the incredible Piton views, the impeccable service. **Cons:** The sky-high rates, the lack of in-room communication (although many consider that a plus), not appropriate for anyone with disabilities. ⊠*Anse Chastanet, Soufrière,* ⌂*Box 7000, Soufrière* ☎*758/459–4000* ⊕*www.jade mountainstlucia.com* ⇨*28 sanctuaries* ♿*In-room: no a/c, no phone, refrigerator, no TV. In-hotel: restaurant, room service, bar, gym, spa, beachfront, diving, water sports, bicycles, no elevator, laundry service, concierge, public Internet, no kids under 15* ⊺⊙⃒*EP.*

$$$$ ⊠**Jalousie Plantation.** Located on the most dramatic 192 ⏱ acres in St. Lucia, this resort flows down Val des Pitons—★ the steep valley smack between the Pitons—on the remains of an 18th-century sugar plantation 2 mi (3 km) south of Soufrière. Sugar Mill rooms are large and close to the beach. Clusters of private villas have elegant furnishings, huge bathrooms, and plunge pools; villa suites also have sitting rooms. Shuttles around the property save a climb up and down the hill. Meals range from fine dining to a beach buffet. Swimming and snorkeling at the beach is magical because of the incomparable Piton view above and the abundant sealife underwater. Dive, windsurf, or sail; play tennis, squash, or pitch-and-putt golf. Take a nature walk, climb Gros Piton (with a guide), or chill by the pool. The spa offers outdoor massage, aromatherapy, and beauty treatments; there are also fitness classes and weight-training sessions. And weddings are complimentary with stays of 10 or more nights—now that's a deal. **Pros:** Incomparable scenery, wonderful spa, lots of water sports. **Cons:** Fairly isolated, cottages are in the jungle, so bring mosquito spray. ⊠*Val des Pitons, Soufrière* ⌂*Box 251, Soufrière* ☎*800/544–2883 or 758/459–7666* 🖷*758/459–7667* ⊕*www.jalousieplantation.com* ⇨*12 rooms, 65 villas, 35* *villa suites* ⟨In-room: safe, refrigerator, VCRs (some), dial-up. In-hotel: 4 restaurants, room service, bars, golf course, tennis courts, pool, gym, spa, beachfront, diving, water sports, no elevator, children's programs (ages 5–12), public Internet, airport shuttle, no-smoking rooms ═AE, MC, V ⦿EP.*

$$$$ **Fodor'sChoice** ⭐ ▣**Ladera.** One of the most sophisticated small inns in the Caribbean, the elegantly rustic Ladera is perched 1,100 feet above the sea, high in the rain forest between the Pitons. An eco-hotel, with a local approach to furnishings, food, and staff, each tree house–style suite or villa is uniquely decorated with colonial antiques and local craftsmanship. Each unit has an open fourth wall with a dazzling view of the Pitons as a backdrop for your private plunge pool—some with a waterfall. And the bathrooms are fitted with individually designed tile work and whimsical fixtures—a conch-shell faucet, for example. Cooling breezes really do preclude the need for air-conditioning. The Ti Kai Posé Spa (Creole for "Little House of Rest") offers relaxing and therapeutic massages, beauty services, and restorative bathing pools containing mineral water drawn directly from the source at Diamond Mineral Baths near Soufrière. Dasheene, the open-air restaurant, has the most stunning view of the Pitons—fabulous by day and stupendous at sunset. The inn provides shuttle service to Soufrière and its private, fully staffed beach at Anse Jambette, a 20-minute boat ride from the Soufrière dock. Diving and other activities can be arranged. Children ages 7–14 are allowed only during the Christmas holiday period; the resort is not suitable for very young children due of the open-to-the-view design of the rooms, the in-room pools, and the hillside perch. **Pros:** The Pitons vista—honeymooners and celebs love this place, the in-room pools, the excellent Dasheene Restaurant. **Cons:** Birds may fly into your open-air suite. ✉ *Val de Pitons, Soufrière* ⓓ*Box 225, Soufrière* ☎758/459–7323, 800/223–9868, or 800/738–4752 ⓕ758/459–5156 ⊕*www.ladera-stlucia.com* ⟳*26 suites, 6 villas* ⟨In-room: no a/c, refrigerator, no TV. In-hotel: restaurant, bars, pool, gym, spa, no elevator, public Internet, airport shuttle, no kids under 14 ═AE, D, MC, V ⦿BP.*

$$$ ▣**Stonefield Estate Villa Resort.** Ali Brown and his family warmly welcome guests to their rambling resort on the site of a former cocoa plantation at the base of Petit Piton. One 18th-century plantation house and several gingerbread-style cottage villas dot this property. All accommodations

have oversized, handcrafted furniture (built by the senior Mr. Brown) and one or two bathrooms—some villas also have outdoor garden showers and plunge pools. Living/dining rooms open onto verandas with double hammocks and panoramic views, perfectly romantic at sunset. A nature trail leads to ancient petroglyphs and palm-lined Malgretoute Beach. A complimentary shuttle goes to Soufrière or to Jalousie Beach for snorkeling and scuba diving. **Pros:** Very private, lovely pool, good breakfasts, great sunset views from villa decks. **Cons:** Meal quality at dinner is inconsistent ⊠*Soufrière* ⊕*Box 228, Soufrière* ☎*758/459–5648 or 758/459–7037* ⊟*758/459–5550* ⊕*www.stonefieldvillas. com* ⤳*16 1- to 3-bedroom villas* ⚷*In-room: no a/c (some), no phone (some), safe, kitchen, refrigerator, VCR (some), no TV (some). In-hotel: restaurant, bar, pool, no elevator, laundry service, public Internet* ⊟*AE, D, MC, V* ⫿○⫿*EP.*

$$–$$$ ⌸**Ti Kaye Village.** Ti Kaye is about halfway between Cas-
★   tries and Soufrière and down a mile-long dirt road off the main highway. Once you're there, however, you recognize the specialness of this aerie overlooking Anse Cochon Beach. Gingerbread-style cottages are surrounded by lush greenery and furnished with handcrafted furniture, including four-poster beds with gauzy canopies. Each room has a private garden shower, a large balcony with double hammock, and wooden louvers in doors and windows to catch every breeze; some have private plunge pools. Dine with a view at Kai Manje, socialize at the friendly bar, and cool off in the pool. Or you can maneuver the 166-step wooden stairway down the cliff to the beach—which is one of the best snorkeling sites in St. Lucia. **Pros:** Perfect for a honeymoon or private getaway, garden showers are fabulous, beautiful sunsets, excellent restaurant. **Cons:** Far from anywhere (although that may be a plus), all those steps down to—but mostly up from—the beach. ⊠*Anse Cochon, Anse la Raye* ⊕*Box GM669 Castries* ☎*758/456–8101* ⊟*758/456–8105* ⊕*www.tikaye.com* ⤳*33 rooms* ⚷*In-room: safe, refrigerator, no TV. In-hotel: restaurant, bars, pool, gym, beachfront, water sports, no elevator, laundry service, public Internet, no kids under 12* ⊟*AE, D, DC, MC, V* ⫿○⫿*BP.*

$$ ⌸**La Haut Plantation.** It's all about the view—the Pitons, of course—and the appeal of staying in an intimate and affordable family-run inn that happens to have that view. Nestled into what was a mountaintop cocoa and coconut estate 100 years ago, just north of the town of Soufrière,

the six-room guesthouse was once the cocoa house, where cocoa beans were fermented and dried. A separate cottage had been the copra house, where the coconuts were processed. Each room has a private balcony with a "to-die-for" view, king beds draped with rather romantic mosquito netting, and shutters or French doors that open to the breeze. A two-bedroom unit is ideal for families or two couples. The two-story cottage has a huge upstairs balcony, where you can gaze at the Pitons, the rain forest, or the sunset; it's perfect for honeymooners. When they're not taking a dip in the infinity pool or the free shuttle to Anse Chastanet Beach, guests are encouraged to roam the 52-acres of grounds and are likely to come across goats, cows, birds, and a couple of donkeys. The La Haut restaurant employs local seafood, fruits and vegetables, and herbs and spices in its excellent Creole cuisine and international dishes. **Pros:** Lovely for weddings and honeymoons, stunning Piton views, excellent restaurant, excellent value. **Cons:** Very quiet, especially at night, unless that's the point. ⊠*Soufrière* ⬠*Box 304, Soufrière* ☎*758/459–7008* ⊕*www.lahaut.com* ⤳*13 rooms, 1 cottage* ⚙*In-room: no a/c (some), no phone, safe, refrigerator, no TV. In-hotel: restaurant, bar, tennis, pools, no elevator, public Internet* ⊟*AE, MC, V* ⊠*EP.*

$–$$ ⌂**Hummingbird Beach Resort.** Unpretentious and welcoming, rooms in this delightful little inn on Soufrière Harbour are in small seaside cabins—most of which have views of the Pitons. Rooms are simply furnished—a primitive motif emphasized by African wood sculptures. Four rooms have mahogany four-poster beds hung with sheer mosquito netting. Most rooms have modern baths; two rooms and a suite share a bath. A two-bedroom country cottage—with a sitting room, kitchenette, and spectacular Piton view—is suitable for a family or two couples vacationing together. The Hummingbird's Lifeline Restaurant is a favorite lunch stop for locals and visitors touring Soufrière. **Pros:** Local island atmosphere, small and quiet, fabulous Piton views, good local food. **Cons:** Beach is not great. ⊠*Anse Chastanet Rd., Soufrière* ⬠*Box 280, Soufrière* ☎*758/459–7232 or 800/223–9815* ⎙*758/459–7033* ⊕*www.nvo.com/piton resort* ⤳*9 rooms (7 with bath), 1 suite, 1 cottage* ⚙*In-room: no a/c (some). In-hotel: restaurant, bar, pool, beachfront, no elevator, public Internet* ⊟*AE, D, MC, V* ⊠*BP.*

PRIVATE VILLAS

$$$$ ⌂**Arc en Ciel.** Architect Lane Pettigrew has put his stamp on many fabulous homes and resorts throughout the Carib-

bean, and Arc en Ciel is another example. The exterior of the house incorporates Caribbean verandahs, jalousie shutters, and traditional wooden railings as well as hand-chipped stones reminiscent of the old French forts found on St. Lucia. Spectacularly situated on Beau Estate, just south of Petit Piton, this lovely villa accommodates up to 10 guests in its five air-conditioned bedrooms. Each bedroom, as well as the centrally located living/dining area, has its own TV, DVD, and stereo system. (TV reception ranges from bad to nonexistent; there's a library of DVDs or you can bring your own.) The master bedroom, which faces Petit Piton, has a glass wall in its ensuite bathroom, so you can take advantage of the unparalleled view as you enjoy a shower or soak in the Jacuzzi. In fact, all bedrooms have Jacuzzis in their en-suite bathrooms, as well as private patios or gardens. The sitting room opens onto a patio and dining gazebo, with a wonderful view as a backdrop. On the lower level, two of the bedrooms face an infinity-edge pool—which weaves its way around a series of patios and sundecks and through a stone cave with a waterfall. Anse des Pitons Beach, The Jalousie Plantation resort, and Ladera are nearby; the Drive-in Volcano, Diamond Botanical Gardens, and the town of Soufrière are just a short drive away. The resident staff is available seven days a week. **Pros:** The Piton view, perfect for a big family or group. **Cons:** No TV reception, but there is a DVD library. ⊠*Beau Estate, Soufrière (Tropical Villas* ☎*758/450–8240* ⊕*www. tropicalvillas.net)* ⤳*5 bedrooms, 5 bathrooms* ⟠*no a/c (some rooms), safe, dishwasher, DVD, on-site security, fully staffed, pools, laundry facilities* ▤*AE, MC, V.*

$$$$ ▦**Bananaquit House.** Named for the little black-and-yellow birds that frequent open-air alfresco breakfast tables, Bananaquit House is located in a garden setting along the dirt road from Soufrière to Anse Chastanet Resort. The view of the sea and the Pitons is unparalleled, and Anse Chastanet and Anse Mamim beaches are five minutes away. The five bedrooms can sleep 11 people comfortably; the house is also equipped with two cribs and two high chairs. The large sitting/dining area has a small library of books, games, and puzzles, as well as a stereo system and a TV with a DVD player. Because of the mountains, TV reception is virtually nonexistent in this area. You enter the living area through a pool terrace, with a fenced-in swimming pool—making it safe for families with small kids. The caretaker, who will provide security at no charge if you wish, has a dog that that he will remove from the property upon request. **Pros:** Family-friendly, great views, cozy and charming yet big enough for a large family or group. **Cons:** Bad or no TV reception, no air-conditioning, although bedrooms have fans. ⊠ *Anse Chastanet Rd., Soufrière (Tropical Villas* ☎758/450–8240 ⊕*www.tropicalvillas. net)* ⚲*5 bedrooms, 3 bathrooms* ⚬*no a/c, safe, DVD, daily maid service, on-site security, pool, laundry facilities* ⊟*AE, MC, V.*

$$$–$$$$ ⊡**St. Remy Plantation.** If you prefer ambience to amenities, then spending your vacation in an historic plantation estate near a colonial town may have more appeal than a modern beachfront resort. St. Remy Plantation is a restored, 150-year-old estate house, with wooden floors, traditional furniture, and a veranda that wraps around three sides of the house. High in the hills just outside the town of Soufrière, the house is surrounded by beautiful gardens that are visited by countless species of birds. Don't expect to get any TV reception, but the house's sitting/dining room has an entertainment center with a video library. There are two double bedrooms, a bathroom, and a shower room. A separate guest cottage with two single beds is available upon request. The pool has a sundeck; Anse Chastanet Beach is nearby. Each St. Remy Plantation guest is treated to a complimentary visit to Diamond Mineral Baths. The housekeeper and cook are available daily until 5 PM, but will stay to cook and serve dinner upon request (and at additional cost). **Pros:** Perfect spot for a honeymoon, great for birdwatchers and nature lovers. **Cons:** No a/c, although hillside location catches the breeze. ⊠*Soufrière (Tropical Villas* ☎758/450–8240 ⊕*www.tropicalvillas.net)* ⚲*2 bedrooms, 2 bathrooms* ⚬*DVD, pool, cook, daily maid service, fully staffed, on-site security, laundry facilities, no kids under 12* ⊟*AE, MC, V* ⦿*BP.*

VIEUX FORT

Hotel locations can be found on the St. Lucia map.

$$$–$$$$ ⊡**Coconut Bay.** The only resort in Vieux Fort (so far), Coconut Bay is a sprawling seaside retreat on 85 beachfront acres just minutes from St. Lucia's Hewanorra International Airport. The ocean views are beautiful, and the beach has lovely white sand, but the resort faces the Atlantic Ocean, so swimming in the sea is not advised. Instead, you'll find three swimming pools and a water park with a lazy river,

waterslides, and a swim-up bar. The Frégate Island and Maria Islands are just offshore, and St. Lucia's Pitons and other natural attractions in Soufrière are just 30 minutes by car. Otherwise, you'll have to be content with the activities in and around the resort—four restaurants, a full-service spa, and plenty of space to relax and socialize. **Pros:** Great for families, perfect for windsurfers, friendly and sociable atmosphere. **Cons:** Rough surf precludes ocean swimming and water sports. ⊠ *Vieux Fort* ✉ *Box 246, Vieux Fort* ☎ *758/459–6000* 🖷 *758/456–9900* ⊕ *www.coconutbay resortandspa.com* ⇆ *254 rooms* 🕭 *In-room: safe. In-hotel: 4 restaurants, bars, tennis courts, pools, gym, spa, beachfront, children's programs (ages 3–12), public Internet* ▤ *AE, MC, V* ⦿ *AI.*

NIGHTLIFE

Most resort hotels have entertainment—island music, calypso singers, and steel bands, as well as disco, karaoke, and talent shows—every night in high season and a couple of nights per week in the off-season. Otherwise, Rodney Bay is the best bet for nightlife. The many restaurants and bars there attract a crowd nearly every night.

BARS

The **Captain's Cellar** (⊠ *Pigeon Island, Rodney Bay* ☎ *758/ 450–0253*) is a cozy Old English–style pub with live jazz on weekends.

DANCE CLUBS

Most dance clubs with live bands have a cover charge of $6 to $8 (EC$15 to EC$20), and the music usually starts at 11 PM. At **Aqua** (⊠ *Rodney Bay* ☎ *758/452–0284*), dance inside or outside on the party deck, starting at 8 PM.

Doolittle's (⊠ *Marigot Bay* ☎ *758/451–4974*) has live bands and dance music—calypso, soul, salsa, steel-band, reggae, and limbo—that changes nightly.

At **Indies** (⊠ *Rodney Bay* ☎ *758/452–0727*) you can dance to the hottest rhythms Wednesday, Friday, and Saturday; dress is casual though smart—no hats or sandals, no shorts or sleeveless shirts for men. There's shuttle-bus service to and from most major hotels.

Rumours (✉*Rodney Bay* ☎*758/452–9249*) is a popular nightspot that rocks well into the night.

The **The Lime and Upper Level at The Lime** (✉*Reduit Beach, Rodney Bay* ☎*758/452–0761*) is a particular favorite of St. Lucians; it's air-conditioned and intimate, with live music, a DJ, or karaoke every night but Tuesday.

STREET PARTIES

★ For a taste of St. Lucian village life, head for the **Anse La Raye "Seafood Friday "** street festival any Friday night. Beginning at 6:30 PM, the main street in this tiny fishing village—about halfway between Castries and Soufrière—is closed to vehicles, and the residents prepare what they know best: fish cakes, grilled or stewed fish, hot bakes (biscuits), roasted corn, boiled crayfish, even grilled-before-your-eyes lobster. Prices range from a few cents for a fish cake or bake to $10 or $15 for a whole lobster, depending on its size. Walk around, eat, chat with the local people, and listen to live music until the wee hours of the morning.

★ A Friday-night ritual for locals and visitors alike is to head for the **Gros Islet Jump-Up,** the island's largest street party. Huge speakers are set up on the village's main street and blast out Caribbean music all night long. Sometimes there are live bands. When you take a break from dancing, you can buy barbecued fish or chicken, rotis, beer, and soda from villagers who set up cookers right along the roadside. It's the ultimate "lime" experience.

BEACHES

Beaches are all public, but many along the northwest coast, particularly north of Castries, are flanked by hotels. A few secluded stretches of beach on the west coast south of Marigot Bay are accessible primarily by boat and are a popular swimming and snorkeling stop on catamaran or powerboat sightseeing trips. Don't swim along the windward (east) coast, as the Atlantic Ocean is too rough—but the views are spectacular. Beaches on St. Lucia are quite beautiful, but none has really soft white sand; given the island's volcanic origins, this shouldn't be surprising, but those looking for powdery soft beaches may be disappointed.

Anse Chastanet. In front of the resort of the same name, just north of the city of Soufrière, this palm-studded dark-sand beach has a backdrop of green hills, brightly painted fishing skiffs bobbing at anchor, and the island's best reefs for snorkeling and diving. The resort's gazebos are nestled among the palms; its dive shop, restaurant, and bar are on the beach and open to the public. ⊠ *1 mi (1½ km) north of Soufrière.*

Anse Cochon. This remote dark-sand beach is reached only by boat or via Ti Kaye Village's mile-long access road. The water and adjacent reef are superb for swimming, diving, and snorkeling. Moorings are free, and boaters can enjoy lunch or dinner at Ti Kaye—if you're willing to climb 166 steps up the hillside. ⊠ *3 mi (5 km) south of Marigot Bay.*

Anse des Pitons. Between the Pitons on Jalousie Bay, the white sand on this crescent beach was imported and spread over the natural black sand. Accessible from Jalousie Plantation resort (whose management prefers to call the beach "Forbidden Beach," although it is a public beach like all others on the island) or by boat, the beach offers good snorkeling, diving, and breathtaking scenery. ⊠ *Jalousie Bay, 1 mi (1½ km) south of Soufrière.*

Anse des Sables. This long, white-sand beach at the southern tip of the island is washed by Atlantic surf and is the place to go windsurfing or kitesurfing. Refreshments are available at The Reef. ⊠ *Vieux Fort.*

Marigot Beach. Calm waters rippled only by passing yachts lap a sliver of sand studded with palm trees on the north side of Marigot Bay. The beach is accessible by a ferry that operates continually from one side of the bay to the other, and you can find refreshments at adjacent restaurants. ⊠ *Marigot Bay.*

Pigeon Point. At this small beach within Pigeon Island National Park, on the northwestern tip of St. Lucia, a restaurant serves snacks and drinks, but this is also a perfect spot for picnicking. ⊠ *Pigeon Island.*

★ **Reduit Beach.** This long stretch of golden sand frames Rodney Bay and is within walking distance of many small hotels and restaurants in Rodney Bay Village. The Rex St. Lucian Hotel, which faces the beach, has a water-sports center, where you can rent sports equipment and beach chairs and take windsurfing or waterskiing lessons. Many feel that Reduit (pronounced red-*wee*) is the island's finest beach. ⊠ *Rodney Bay.*

Vigie Beach. This 2-mi (3-km) strand runs parallel to the George F. L. Charles Airport runway in Castries, and continues on to become Malabar Beach, the beachfront in front of the Rendezvous resort. ⊠*Castries, next to the airport.*

SPORTS & THE OUTDOORS

Cricket: Is it a passion or an obsession? In either case, the country nearly shuts down when an important local or international match takes place. International and test-series cricket matches are played at the Beausejour Cricket Ground in Gros Islet and at the impressive National Stadium in Vieux Fort. Contact the tourist board for details on schedules and tickets.

St. Lucia is particularly noted for having a great women's team. In 1986 Verna Felicien founded the first St. Lucia women's cricket team. In 1998 St. Lucia—with Felicien as captain—won the Caribbean Women's Cricket Championships and retained the title for five years. During that time, 10 St. Lucians—including Captain Felicien—also played on the West Indies Women's team. In 2005 Felicien represented St. Lucia in the World Cup tournament, which was held in South Africa.

BIKING

★ Although the terrain is pretty rugged, two tour operators have put together fascinating bicycle and combination bicycle-hiking tours that appeal to novice riders as well as those who enjoy a good workout. Prices range from $60 to $100 per person. **Bike St. Lucia** (⊠*Anse Chastanet, Soufrière* ☎*758/451–2453* ⊕*www.bikestlucia.com*) takes small groups of bikers on Jungle Biking™ tours along trails that meander through the remnants of an 18th-century plantation near Soufrière. Stops are made to explore the French colonial ruins, study the beautiful tropical plants and fruit trees, enjoy a picnic lunch, and take a dip in a river swimming hole or a swim at the beach. If you're staying in the north, you can get a tour that includes transportation to the Soufrière area.

Palm Services Bike Tours (⊠*Castries* ☎*758/458–0908* ⊕*www .adventuretoursstlucia.com*) is suitable for all fitness levels. Jeep or bus transportation is provided across the central mountains to Dennery, on the east coast. After a 3-mi

(5-km) ride through the countryside, bikes are exchanged for shoe leather. The short hike into the rain forest ends with a picnic and a refreshing swim next to a sparkling waterfall—then the return leg to Dennery. All gear is supplied.

BOATING & SAILING

Rodney Bay and Marigot Bay are centers for bareboat and crewed yacht charters. Their marinas offer safe anchorage, shower facilities, restaurants, groceries, and maintenance for yachts sailing the waters of the eastern Caribbean. Charter prices range from $1,750 to $10,000 per week, depending on the season and the type and size of vessel, plus $250 extra per day if you want a skipper and cook. **Bateau Mygo** (⊠*Marigot Bay* ☎*758/451–4772* ⊕*www. bateaumygo.com*) specializes in customized, crewed charters on its 40- to 44-foot yachts for either a couple of days or a week.

Destination St. Lucia (DSL) Ltd. (⊠*Rodney Bay Marina, Gros Islet* ☎*758/452–8531* ⊕*www.dsl-yachting.com*) offers bareboat yacht charters; vessels range in length from 38 to 51 feet.

Moorings Yacht Charters (⊠*Marigot Bay* ☎*758/451–4357 or 800/535–7289* ⊕*www.moorings.com*) rents bareboat and crewed yachts ranging from Beneteau 39s to Morgan 60s.

CAMPING

Bay of Freedom Camp Site (☎*758/452–5005 or 758/454–5014*), St. Lucia's only campsite, is 133 acres of sloping terrain at Anse La Liberté (French for "Bay of Freedom"), on the west coast near the village of Canaries. It's accessible by boat or by car (a 45-minute drive south from Castries or 15 minutes north from Soufrière). Rough campsites and platforms for tents are available, along with communal toilets and showers, a cooking center, 6 mi (10 km) of hiking trails, and a small secluded beach. Camping fees are inexpensive, but reservations are required. The facility is on one of the many sites where former slaves celebrated their emancipation in 1834; it's administered by the St. Lucia National Trust.

DIVING & SNORKELING

★ **Anse Chastanet,** near the Pitons on the southwest coast, is the best beach-entry dive site. The underwater reef drops from 20 feet to nearly 140 feet in a stunning coral wall.

A 165-foot freighter, *Lesleen M*, was deliberately sunk in 60 feet of water near **Anse Cochon** to create an artificial reef; divers can explore the ship in its entirety and view huge gorgonians, black coral trees, gigantic barrel sponges, lace corals, schooling fish, angelfish, sea horses, spotted eels, stingrays, nurse sharks, and sea turtles.

Anse-La-Raye, midway up the west coast, is one of St. Lucia's finest wall and drift dives and a great place for snorkeling.

At the base of **Petit Piton** a spectacular wall drops to 200 feet. You can view an impressive collection of huge barrel sponges and black coral trees; strong currents ensure good visibility.

At the **Pinnacles,** four coral-encrusted stone piers rise to within 10 feet of the surface.

Depending on the season and the particular trip, prices range from about $40 to $60 for a one-tank dive, $175 to $260 for a six-dive package over three days, and $265 to $450 for a 10-dive package over five days. Dive shops provide instruction for all levels (beginner, intermediate, and advanced). For beginners, a resort course (pool training), followed by one open-water dive, runs from $65 to $90. Snorkelers are generally welcome on dive trips and usually pay $25 to $50, which includes equipment and sometimes lunch and transportation.

Buddies (⊠*Rodney Bay Marina, Rodney Bay* ☎758/452–8406) offers wall, wreck, reef, and deep dives; resort courses and open-water certification with advanced and specialty courses are taught by PADI-certified instructors.

Dive Fair Helen (⊠*Vigie Marina, Castries* ☎758/451–7716, *888/855–2206 in U.S. and Canada* ⊕*www.divefairhelen. com*) is a PADI center that offers half- and full-day excursions to wreck, wall, and marine reserve areas, as well as night dives.

Scuba St. Lucia (⊠*Anse Chastanet, Soufrière* ☎758/459–7755 ⊕*www.scubastlucia.com*) is a PADI five-star training facility. Daily beach and boat dives and resort and certification courses are offered; underwater photography and snorkeling equipment are available. Day trips from the north of the island include round-trip speedboat transportation.

FISHING

Among the deep-sea creatures you can find in St. Lucia's waters are dolphin (also called dorado or mahimahi), barracuda, mackerel, wahoo, kingfish, sailfish, and white and blue marlin. Sportfishing is generally done on a catch-and-release basis, but the captain may permit you to take a fish back to your hotel to be prepared for your dinner. Neither spearfishing nor collecting live fish in coastal waters is permitted. Half- and full-day deep-sea fishing excursions can be arranged at either Vigie Marina or Rodney Bay Marina. A half-day of fishing on a scheduled trip runs about $75–$80 per person. Beginners are welcome. **Captain Mike's** (⊠ *Vigie Marina* ☎ *758/452–1216 or 758/452–7044* ⊕ *www.captmikes.com*) has a fleet of Bertram power boats (31 to 38 feet) that accommodate as many as eight passengers; tackle and cold drinks are supplied.

Hackshaw's Boat Charters (⊠ *Vigie Marina* ☎ *758/453–0553 or 758/452–3909* ⊕ *www.hackshaws.com*), in business since 1953, runs charters on boats ranging from the 31-foot *Blue Boy* or *Miss T.* to the 50-foot, custom-built *Lady Hack.*

Mako Watersports (⊠ *Rodney Bay Marina, Rodney Bay* ☎ *758/452–0412*) takes fishing enthusiasts out on the well-equipped six-passenger *Annie Baby.*

GOLF

Although St. Lucia has only one 18-hole championship course at this writing, two more are on the drawing board and/or under construction. One will be in Praslin, on the east coast, as part of a new resort development; the other will be near the existing course in Cap Estate. **Sandals Regency Golf Resort & Spa** has a 9-hole course for its guests. **The Jalousie Plantation** has a par-3 Executive course.

St. Lucia & Country Golf Club (⊠ *Cap Estate* ☎ *758/452–8523* ⊕ *www.stluciagolf.com*), the only public course, is at the island's northern tip and offers panoramic views of both the Atlantic and the Caribbean. It's an 18-hole championship course (6,836 yards, par 71). The clubhouse has a fine-dining restaurant called the Cap Grill that serves breakfast, lunch, and dinner; the Sports Bar is a convivial meeting place any time of day. You can rent clubs and shoes and arrange lessons at the pro shop and perfect your swing at the 350-yard driving range. Depending on the season, greens fees range from $75 for 9 holes to $125 for 18 holes; carts are required and included; club and shoe rentals are available. Reservations are essential. Complimentary transportation from your hotel or cruise ship is provided for parties of three or more people. The St. Lucia Golf Open, a two-day tournament held in March, is open to amateurs; it's a handicap event, and prizes are awarded.

HIKING

The island is laced with trails, but you shouldn't attempt the more challenging ones on your own. Seasoned hikers may aspire to climb the Pitons, the two volcanic cones rising 2,460 feet and 2,619 feet, respectively, from the ocean floor just south of Soufrière. Hiking is recommended only on Gros Piton, which offers a steep but safe trail to the top. Tourists are permitted to hike Petit Piton, but the second half of the hike requires a good deal of rock climbing, and you'll need to provide your own safety equipment. Hiking the Pitons requires the permission of the St. Lucia Forest & Lands Department and a knowledgeable guide from the **Pitons Tour Guide Association** (☎758/459–9748).

The **St. Lucia Forest & Lands Department** (☎758/450–2231 or 758/450–2078) manages trails throughout the rain forest and provides guides who explain the plants and trees you'll encounter and keep you on the right track for a small fee.

The **St. Lucia National Trust** (☎758/452–5005 ⊕www.sluna trust.org) maintains two trails: one is at Anse La Liberté, near Canaries on the Caribbean coast; the other is on the Atlantic coast, from Mandélé Point to the Frégate Islands Nature Reserve. Full-day excursions with lunch cost about $50 to $85 per person and can be arranged through hotels or tour operators.

HORSEBACK RIDING

Creole horses, a breed indigenous to South America and popular on the island, are fairly small, fast, sturdy, and even-tempered animals suitable for beginners. Established stables can accommodate all skill levels and offer countryside trail rides, beach rides with picnic lunches, plantation tours, carriage rides, and lengthy treks. Prices run about $40 for one hour, $50 for two hours, and $70 for a three-hour beach ride and barbecue. Transportation is usually provided between the stables and nearby hotels. Local people sometimes appear on beaches with their steeds and offer 30-minute rides for $10; ride at your own risk.

Atlantic Shores Riding Stable (⊠ *Savannes Bay, Vieux Fort* ☎ *758/454–8668 or 758/484–9769*) is in south St. Lucia; trails take in Honeymoon Beach, mangroves, grassy fields, and the rugged Atlantic coast.

Country Saddles (⊠ *Marquis Estate, Babonneau* ☎ *758/450– 5467 or 758/450–0197*), 45 minutes east of Castries, guides beginners and advanced riders through banana plantations, forest trails, and along the Atlantic coast.

International Riding Stables (⊠ *Beauséjour Estate, Gros Islet* ☎ *758/452–8139 or 758/450–8665*) offers English- and western-style riding. The beach-picnic ride includes time for a swim—with or without your horse.

Trim's National Riding Stable (⊠ *Cas-en-Bas, Gros Islet* ☎ *758/452–8273 or 758/450–9971*), the island's oldest riding stable, offers four sessions per day, plus beach tours, trail rides, and carriage tours to Pigeon Island.

SEA EXCURSIONS

A day sail or sea cruise to Soufrière and the Pitons is a wonderful way to see St. Lucia and a great way to get to the island's distinctive natural sites. Prices for a full-day sailing excursion to Soufrière run about $75 to $90 per person and include a land tour to the Sulphur Springs and the Botanical Gardens, lunch, a stop for swimming and snorkeling, and a visit to pretty Marigot Bay. Two-hour sunset cruises along the northwest coast cost about $45 per person. Most boats leave from either Vigie Cove in Castries or Rodney Bay.

☽ The 140-foot tall ship **Brig Unicorn** (⊠ *Vigie Cove, Castries* ☎ *758/452–8644*), used in the filming of the TV miniseries *Roots* and more recently the movie *Pirates of the Carib- bean,* is a 140-foot replica of a 19th-century sailing ship. Day trips along the coast are fun for the whole family. Sev- eral nights each week a sunset cruise, with drinks and a live steel band, sails to Pigeon Point and back. Customized pleasure trips and snorkeling charters can be arranged for small groups (four to six people) through **Captain Mike's** (✉ *Vigie Cove, Castries* ☎ *758/452–0216 or 758/452–7044* ⊕ *www.captmikes.com*).

Mystic Man Tours (✉ *Bay St., Soufrière* ☎ *758/459–7783 or 758/455–9634*) operates whale- and dolphin-watching tours, which are fun for the whole family.

On **Endless Summer** (✉ *Rodney Bay Marina, Rodney Bay* ☎ *758/450–8651*), a 56-foot "party" catamaran, you can take a day trip to Soufrière or a half-day swimming and snorkeling trip. For romantics, there's a weekly sunset cruise, with dinner and entertainment.

Surf Queen (✉ *Vigie Cove, Castries* ☎ *758/452–8232*), a trimaran, runs a fast, sleek sail and has a special tour for German-speaking passengers.

L'Express des Iles (✉ *La Place Carenage, Castries* ☎ *758/452–2211*) offers an interesting day trip to the French island of Martinique. A hydrofoil departs daily for the 20-mi (32-km) voyage. As you approach Martinique, be sure to be among the first to disembark. There's usually only one immigration-customs agent on duty, and it can take an hour to clear if you're at the end of the line.

From Pigeon Island, north of Rodney Bay, you can take a more intimate cruise to the Pitons aboard the 57-foot luxury cruiser **MV Vigie** (✉ *Pigeon Island* ☎ *758/452–8232*).

For a boat trip to Pigeon Island, the **Rodney Bay Ferry** (✉ *Rodney Bay Marina, Rodney Bay* ☎ *758/452–8816*) departs from the ferry slip adjacent to the Lime restaurant twice daily for $50 round-trip, which includes the entrance fee to Pigeon Island and lunch; snorkel equipment can be rented for $12.

SIGHTSEEING TOURS

Taxi drivers are well informed and can give you a full tour—and often an excellent one, thanks to government-sponsored training programs. From the Castries area, full-day island tours cost $140 for up to four people; sightseeing trips to Soufrière, $120. If you plan your own day, expect to pay the driver $20 per hour plus tip.

★ **Jungle Tours** (✉ *Cas en Bas, Gros Islet* ☎ *758/715–3438* ⊕ *www.jungletoursstlucia.com*) specializes in rain-forest hiking tours for all levels of ability. You're required only to bring hiking shoes or sneakers and have a willingness to get wet and have fun. Prices range from $80 to $90 and include lunch, fees, and transportation via open Land Rover truck.

St. Lucia Helicopters (✉ *Pointe Seraphine, Castries* ☎ *758/453–6950* 🖷 *758/452–1553* ⊕ *www.stluciahelicopters.com*) offers a bird's-eye view of the island. A 10-minute North Island tour ($55 per person) leaves from Pointe Seraphine, in Castries, continues up the west coast to Pigeon Island, then flies along the rugged Atlantic coastline before returning inland over Castries. The 20-minute South Island tour ($85 per person) starts at Pointe Seraphine and follows the western coastline, circling picturesque Marigot Bay, Soufrière, and the majestic Pitons before returning inland over the volcanic hot springs and tropical rain forest. A complete island tour combines the two and lasts 30 minutes ($130 per person).

St. Lucia Heritage Tours (✉ *Pointe Seraphine, Castries* ☎ *758/451–6058* ⊕ *www.heritagetoursstlucia.org*) has put together an "authentic St. Lucia experience," specializing in the local culture and traditions. Groups are small, and some of the off-the-beaten-track sites visited are a 19th-century plantation house surrounded by nature trails, a 20-foot waterfall hidden away on private property, and a living museum presenting Creole practices and traditions. Plan on paying $65 per person for a full-day tour.

Sunlink Tours (✉ *Reduit Beach Ave., Rodney Bay* ☎ *758/452–8232 or 800/786–5465* ⊕ *www.sunlinktours.com*) offers dozens of land, sea, and combination sightseeing tours, as well as shopping tours, plantation, and rain forest adventures via Jeep safari, deep-sea fishing excursions, and day trips to other islands. Prices range from $20 for a half-day shopping tour to $120 for a full-day land-and-sea Jeep safari to Soufrière.

TENNIS & SQUASH

People staying at small inns without on-site tennis courts or those who wish to play squash can access private facilities for a small hourly fee; reservations are required. **St. Lucia Racquet Club** (✉ *Cap Estate* ☎ *758/450–0106*) is the best private tennis facility on the island, with seven floodlit, hard-surface tennis courts and a squash court, pro shop, restaurant, and bar. It is also the site of the St. Lucia Open each December.

St. Lucia Yacht Club (⊠*Reduit Beach, Rodney Bay* ☎*758/ 452–8350*) has two squash courts, and you can rent racquets.

WINDSURFING & KITEBOARDING

2

Windsurfers and kiteboarders congregate at Anse de Sables Beach, at the southeastern tip of St. Lucia, to take advantage of the blue-water and high-wind conditions that the Atlantic Ocean provides. **The Reef Kite & Surf Centre** (⊠*Anse de Sables, Vieux Fort* ☎*758/454–3418* ⊕*www.slucia.com/ kitesurf*) rents equipment and offers lessons from certified instructors in both windsurfing and kiteboarding. A three-hour beginner's course in windsurfing costs $90 plus $45 to rent equipment for a half-day. For kiteboarding, the three-hour starter course costs $125, including equipment. Kiteboarding is particularly strenuous, so participants must be excellent swimmers and in good physical health.

SHOPPING

The island's best-known products are artwork and wood carvings; clothing and household articles made from batik and silk-screened fabrics that are designed and produced in island workshops; straw mats and clay pottery. You can also take home straw hats and baskets and locally grown cocoa, coffee, and spices.

AREAS & MALLS

★ Along the harbor in Castries you can see rambling structures with bright-orange roofs that house several markets, which are open from 6 AM to 5 PM Monday through Saturday. Saturday morning is the busiest and most colorful time to shop. For more than a century, farmers' wives have gathered at the **Castries Market** to sell produce—which, alas, you can't import to the United States. But you can bring back spices (such as cocoa, turmeric, cloves, bay leaves, ginger, peppercorns, cinnamon sticks, nutmeg, mace, and vanilla essence), as well as bottled hot pepper sauces—all of which cost a fraction of what you'd pay back home.

The **Craft Market,** adjacent to the produce market, has aisles and aisles of baskets and other handmade straw work, rustic brooms made from palm fronds, wood carvings and

CLOSE UP

Cocoa Tea

The homemade chocolate balls or sticks that vendors sell in the market are formed from locally grown and processed cocoa beans. The chocolate is used locally to make cocoa tea—a beverage that actually originated in Soufrière but has since become a popular drink wherever cocoa is grown throughout the Caribbean. The chocolate is grated and steeped in boiling water, along with a bay leaf and cinnamon stick. Sugar is added, along with a little milk or cream, and some vanilla. Some people add nutmeg, as well, and some cornstarch to make it thicker and more filling. Cocoa tea began as a breakfast treat but is now enjoyed with a slice of bread as a snack or even as a dessert. Be sure to bring some chocolate sticks or balls home with you. One sniff and you won't be able to resist buying a packet ($2 to $4).

leather work, clay pottery, and souvenirs—all at affordable prices.

The **Vendor's Arcade,** across the street from the Craft Market, is a maze of stalls and booths where you can find handicrafts among the T-shirts and costume jewelry.

Gablewoods Mall, on the Gros Islet Highway in Choc Bay, a couple of miles north of downtown Castries, has about 35 shops that sell groceries, wines and spirits, jewelry, clothing, crafts, books and overseas newspapers, music, souvenirs, household goods, and snacks.

Along with 54 boutiques, restaurants, and other businesses that sell services and supplies, a large supermarket is the focal point of each **J.Q.'s Shopping Mall**; one is at Rodney Bay and another at Vieux Fort.

The duty-free shopping areas are at **Pointe Seraphine,** an attractive Spanish-motif complex on Castries Harbour with more than 20 shops, and **La Place Carenage,** an inviting three-story complex on the opposite side of the harbor. You can also find duty-free items in a few small shops at the arcade at the Rex St. Lucian hotel in Rodney Bay and, of course, in the departure lounge at Hewanorra International Airport. You must present your passport and airline ticket to purchase items at the duty-free price.

Marigot Marina Village, on Marigot Bay, has shops and services for boaters and landlubbers alike, including a bank, grocery store, business center, art gallery, an assortment of boutiques, and a French bakery/coffee shop.

Vieux Fort Plaza, near Hewanorra International Airport in Vieux Fort, is the main shopping center in the southern part of St. Lucia. You'll find a bank, supermarket, bookstore, toy shop, and several clothing stores there.

SPECIALTY ITEMS

ART

Art & Antiques (⊠*Point Seraphine, Castries* ☎*758/451–4150*) is a museum-type shop begun by artist Llewellyn Xavier and his wife. You'll find everything here from fine art to antique maps and prints, from sterling silver and crystal to rich linens, and from objets d'art to mere collectibles.

World-renowned St. Lucian artist **Llewellyn Xavier** (⊠*Cap Estate* ☎*758/450–9155*) creates modern art, ranging from vigorous oil abstracts that take up half a wall to small objects made from beaten silver and gold. Much of his work has an environmental theme, created from recycled materials. Xavier's work is on permanent exhibit at major museums in New York and Washington, D.C. Call to arrange a visit to the studio.

Modern Art Gallery (⊠*Gros Islet Hwy., Bois d'Orange* ☎*758/452–9079*) is a home studio, open by appointment only, where you can buy contemporary and avant-garde Caribbean art.

Artsibit Gallery (⊠*Brazil and Mongiraud Sts., Castries* ☎*758/452–7865*) exhibits and sells moderately priced pieces by St. Lucian painters and sculptors.

Caribbean Art Gallery (⊠*Rodney Bay Yacht Marina, Rodney Bay* ☎*758/452–8071*) sells original artwork by local artists, along with antique maps and prints and hand-painted silk.

BOOKS & MAGAZINES

Sunshine Bookshop (⊠*Gablewoods Mall, Castries* ☎*758/452–3222*) has novels and titles of regional interest, including books by Caribbean authors—among them the works of the St. Lucian Nobel laureate, poet Derek Walcott. You can also find current newspapers and magazines.

Valmont Books (✉*Jeremie and Laborie Sts., Castries* ☎*758/452–3817*) has West Indian literature and picture books, as well as stationery.

CLOTHES & TEXTILES

★ **Bagshaw Studios** (✉*La Toc Rd., La Toc Bay, Castries* ☎*758/452–2139 or 758/451–9249*) sells clothing and table linens in colorful tropical patterns using Stanley Bagshaw's original designs. The fabrics are silk-screened by hand in the adjacent workroom. You can also find Bagshaw boutiques at Pointe Seraphine, La Place Carenage, and Rodney Bay, and a selection of items in gift shops at Hewanorra Airport. Visit the workshop to see how designs are turned into colorful silk-screen fabrics, which are then fashioned into clothing and household articles. It's open weekdays from 8:30 to 5, Saturday 8:30 to 4, and Sunday 10 to 1. Weekend hours may be extended if a cruise ship is in port.

Batik Studio (✉*Hummingbird Beach Resort, on the bay-front, north of the wharf, Soufrière* ☎*758/459–7232*) has superb batik sarongs, scarves, and wall panels designed and created on-site by Joan Alexander and her son David.

At **Caribelle Batik** (✉*La Toc Rd., Morne Fortune, Castries* ☎*758/452–3785*), craftspeople demonstrate the art of batik and silk-screen printing. Meanwhile, seamstresses create clothing and wall hangings, which you can purchase in the shop. The studio is in an old Victorian mansion, high atop the Morne overlooking Castries. There's a terrace where you can have a cool drink, and there's a garden full of tropical orchids and lilies. Caribelle Batik creations are featured in many gift shops throughout St. Lucia.

Sea Island Cotton Shop (✉*Bridge St., Castries* ☎*758/452–3674* ✉*Gablewoods Mall, Choc Bay* ☎*758/451–6946* ✉*J. Q.'s Shopping Mall, Rodney Bay* ☎*758/458–4220*) sells quality T-shirts, Caribelle Batik clothing and other resort wear, and colorful souvenirs.

GIFTS & SOUVENIRS

Caribbean Perfumes (✉*Jacques Restaurant, Vigie Marina, Castries* ☎*758/453–7249*) blends a half-dozen lovely scents for women and two aftershaves for men from exotic flowers, fruits, tropical woods, and spices. Fragrances are all made in St. Lucia, reasonably priced, and available at the perfumery (adjacent to Jacques Waterside Dining Restaurant) and at many hotel gift shops.

Noah's Arkade (⊠*Jeremie St., Castries* ☎*758/452–2523* ⊠*Pointe Seraphine, Castries* ☎*758/452–7488*) has hammocks, wood carvings, straw mats, T-shirts, books, and other regional goods.

HANDICRAFTS

On the southwest coast, halfway between Soufrière and Vieux Fort, you can find locally made clay and straw pieces at the **Choiseul Arts & Crafts Centre** (⊠*La Fargue* ☎*758/454–3226*). Many of St. Lucia's artisans come from this area.

Eudovic Art Studio (⊠*Morne Fortune, Castries* ☎*758/452–2747*) is a workshop and studio where you can buy trays, masks, and figures sculpted from local mahogany, red cedar, and eucalyptus wood.

At **Zaka** (⊠*Malgretoute, Soufrière* ☎*758/457–1504*), you're likely to get a chance to talk with artist and craftsman Simon Gajhadhar, who fashions totems and masks from driftwood and other environmentally friendly sources of wood—taking advantage of all the natural nibs and knots that distinguish each piece. Once the "face" is carved, it is painted in vivid colors to highlight the exaggerated features and provide expression. Each piece is a unique work of art.

Barbados & St. Lucia Essentials

PLANNING TOOLS, EXPERT INSIGHT, GREAT CONTACTS

There are planners and there are those who, excuse the pun, fly by the seat of their pants. We happily place ourselves among the planners. Our writers and editors try to anticipate all the issues you may face before and during any journey, and then they do their research. This section is the product of their efforts. Use it to get excited about your trip to Book Title, to inform your travel planning, or to guide you on the road should the seat of your pants start to feel threadbare.

www.fodors.com/forums

GETTING STARTED

We're very proud of our Web site: Fodors.com is a great place to begin any journey. Scan Travel Wire for suggested itineraries, travel deals, restaurant and hotel openings, and other up-to-the-minute info. Check out Booking to research prices and book plane tickets, hotel rooms, rental cars, and vacation packages. Head to Talk for on-the-ground pointers from travelers who frequent our message boards. You can also link to loads of other travel-related resources.

▮ RESOURCES

ONLINE TRAVEL TOOLS
To get a good understanding of news, current events, and regional happenings before you take your trip, check out the Web sites of local island newspapers. In Barbados the major newspapers are *The Nation* and *Barbados Advocate.* In St. Lucia the major newspaper is *The Star.*

For a snapshot of island history, the BBC News Web site offers an interesting chronology of key events from 1536 to the present in the case of Barbados and from 1501 to the present in the case of St. Lucia.

The Barbados Government Information Service (BGIS) is the official communications arm of the Barbados government and is responsible for the dissemination of public information to the vari-

ous news media and the general public. It posts the "official" news of the day on its Web site.

All About Barbados Barbados Government Information Service (⊕www.barbados.gov.bb/bgis.htm). **Barbados Advocate** (⊕www.barbadosadvocate.com). **Barbados National Trust** (⊕www.barbadosadvocate.com). **BBC News–Barbados** (⊕news.bbc.co.uk/2/hi/americas/1154227.stm). **The Nation** (⊕www.nationnews.com).

All About St. Lucia BBC News–St. Lucia (⊕news.bbc.co.uk/2/hi/americas/country_profiles/1210528.stm). **St. Lucia Star** (⊕www.stluciastar.com).

TIME ZONES
Barbados and St. Lucia are both in the Atlantic Standard Time zone, which is one hour later than Eastern Standard Time and four hours earlier than GMT. As is true throughout the Caribbean, neither island observes daylight saving time, so Atlantic Standard is the same time as Eastern Daylight Time during that period (March through October).

Timeanddate.com (⊕www.time-anddate.com/worldclock) can help you figure out the correct time anywhere.

Weather **Accuweather.com** (⊕www.accuweather.com) is an independent weather-forecasting service with good coverage of hurricanes. **Weather.com** (⊕www.weather.com) is the Web site for the Weather Channel.

VISITOR INFORMATION
Both Barbados and St. Lucia have tourist offices in the U.S., where you can get brochures and maps in advance of your trip.

Contacts **Barbados Tourism Authority** (⊠New York, NY ☎212/986–6516 or 800/221–9831 ⊕www.visitbarbados.org ⊠Coral Gables, FL ☎305/442–7471 🖷305/567–2844 ⊠Los Angeles, CA ☎213/380–2198). **St. Lucia Tourist Board** (⊠New York, NY ☎212/867–2950 or 800/456–3984 ⊕www.stlucia.org).

▌ THINGS TO CONSIDER

PASSPORTS & VISAS
All visitors to both Barbados and St. Lucia must have a valid passport and a return or ongoing ticket. A birth certificate and photo ID are *not* sufficient proof of citizenship.

U.S. Passport Information **U.S. Department of State** (☎877/487–2778 ⊕travel.state.gov/passport).

SHOTS & MEDICATIONS
No specific immunizations are required to enter Barbados or St. Lucia, but all individuals,

particularly children, should be up-to-date with their routine and recommended vaccinations, which include all the childhood diseases, tetanus (booster every 10 years), as well as an annual flu shot.

For more information see Health under On the Ground in Barbados & St. Lucia, below.

■TIP➔ **If you travel a lot internationally—particularly to developing nations—refer to the CDC's** *Health Information for International Travel* **(aka Traveler's Health Yellow Book). Info from it is posted on the CDC Web site (www.cdc.gov/travel), or you can buy a copy from your local bookstore for $24.95.**

Health Warnings **National Centers for Disease Control & Prevention** (CDC ☎877/394–8747 international travelers' health line ⊕www.cdc.gov/travel). **World Health Organization** (WHO ⊕www.who.int).

TRIP INSURANCE
What kind of coverage do you honestly need? Do you need trip insurance at all? Take a deep breath and read on.

We believe that comprehensive trip insurance is especially valuable if you're booking a very expensive or complicated trip (particularly to an isolated region) or if you're booking far in advance. Who knows what could happen six months down the road? But whether or not you get insurance has more to do

Trip Insurance Resources

INSURANCE COMPARISON SITES		
Insure My Trip.com	800/487-4722	www.insuremytrip.com
Square Mouth.com	800/240-0369 or 727/490-5803	www.squaremouth.com
COMPREHENSIVE TRAVEL INSURERS		
Access America	866/729-6021	www.accessamerica.com
CSA Travel Protection	800/873-9855	www.csatravelprotection.com
HTH Worldwide	610/254-8700	www.hthworldwide.com
Travelex Insurance	888/228-9792	www.travelex-insurance.com
AIG Travel Guard	800/826-4919	www.travelguard.com
Travel Insured International	800/243-3174	www.travelinsured.com
MEDICAL-ONLY INSURERS		
International Medical Group	800/628-4664	www.imgglobal.com
International SOS		www.internationalsos.com
Wallach & Company	800/237-6615 or 504/687-3166	www.wallach.com

with how comfortable you are assuming all that risk yourself.

Comprehensive travel policies typically cover trip-cancellation and interruption, letting you cancel or cut your trip short because of a personal emergency, illness, or, in some cases, acts of terrorism in your destination. Such policies also cover evacuation and medical care. Some also cover you for trip delays because of bad weather or mechanical problems as well as for lost or delayed baggage. Another type of coverage to look for is financial default—that is, when your trip is disrupted because a tour operator, airline, or cruise line goes out of business. General-

ly you must buy this when you book your trip or shortly thereafter, and it's only available to you if your operator isn't on a list of excluded companies.

If you're going abroad, consider buying medical-only coverage at the very least. Neither Medicare nor some private insurers cover medical expenses anywhere outside of the United States (including time aboard a cruise ship, even if it leaves from a U.S. port). Medical-only policies typically reimburse you for medical care (excluding that related to preexisting conditions) and hospitalization abroad, and provide for evacuation. You still have to pay the bills and await reimbursement from the insurer, though.

Expect comprehensive travel insurance policies to cost about 4% to 7% or 8% of the total price of your trip (it's more like 8%–12% if you're over age 70). A medical-only policy may or may not be cheaper than a comprehensive policy. Always read the fine print of your policy to make sure that you are covered for the risks that are of most concern to you. Compare several policies to make sure you're getting the best price and range of coverage available.

■TIP→ OK. You know you can save a bundle on trips to warm-weather destinations by traveling in rainy season. But there's also a chance that a severe storm will disrupt your plans. The solution? Look for hotels and resorts that offer storm/hurricane guarantees. Although they rarely allow refunds, most guarantees do let you rebook later if a storm strikes.

BOOKING YOUR TRIP

Unless your cousin is a travel agent, you're probably among the millions of people who make most of their travel arrangements online.

But have you ever wondered just what the differences are between an online travel agent (a Web site through which you make reservations instead of going directly to the airline, hotel, or car-rental company), a discounter (a firm that does a high volume of business with a hotel chain or airline and accordingly gets good prices), a wholesaler (one that makes cheap reservations in bulk and then re-sells them to people like you), and an aggregator (one that compares all the offerings so you don't have to)?

Is it truly better to book directly on an airline or hotel Web site? And when does a real live travel agent come in handy?

▌ ONLINE

You really have to shop around. A travel wholesaler such as Hotels.com or HotelClub.net can be a source of good rates, as can discounters such as Hotwire or Priceline, particularly if you can bid for your hotel room or airfare. Indeed, such sites sometimes have deals that are unavailable elsewhere. They do, however, tend to work only with hotel chains (which makes them just plain useless for getting hotel reservations outside of major cities) or big airlines (so that often leaves out upstarts like jetBlue and some foreign carriers like Air India).

Also, with discounters and wholesalers you must generally prepay, and everything is non-refundable. And before you fork over the dough, be sure to check the terms and conditions, so you know what a given company will do for you if there's a problem and what you'll have to deal with on your own.

▌TIP→ **To be absolutely sure everything was processed correctly, confirm reservations made through online travel agents, discounters, and wholesalers directly with your hotel before leaving home.**

Booking engines like Expedia, Travelocity, and Orbitz are actually travel agents, albeit high-volume, online ones. And airline travel packagers like American Airlines Vacations and Virgin Vacations—well, they're travel agents, too. But they may still not work with all the world's hotels.

An aggregator site will search many sites and pull the best prices for airfares, hotels, and rental cars from them. Most aggregators compare the major travel-booking sites such as Expedia, Travelocity, and Orbitz; some also look at airline Web sites, though rarely the sites of smaller budget airlines. Some aggregators also compare other travel products, including complex packages—a good thing, as you can sometimes get the best overall deal by booking an air-and-hotel package.

▌ WITH A TRAVEL AGENT

If you use an agent—brick-and-mortar or virtual—you'll pay a fee for the service. And know that the service you get from some online agents isn't comprehensive. For example Expedia and Travelocity don't search for prices on budget airlines like jetBlue, Southwest, or small foreign carriers. That said, some agents (online or not) *do* have access to fares that are difficult to find otherwise, and the savings can more than make up for any surcharge.

A knowledgeable brick-and-mortar travel agent can be a godsend if you're booking a cruise, a package trip that's not available to you directly, an air pass, or a complicated itinerary including several overseas flights. What's more, travel agents that specialize in a destination may have exclusive access to certain deals and insider information on things such as charter flights. Agents who specialize in types of travelers (senior citizens, gays and lesbians, naturists) or types of trips (cruises, luxury travel, safaris) can also be invaluable.

A top-notch agent will help arrange all the details you don't want (or wouldn't think) to arrange yourself. And complain about the surcharges all you like, but when things don't work out the way you'd hoped, it's nice to have an agent to put things right.

▌ ACCOMMODATIONS

In Barbados, visitors may choose an appropriate vacation retreat from among hundreds of choices: full-service resorts, large hotels, boutique hotels, small inns, serviced apartments, or private villas. The island offers something to suit every taste and every pocketbook. The fashionable west coast, north of Bridgetown, is known for its very luxurious (and pricey) resorts and villas. Christ Church Parish on the south coast is the location of many hotels and resorts, both large and small, which are less secluded and more reasonably priced. Generally speaking, British visitors and those seeking a more quiet retreat tend to prefer the west coast; Americans tend to congregate on the action-packed south coast. On the remote east and southeast coasts, a few small inns are, what you might call, off the beaten track.

St. Lucia prides itself in being the most romantic Caribbean island, and many of its all-inclusive resorts cater to that market. The island also has its eyes on return visitors—lovers and others who may have spent a honey-

Online Booking Resources

AGGREGATORS

Kayak	www.kayak.com	looks at cruises and vacation packages.
Mobissimo	www.mobissimo.com	examines airfare, hotels, cars, and tons of activities.
Qixo	www.qixo.com	compares cruises, vacation packages, and even travel insurance.
Sidestep	www.sidestep.com	compares vacation packages and lists travel deals and some activities.
Travelgrove	www.travelgrove.com	compares cruises and packages and lets you search by themes.

BOOKING ENGINES

Cheap Tickets	www.cheaptickets.com	discounter.
Expedia	www.expedia.com	large online agency that charges a booking fee for airline tickets.
Hotwire	www.hotwire.com	discounter.
lastminute.com	www.lastminute.com	specializes in last-minute travel; the main site is for the U.K., but it has a link to a U.S. site.
Luxury Link	www.luxurylink.com	has auctions (surprisingly good deals) as well as offers on the high-end side of travel.
Onetravel.com	www.onetravel.com	a discounter for hotels, car rentals, airfares, and packages.
Orbitz	www.orbitz.com	charges a booking fee for airline tickets, but gives a clear breakdown of fees and taxes before you book.
Priceline.com	www.priceline.com	discounter that also allows bidding.
Travel.com	www.travel.com	allows you to compare its rates with those of other booking engines.
Travelocity	www.travelocity.com	charges a booking fee for airline tickets, but promises good problem resolution.

ONLINE ACCOMMODATIONS

Hotelbook.com	www.hotelbook.com	focuses on independent hotels worldwide.
Hotel Club	www.hotelclub.net	good for major cities worldwide and some resort areas.
Hotels.com	www.hotels.com	Expedia-owned wholesaler that offers rooms in hotels all over the world.
Quikbook	www.quikbook.com	offers "pay when you stay" reservations that allow you to settle your bill when you check out, not when you book; best for trips to U.S. and Canadian cities.

OTHER RESOURCES

Bidding For Travel	www.biddingfor-travel.com	good place to figure out what you can get and for how much before you start bidding on, say, Priceline.

moon or romantic vacation here and who now want a reprise in one of the luxury resorts or who may be interested in investing in a vacation property. Luxury villa communities and condo complexes have sprouted up all over the northern tip of St. Lucia and in Marigot Bay—and it looks like there's no end in sight. New developments are underway on the east coast—virtually untouched until now by the tourist market—and the southern coast will probably be next. In the meantime, visitors to the island have a huge array of wonderful all-inclusive resorts, luxury hotels, boutique inns, and small apartments from which to choose in the areas north and south of Castries and in and around Soufrière.

Most hotels and other lodgings require you to give your credit-card details before they will confirm your reservation. If you don't feel comfortable e-mailing this information, ask if you can fax it (some places even prefer faxes). However you book, get confirmation in writing and have a copy of it handy when you check in.

Be sure you understand the hotel's cancellation policy. Some places allow you to cancel without any kind of penalty—even if you prepaid to secure a discounted rate—if you cancel at least 24 hours in advance. Others require you to cancel a week in advance or penalize you the cost of one night. Small inns and B&Bs are most likely to require you to cancel far in advance. Most hotels allow children under a certain age to stay in their parents' room at no extra charge, but others charge for them as extra adults; find out the cutoff age for discounts.

■TIP→ **Assume that hotels operate on the European Plan (EP, no meals) unless we specify that they use the Breakfast Plan (BP, with full breakfast), Continental Plan (CP, Continental breakfast), Full American Plan (FAP, all meals), or Modified American Plan (MAP, breakfast and dinner), or are all-inclusive (AI, all meals and most activities).**

▌AIRLINE TICKETS

Most domestic airline tickets are electronic; international tickets may be either electronic or paper. With an e-ticket the only thing you receive is an e-mailed receipt citing your itinerary and reservation and ticket numbers.

The greatest advantage of an e-ticket is that if you lose your receipt, you can simply print out another copy or ask the airline to do it for you at check-in. You usually pay a surcharge (up to $50) to get a paper ticket, if you can get one at all.

The sole advantage of a paper ticket is that it may be easier to endorse over to another airline if your flight is canceled and the airline with which you booked can't accommodate you on another flight.

▮ RENTAL CARS

To rent a car in Barbados you must present a valid driver's license and major credit card. Most agencies require renters to be between 21 and 75 years of age. Those over 75 may need a certified doctor's note indicating a continuing ability to drive safely. A local driver's permit, which costs $5, is obtained through the rental agency. More than 75 agencies rent cars, Jeeps, or minimokes (small, open-sided vehicles), and rates are expensive—about $55 per day for a minimoke to $85 or more per day for a four-wheel-drive vehicle (or $400 to $500 or more per week) in high season, depending on the vehicle and whether it has air-conditioning. Most firms also offer discounted three-day rates. The rental generally includes insurance, pickup and delivery service, maps, 24-hour emergency service, and unlimited mileage. Baby seats are usually available upon request.

To rent a car in St. Lucia you must be at least 25 years old and provide a valid driver's license and a credit card. If you don't have an international driver's license, you must buy a temporary St. Lucian driving permit at car-rental firms, the immigration office at either airport, or the Gros Islet police station. The permit costs $20 (EC$54) and is valid for three months. Car-rental rates are usually quoted in U.S. dollars and range from $50 to $80 per day or $300 to $425 per week, depending on the car. Car-rental agencies generally include free pickup at your hotel and unlimited mileage.

CAR RENTAL RESOURCES
Local Agencies in Barbados
Coconut Car Rentals (✉Bay St., Bridgetown, St. Michael ☎246/437–0297). **Courtesy Rent-A-Car** (✉Grantley Adams International Airport, Christ Church ☎246/431–4160). **Drive-a-Matic Car Rental** (✉Lower Carlton, St. James ☎246/422–3000).**National Car Rentals** (✉Lower Carlton, St. James ☎246/426–0603). **Sunny Isle Sixt Car Rentals** (✉Worthing, Christ Church ☎246/435–7979). **Sunset Crest Car Rental** (✉Sunset Crest, Holetown, St. James ☎246/432–2222).

Local Agencies in St. Lucia Cool Breeze Jeep/Car Rental (✉Soufrière ☎758/459–7729 ⊕www. coolbreezecarrental.com/stlucia). **Courtesy Car Rental** (✉Bois d'Orange, Gros Islet ☎758/452–8140 ⊕www.courtesycarrentals. com).

TRANSPORTATION

▮ BY AIR

Several carriers offer frequent nonstop or direct flights between North America and both Barbados, which is a regional Caribbean airline hub, and St. Lucia's Hewanorra International Airport (St. Lucia's smaller Vigie airport only accommodates smaller interisland planes). Flying time from New York is about 4½ hours to either island.

AIRPORTS

Barbados's Grantley Adams International Airport (BGI) is a stunning, modern facility located in Christ Church Parish, on the south coast. The airport is about 15 minutes from hotels situated along the south or east coasts, 45 minutes from the west coast, and about 30 minutes from Bridgetown.

St. Lucia has two airports. Hewanorra International Airport (UVF) accommodates large jet aircraft and is located at the southeastern tip of the island in Vieux Fort. George F.L. Charles Airport (SLU, often referred to as Vigie Airport) is located at Vigie Point in Castries, in the northwestern part of the island, and accommodates only prop aircraft due to its location and runway limitations.

Airport Information **George F.L. Charles Airport** (☎758/452–1156). **Grantley Adams International**

Airport (BGI ☎246/428–7101). **Hewanorra International Airport** (☎758/454–6355).

GROUND TRANSPORTATION

In Barbados, ground transportation is available immediately outside the customs area of the airport. Taxis aren't metered, but fares are regulated (about $30 to Speightstown, $20 to $22 to west coast hotels, $10 to $12 to south coast ones). Always confirm the price before getting in the taxi.

From Hewanorra, the one-way taxi fare for the long—though scenic—30- to 90-minute ride (depending on whether you're headed to Soufrière or Castries) is expensive—$55 to $75 for up to four passengers. If you land instead at George F.L. Charles Airport, it's a short drive to resorts in the north, about 20 minutes to Marigot Bay, but more than an hour to Soufrière.

In St. Lucia, some people opt for a helicopter transfer between Hewanorra and either Castries or Soufrière, a quick seven- to ten-minute ride with a beautiful view at a one-way cost of $120 to $140 per passenger.

Information **St. Lucia Helicopters** (✉Pointe Seraphine, Castries ☎758/453–6950 ⊕www.stluciahelicopters.com).

FLIGHTS

Airlines serving Barbados and St. Lucia include Air Jamaica (Barbados only), American Airlines (which also has connecting service through San Juan), British Airways, Caribbean Airlines, Continental, Delta, and USAirways.

Barbados and George F.L. Charles Airport in St. Lucia are also well connected to other Caribbean islands via LIAT.

Airline Contacts Air Jamaica (☎246/428–1660 in Barbados, 758/453–6611 in St. Lucia, or 800/523–5585 ⊕www.airjamaica. com). **American Airlines/American Eagle** (☎246/428–4170 in Barbados, 758/452–1820 or 758/454–6777 in St. Lucia, or 800/744–0006 ⊕www.aa.com). **Caribbean Airlines** (☎246/428–1950 in Barbados or 800/920–4225 ⊕www.caribbean-airlines.com). **Continental Airlines** (☎800/534–0089 ⊕www.continental.com). **Delta** (☎800/221–1212 ⊕www.delta. com). **LIAT** (☎246/428–0986 in Barbados, 758/452–3056 in St. Lucia, or 888/844–5428 ⊕www.liat.com). **US Airways** (☎758/454–8186 in St. Lucia or 800/622–1015 ⊕www. usairways.com).

▌BY BOAT & FERRY

For visitors to St. Lucia arriving at Rodney Bay on their own or chartered yachts, Rodney Bay Marina is an official port of entry for customs and immigration purposes. A ferry travels between the marina and the shopping complex daily from 9 to 4, on the hour, for $4 per person round-trip.

▌BY BUS

On Barbados, bus service is efficient, inexpensive, and plentiful. Blue buses with a yellow stripe are public, yellow buses with a blue stripe are private, and private "Zed-R" vans (so called for their ZR license-plate designation) are white with a maroon stripe. All buses travel frequently along Highway 1 (St. James Road) and Highway 7 (South Coast Main Road), as well as inland routes. The fare is Bds$1.50 (75¢) for any one destination; exact change in either local or U.S. currency is appreciated. Buses pass along main roads about every 20 minutes. Stops are marked by small signs on roadside poles that say TO CITY or OUT OF CITY, meaning the direction relative to Bridgetown. Flag down the bus with your hand, even if you're standing at the stop. Bridgetown terminals are at Fairchild Street for buses to the south and east and at Lower Green for buses to Speightstown via the west coast.

In St. Lucia, privately owned and operated minivans constitute the bus system, an inexpensive and efficient means of transportation used primarily by local people. Minivan routes cover the entire island and run from early morning until approximately 10 PM. You may find this method of getting around most useful for short distances, between

Castries and the Rodney Bay area, for example; longer hauls can be uncomfortable. The fare between Castries and Gablewoods Mall is EC$1.25; Castries and Rodney Bay, EC$2; Castries and Gros Islet, EC$2.25; Castries and Vieux Fort (a trip that takes more than two hours), EC$7; Castries and Soufrière (a bone-crushing journey that takes even longer), EC$10. Minivans follow designated routes (signs are displayed on the front window); ask at your hotel for the appropriate route number for your destination. Wait at a marked bus stop or hail a passing minivan from the roadside. In Castries, buses depart from the corner of Micoud and Bridge streets, behind the markets.

In addition to the driver, each minivan usually has a conductor, a young man whose job it is to collect fares, open the door, and generally take charge of the passenger area. If you're sure of where you're going, simply tap twice on the metal window frame to signal that you want to get off at the next stop. Otherwise, just let the conductor or driver know where you're going, and he'll stop at the appropriate place.

▎ BY CAR

Both Barbados and St. Lucia are medium-sized islands, and you can do a complete circuit of either island in about four hours—although it would be a very exhausting way to spend the day. You're better off visiting different sections of each island on separate day trips. You can get by on either island using a combination of tours, taxis, and local buses (and on St. Lucia water taxis), but you might also opt for a rental car and explore on your own—although be aware that driving on both islands is on the left (British-style).

The roads in Barbados are quite good, with well-maintained highways linking the major cities and the airport, but the roads in the countryside can be narrow, winding, and confusing. On St. Lucia the roads in the north are comparatively flat and well-marked; the coastal roads, while fairly wellmaintained, are mountainous and filled with reverse curves and steep, narrow inclines.

GASOLINE
In Barbados you can find gasoline stations in and around Bridgetown, on the main highways along the west and south coasts, and in most inland parishes.

In St. Lucia gas stations are found in and around major cities such as Castries, Gros Islet (Rodney Bay), Soufrière, Vieux Fort, and Dennery.

On either island, gas is very expensive—often $6 per gallon or more.

ROAD CONDITIONS
Barbados has nearly 1,000 mi (1,600 km) of paved roads that follow the coastline and meander through the countryside. A

network of main highways facilitates traffic flow into and out of Bridgetown. The Adams-Barrow-Cummins (ABC) Highway bypasses Bridgetown, which saves time getting from coast to coast. Small signs tacked to trees and poles at intersections point the way to most attractions, and local people are helpful if you get lost. Remote roads are in fairly good repair, yet few are lighted at night—and night falls quickly at about 6 PM year-round. Even in full daylight, the tall sugarcane fields lining both sides of the road in interior sections can hinder visibility.

St. Lucia has about 500 mi (800 km) of roads, but only about half (281 mi [450 km]) are paved. All towns and villages are connected to major routes. The highways on both coasts are winding and mountainous—particularly on parts of the West Coast Road north of Soufrière.

RULES OF THE ROAD
Driving in both Barbados and St. Lucia is on the left, British style. Be mindful of pedestrians and, in the countryside, occasional livestock walking on the road. When someone flashes headlights at you at an intersection, it means "after you." Be especially careful negotiating roundabouts (traffic circles). Observe speed limits which, in keeping with the pace of life and the narrow roads, are 30 mph (50 kph) in the country, 20 mph (30 kph) in town. The roads and highways into and out of the capital cities of Bridgetown, in Barbados, and Castries, in St. Lucia, actually have rush hours: 7 to 9 and 4 to 6. On both islands, respect no-parking zones; police issue tickets. And wear your seat belts—it's the law!

▌ BY TAXI

On Barbados, taxis operate 24 hours a day. They aren't metered but charge according to fixed rates set by the government. They carry up to three passengers, and the fare may be shared. For short trips, the rate per mile (or part thereof) should not exceed $1.50. Drivers are courteous and knowledgeable; most will narrate a tour at an hourly rate of about $25 for up to three people. Be sure to settle the price before you start off and agree on whether it's quoted in U.S. or Barbados dollars.

On St. Lucia, taxis are always available at the airports, the harbor, and in front of major hotels. They're unmetered, although nearly all drivers belong to a taxi cooperative and adhere to standard fares. Sample fares for up to four passengers are as follows: Castries to Rodney Bay, $20; Rodney Bay to Cap Estate, $10; Castries to Cap Estate, $25; Castries to Marigot Bay, $25; Castries to Anse-La-Raye, $30: Castries to Soufrière, $70. Always ask the driver to quote the price *before* you get in, and be sure that you both understand whether it's quoted in EC or U.S. dollars. Drivers are careful, knowledgeable, and courteous.

ON THE GROUND

▌ COMMUNICATIONS

INTERNET

On both Barbados and St. Lucia, most hotels and resorts provide Internet access—either free or for a small fee—for their guests. In Barbados you'll also find Internet cafés in and around Bridgetown, in Holetown and Speightstown on the west coast, and at St. Lawrence Gap on the south coast. Rates range from $2 for 15 minutes to $8 or $9 per hour. In St. Lucia, Internet cafés can be found in Castries and at the Rodney Bay Marina; Cable Wireless maintains a public Internet kiosk at Point Seraphine, in Castries, that accepts major credit cards or cash.

Barbados Internet Cafés **Bean-n-Bagel Internet Cafe** (⊠St. Lawrence Gap, Dover, Christ Church ☎246/420–4604). **Bean-n-Bagel Internet Cafe** (⊠West Coast Mall, Holetown, St. James ☎246/432–1103).

Bean-n-Bagel Internet Cafe (⊠The Wharf, Bridgetown, St. Michael ☎246/436–7778).

Clicks-N-Bytes Cafe (⊠144 Roebuck St., Bridgetown, St. Michael ☎246/427–8939). **Connect Internet Cafe** (⊠Shop #9, 27 Broad St., Bridgetown, St. Michael ☎246/228–8648). **ICS Internet Cafe** (⊠St. Lawrence Gap, Dover, Christ Church ☎246/428–1513). **Surf 'n' Lime** (⊠Road View, Main Rd., Speightstown, St. Peter ☎246/422–5871).

St. Lucia Internet Cafés **CIBS Cafe** (⊠Chisel & St. Louis Sts., Castries ☎758/458–2195). **Cyber Connections** (⊠Rodney Bay Marina, Gros Islet ☎758/450–9309). **Destination St. Lucia (DSL) Ltd.** (⊠Rodney Bay Marina, Gros Islet ☎758/452–8531).

PHONES

The area code for Barbados is 246. The area code for St. Lucia is 758.

CALLING WITHIN BARBADOS & ST. LUCIA

In Barbados, local calls are free from private phones; some hotels charge a small fee. For directory assistance, dial 411. Calls from pay phones cost Bds25¢ for five minutes.

Throughout St. Lucia, you can dial local calls directly from your hotel room by connecting to an outside line and dialing the seven-digit number. Some hotels charge a small fee (usually about EC50¢) for local calls. Pay phones accept EC25¢ and EC$1 coins.

CALLING OUTSIDE BARBADOS & ST. LUCIA

The country code for the United States is 1.

From Barbados, direct-dialing to the United States and other countries is efficient and reasonable, but always check with your hotel to see if a surcharge is added. Some toll-free numbers cannot be accessed in Barbados. To charge your overseas call to a major credit card or U.S. calling card without incurring a surcharge, dial 800/225-5872 (1-800/CALL-USA) from any phone.

From St. Lucia you can make direct-dial overseas and interisland calls, and the connections are excellent. You can charge an overseas call to a major credit card with no surcharge. From public phones and many hotels, dial 811 and charge the call to your credit card to avoid expensive rates or hotel surcharges.

Information AT&T (☎800/872-2881). **Cable & Wireless** (☎758/453-9922 in St. Lucia). **Credit Card Charge Call** (☎811 in St. Lucia). **Digicel** (☎758/456-3400 or 758/456-3444 in St. Lucia).

PHONE CARDS
Prepaid phone cards, which can be used for both local and international calls throughout Barbados, St. Lucia, and other Caribbean islands, are available for purchase in various denominations ($5, $10, $25, $50, $100) at shops, attractions, transportation centers, and other convenient retail outlets on both islands. The phone cards can be used from any touch-tone telephone (including pay phones).

MOBILE PHONES
If you have a quad-band GSM cell phone and if your cell company has a roaming agreement with a local company, you can probably use your cell phone in both Barbados and St. Lucia; but be aware that, based on your calling plan, the roaming charges to call home or to make local calls can be extremely expensive—even for just a brief telephone call. Renting a prepaid cell phone if you're planning an extended vacation or expect to make a lot of local calls may be a less expensive alternative than using your own. A cell phone can be rented for as little as $5 a day (minimum one-week rental); then prepaid cards are available at several locations throughout the island and in varying denominations—$5, $10, $25, and $37.50.

Cell phones can be rented from Cable & Wireless offices in Castries, Gablewoods Mall, Rodney Bay Marina, and Vieux Fort; or, if you have an "unlocked" cell phone that uses GSM technology, you can purchase a local SIM card for $20 (which includes an $8 call credit) at Digicel offices in those same areas. The cards can be topped up at hundreds of business locations around the island.

Barbados Cell Phone Rental Global Business Centre (✉West Coast Mall, Sunset Crest, Holetown, St. James ☎246/432-6508 ⊕www.globalbizcentre.com)

St. Lucia Cell Phone Rental Cable & Wireless (✉Bridge St., Castries ☎758/453-9000 ⊠Gablewoods Mall, Castries ☎758/453-9908 ⊠Rodney Bay, Gros Islet

☎758/453–9054 ✉Vieux Fort, Castries ☎758/453–9671 ⊕www.candw.lc)

Digicel (✉Cor. Chisel and St. Louis Sts, Castries ☎758/453–2999 ✉Rodney Bay, Gros Islet ☎758/450–3872 ⊕www.digicelstlucia.com)

▌ CUSTOMS & DUTIES

You're always allowed to bring goods of a certain value back home without having to pay any duty or import tax. But there's a limit on the amount of tobacco and liquor you can bring back duty-free, and some countries have separate limits for perfumes; for exact figures, check with your customs department. The values of so-called "duty-free" goods are included in these amounts. When you shop abroad, save all your receipts, as customs inspectors may ask to see them as well as the items you purchased. If the total value of your goods is more than the duty-free limit, you'll have to pay a tax (most often a flat percentage) on the value of everything beyond that limit.

U.S. Information **U.S. Customs and Border Protection** (⊕www.cbp.gov).

▌ DAY TOURS & GUIDES IN BARBADOS

A sightseeing tour is a good way to get your bearings and to experience the rich Bajan culture. Taxi drivers will give you a personalized tour of Barbados for about $25 per hour for up to three people. Or you can choose a fascinating helicopter ride, an overland horseback or mountain bike journey, a 4x4 safari expedition, or a full-day bus excursion. The prices vary according to the mode of travel and the number and kind of attractions included. Ask your hotel to help you make arrangements.

Bajan Helicopters offers an eagle's-eye view of the island. The air-conditioned jet helicopters accommodate up to five people for a 30-mi (50-km) "Discover Barbados Tour" or a 50-mi (80-km) "Island Tour." Prices start at $97.50 per person. Highland Adventure Centre offers horseback or mountain bike tours for $50 per person, including transportation, guides, and refreshments. Whether it's your first time on a horse or you're an experienced rider, the chance to view plantation houses, three coastlines, and quaint villages astride a thoroughbred is a thrilling opportunity—don't forget your camera! The mountain-bike tour is an exhilarating 7½-mi (12-km) ride (15% uphill) through the picturesque heart of northern Barbados, ending up at Barclays Park on the east coast. Island Safari will take you to all the popular spots via a 4x4 Land Rover—including some gullies, forests, and remote areas that are inaccessible by conventional cars and buses. The cost for half-day or full-day tours ranges from $45 to $77 per person, including snacks or lunch. L. E.

Williams Tour Co. will pick you up at your hotel for a seven-hour narrated bus tour—an 80-mi (130-km) circuit of the best of Barbados. The $62.50 per-person price includes a Bajan buffet lunch and beverages at Atlantis Inn on the rugged east coast.

Information Bajan Helicopters (✉Bridgetown Heliport, Bridgetown, St. Michael ☎246/431–0069 ⊕www.bajanhelicopters.com). **Highland Adventure Centre** (✉Cane Field, St. Thomas ☎246/438–8069 or 246/438–8928). **Island Safari** (✉Main Rd., Bush Hall, St. Michael ☎246/429–5337 ⊕www.islandsafari.bb). **L. E. Williams Tour Co.** (✉Hastings, Christ Church ☎246/427–1043).

■ DAY TOURS & GUIDES IN ST. LUCIA

Taxi drivers are well informed and can give you a full tour—and often an excellent one, thanks to government-sponsored training programs. From the Castries area, full-day island tours cost $140 for up to four people; sightseeing trips to Soufrière, $120. If you plan your own day, expect to pay the driver $20 per hour plus tip.

Jungle Tours specializes in rainforest hiking tours for all levels of ability. You're required only to bring hiking shoes or sneakers and have a willingness to get wet and have fun. Prices range from $80 to $90 and include lunch, fees, and transportation via open Land Rover truck. St. Lucia Helicopters offers a bird's-

eye view of the island. A 10-minute North Island tour ($55 per person) leaves from Pointe Seraphine, in Castries, continues up the west coast to Pigeon Island, then flies along the rugged Atlantic coastline before returning inland over Castries. The 20-minute South Island tour ($85 per person) starts at Pointe Seraphine and follows the western coastline, circling picturesque Marigot Bay, Soufrière, and the majestic Pitons before returning inland over the volcanic hot springs and tropical rain forest. A complete island tour combines the two and lasts 30 minutes ($130 per person). St. Lucia Heritage Tours has put together an "authentic St. Lucia experience," specializing in the local culture and traditions. Groups are small, and some of the off-the-beaten-track sites visited are a 19th-century plantation house surrounded by nature trails, a 20-foot waterfall hidden away on private property, and a living museum presenting Creole practices and traditions. Plan on paying $65 per person for a full-day tour. Sunlink Tours offers dozens of land, sea, and combination sightseeing tours, as well as shopping tours, plantation, and rain-forest adventures via Jeep safari, deep-sea fishing excursions, and day trips to other islands. Prices range from $20 for a half-day shopping tour to $120 for a full-day land-and-sea Jeep safari to Soufrière.

Information Jungle Tours (✉Cas en Bas, Gros Islet ☎758/450–0434).

St. Lucia Helicopters (✉Pointe Seraphine, Castries ☎758/453–6950 🖷758/452–1553 ⊕www.stluciahe-licopters.com). **St. Lucia Heritage Tours** (✉Pointe Seraphine, Castries ☎758/451–6058 ⊕www.heritag-etoursstlucia.org). **Sunlink Tours** (✉Reduit Beach Ave., Rodney Bay ☎758/452–8232 or 800/786–5465 ⊕www.sunlinktours.com).

▌ EATING OUT

Barbados prides itself on its many wonderful restaurants, many of which can compete with top-notch dining experiences anywhere in the world. On the west coast, excellent restaurants are concentrated in St. James Parish along Highway 1, particularly in and around Holetown. In fact, First Street and Second Street in Holetown are lined with restaurants that offer a variety of cuisines and prices that range from inexpensive to plan ahead! On the south coast, St. Lawrence Gap is the mother lode of Barbados restaurants, with about 20 possible choices lining both sides of the street (or "gap").

The bulk of St. Lucia's restaurants—both casual and classy—are concentrated in Rodney Bay Village, although some excellent dining establishments are in the Vigie area of Castries and in pretty Marigot Bay. In Soufrière, the best dining is in small hotels and inns, which always welcome nonguests for both lunch and dinner.

MEALS & MEALTIMES
Resort breakfasts are frequently lavish buffets that offer tropical fruits and fruit juices, cereal, fresh rolls and pastries, hot dishes (such as codfish, corned-beef hash, and potatoes), and prepared-to-order eggs, pancakes, and French toast. Lunch could be a sit-down meal at a beachfront café or a picnic at a secluded cove. But dinner is the highlight, often combining the expertise of internationally trained chefs with local know-how and ingredients.

Of course, you'll want to take advantage of the weekend evening street parties in both Barbados (Oistins) and St. Lucia (Gros Islet and Anse La Raye), where you can buy and try local food barbecued right before your eyes and accompanied by music and conviviality—a wonderful experience for the whole family.

Expect breakfast to be served from 7:30 AM to 10 AM; lunch from noon to 2 PM or so; and dinner from 7 PM to about 10 PM. Some restaurants have specific mealtimes; others serve continuously all day long.

Unless otherwise noted, the restaurants listed in this guide are open daily for lunch and dinner.

PAYING
Major credit cards (American Express, Diners Club, Discover, MasterCard, and Visa) are accepted in most Caribbean restaurants. We note in reviews when credit cards are not accepted. Price charts for restaurants

are included in each destination chapter's Planner.

RESERVATIONS & DRESS

It's always a good idea to make a reservation if you can. In some small or pricey restaurants, it's required. We mention specifically only when reservations are essential (there's no other way you'll ever get a table) or when they are not accepted. For very popular restaurants, book as far ahead as you can (often 30 days), and reconfirm as soon as you arrive. (Large parties should always call ahead to check the reservations policy.) We mention dress only for the very few restaurants where men are required to wear a jacket or a jacket and tie. Shorts and T-shirts at dinner and beach attire anytime are universally frowned upon in restaurants throughout the Caribbean.

ELECTRICITY

Electric current on Barbados is 110 volts–50 cycles, U.S. standard. Hotels generally have plug adapters and transformers available for guests who bring appliances to Barbados from countries that operate on 220-volt current.

The electric current on St. Lucia is 220 volts, 50 cycles with a square, three-pin plug (UK standard). A few large hotels have 110-volt outlets for electric razors only. To use most North American appliances, you'll need a transformer to convert voltage and a plug adapter; dual-voltage computers or appliances will

WORD OF MOUTH

Was the service stellar or not up to snuff? Did the food give you shivers of delight or leave you cold? Did the prices and portions make you happy or sad? Rate restaurants and write your own reviews in Travel Ratings or start a discussion about your favorite places in Travel Talk on www.fodors.com. Your comments might even appear in our books. Yes, you, too, can be a correspondent!

still need a plug adapter. Hotels will sometimes lend you a plug adapter for use during your stay.

Contacts **Steve Kropla's Help for World Traveler's** (⊕www.kropla.com) has information on electrical and telephone plugs around the world. **Walkabout Travel Gear** (⊕www.walkabouttravelgear.com) has a good coverage of electricity under "adapters."

EMERGENCIES

Emergency Services **Ambulance** (☎511 in Barbados, 911 in St. Lucia). **Fire** (☎311 in Barbados, 911 in St. Lucia). **Police** (☎211 for emergencies in Barbados, 242/430–7100 nonemergencies, 999 for emergencies in St. Lucia.).

Hospitals in Barbados **Bayview Hospital** (✉St. Paul's Ave., Bayville, St. Michael ☎246/436–5446). **Queen Elizabeth Hospital** (✉Martindales Rd., Bridgetown, St. Michael ☎246/436–6450).

Hospitals in St. Lucia **Dennery Hospital** (✉Main Rd., Dennery ☎758/453–3310). **St. Jude's**

Hospital (⊠Airport Rd., Vieux
Fort ☎758/454–6041). **Soufrière
Hospital** (⊠W. Quinlan St., Sou-
frière ☎758/459–7258). **Victoria
Hospital** (⊠Hospital Rd., Castries
☎758/452–2421).

Pharmacies in Barbados Grant's
(⊠Fairchild St., Bridgetown, St. Mi-
chael ☎246/436–6120 ⊠Main Rd.,
Oistins, Christ Church ☎246/428–
9481). **Knight's** (⊠Lower Broad
St., Bridgetown, St. Michael
☎246/426–5196 ⊠Super Centre
Shopping Center, Main Rd., Oistins,
Christ Church ☎246/428–6057
⊠Suncrest Mall, Hwy. 1, Hole-
town, St. James ☎246/432–1290
⊠Hwy. 1, Speightstown, St. Peter
☎246/422–0048).

**Pharmacies in St. Lucia M & C
Drugstore** (⊠Bridge St., Castries
☎758/452–2811 ⊠J. Q.'s Shopping
Mall, Rodney Bay ☎758/458–0178
⊠Gablewoods Mall, Gros Islet
Hwy., Choc Bay ☎758/451–7808
⊠New Dock Rd., Vieux Fort
☎758/454–3760). **Williams
Pharmacy** (⊠Bridge St., Castries
☎758/452–2797).

**Other Emergencies in Barbados
Coast Guard Defence Force (24-
hour hyperbaric chamber)** (⊠St.
Ann's Fort, Garrison, St. Michael
☎246/427–8819 emergencies,
246/436–6185 nonemergen-
cies). **Divers' Alert Network**
(☎246/684–8111 or 246/684–
2948).

**Other Emergencies in St. Lucia
Marine police** (☎758/453–0770
or 758/452–2595). **Sea-Air Rescue**
(☎758/452–2894, 758/452–1182,
or 758/453–6664).

▌ HEALTH

Dengue fever is one of the common viral diseases transmitted to
humans by the bite of mosqui-
toes, and the Caribbean—including the islands of Barbados and
St. Lucia—is one of the regions
of the world that is considered
a "risk area" by the CDC. No
vaccine is available to prevent
dengue fever, but travelers are
advised to protect against mosquito bites by using insect repel-
lent and protective clothing when
in swampy or forested areas.

HIV is also a growing problem
throughout the Caribbean, and
visitors to the region should take
appropriate precautions to prevent contracting the virus.

Tap water in both Barbados
and St. Lucia is generally safe to
drink, although bottled water is
always available if you prefer.

The major health risk in the
Caribbean is sunburn or sun-
stroke. Protect your skin, wear a
hat, and use sunscreen.

Swimming on the windward
(Atlantic Ocean) side of either
island is not recommended—
even for experienced swimmers.
Tricky currents, powerful waves,
strong undertows, and rocky
bottoms can be extremely dangerous—and lifeguards are nonexistent.

Watch out for black, spiny sea
urchins that live on the rocky sea
floor in both shallow and deep
waters. Stepping on one is guaranteed to be painful for quite
some time, as the urchin releases

its spikes into the offending body. To remove a spike simply pull it out and apply an antiseptic. To remove an embedded spike, first apply some warm oil (preferably olive oil) to soften and dilate the skin, then remove the spike with a sterile needle.

The worst insect problem may well be the tiny "no-see-ums" (sand flies) that appear after a rain, near swampy ground, and at the beach around sunset.

On the west coast of Barbados in particular, beware of the manchineel tree, which grows near the beach and has fruit that looks like little green apples—but is poisonous—and bark and leaves that can burn the skin if you touch them; even the droplets of water that might reach your skin if you seek protection under the tree during a shower can burn you.

Do not fly within 24 hours of scuba diving.

∎ HOURS OF OPERATION

In Barbados, banks are open Monday through Thursday from 8 to 3, Friday from 8 to 5 (some branches in supermarkets are open Saturday morning from 9 to noon). At the airport, the Barbados National Bank is open from 8 AM until the last plane leaves or arrives, seven days a week (including holidays). The General Post Office in Cheapside, Bridgetown, is open weekdays from 7:30 to 5; the Sherbourne Conference Center branch is open weekdays from 8:15 to 4:30 during conferences; and branches in each parish are open weekdays from 8 to 3:15. Most stores in Bridgetown are open weekdays from 8:30 or 9 to 4:30 or 5, Saturday from 8:30 to 1 or 2. Stores in shopping malls outside of Bridgetown may stay open later. Some supermarkets are open daily from 8 to 6 or later.

In St. Lucia, banks are open Monday through Thursday from 8 to 2, Friday 8 to 5; a few branches in Rodney Bay are also open Saturday from 9 to noon. Post offices are open weekdays from 8:30 to 4:30. Most stores are open weekdays from 8:30 to 4:30, Saturday from 8 to 12:30; Gablewoods Mall shops are open Monday through Saturday from 9 to 7; J. Q.'s Shopping Mall shops are open weekdays from 9 to 7 and Saturdays from 9 to 8; Pointe Seraphine shops are open weekdays from 9 to 5, Saturday 9 to 2. Some hotel gift shops may be open on Sunday.

HOLIDAYS

In Barbados, public holidays are New Year's Day (Jan. 1), Errol Barrow Day (Jan. 21), Good Friday (Fri. before Easter), Easter Monday (day after Easter), National Heroes Day (Apr. 28), Labour Day (May 1), Whitmonday (7th Mon. after Easter), Emancipation Day (Aug. 1), Kadooment Day (1st Mon. in Aug.), Independence Day (Nov. 30), Christmas (Dec. 25), and Boxing Day (Dec. 26).

In St. Lucia, public holidays are New Year's Day (Jan. 1), Independence Day (Feb. 22), Good Friday, Easter Monday, Labour Day (May 1), Whitmonday (7th Mon. after Easter), Corpus Christi (8th Thurs. after Easter), Emancipation Day (1st Mon. in Aug.), Carnival (3rd Mon. and Tues. in July), Thanksgiving Day (Oct. 25), National Day (Dec. 13), Christmas (Dec. 25), and Boxing Day (Dec. 26).

LANGUAGE

English is the official language of both Barbados and St. Lucia and is spoken everywhere, but you may hear local St. Lucians speaking a French-Creole patois (Kwéyòl) among themselves.

▌ MAIL

An airmail letter from Barbados to the United States or Canada costs Bds$1.15 per half ounce; an airmail postcard, Bds45¢. Letters to the United Kingdom cost Bds$1.40; postcards, Bds70¢. When sending mail to Barbados, be sure to include the parish name in the address.

In St. Lucia the General Post Office is on Bridge Street in Castries and is open weekdays from 8:30 to 4:30; all towns and villages have branches. Postage for airmail letters to the United States, Canada, and the United Kingdom is EC95¢ per ½ ounce; postcards are EC65¢.

▌ MONEY

The Barbados dollar is pegged to the U.S. dollar at the rate of Bds$1.98 to $1. U.S. paper currency, major credit cards, and traveler's checks are all accepted islandwide. Be sure you know which currency is being quoted when making a purchase. Major credit cards readily accepted throughout Barbados include American Express, Diners Club, EnRoute, Eurocard, MasterCard, and Visa.

In St. Lucia, the official currency is the Eastern Caribbean dollar (EC$). It's linked to the U.S. dollar at EC$2.67, but, simply for convenience, stores and hotels often exchange at EC$2.50 or EC$2.60. U.S. currency is readily accepted, but you'll receive change in EC dollars—so use your smallest-denomination U.S. bill when making a purchase. Major credit cards and traveler's checks are widely accepted, as well.

Prices throughout this guide are given for adults. Substantially reduced fees are almost always available for children, students, and senior citizens.

ATMS & BANKS

On both Barbados and St. Lucia, ATMs are available 24 hours a day at bank branches, transportation centers, shopping centers, gas stations, and other convenient spots throughout the island where you can use major credit cards to obtain cash (in local currency only).

Barbados National Bank has a branch at Grantley Adams International Airport that's open every day from 8 AM until the last plane lands or departs. First Caribbean International Bank has a network of operations on the Caribbean islands, including several branches and ATMs in Barbados. The Bank of Nova Scotia, or Scotiabank, is a major Canadian bank that is represented throughout the Caribbean. Caribbean Commercial Bank has convenient Saturday morning hours at its branch at Sunset Crest Mall, in Holetown. ATMs are available 24 hours a day at bank branches, transportation centers, shopping centers, gas stations, and other convenient spots throughout the island.

On St. Lucia, major banks include the Bank of Nova Scotia, FirstCaribbean International Bank, National Commercial Bank of St. Lucia, and the Royal Bank of Canada.

CREDIT CARDS

Throughout this guide, the following abbreviations are used: **AE**, American Express; **D**, Discover; **DC**, Diners Club; **MC**, MasterCard; and **V**, Visa.

It's a good idea to inform your credit-card company before you travel, especially if you're going abroad and don't travel internationally very often. Otherwise, the credit-card company might put a hold on your card owing to unusual activity—not a good thing halfway through your trip.

Reporting Lost Cards **American Express** (☎800/528–4800 in the U.S. or 336/393–1111 collect from abroad ⊕www.americanexpress.com). **Diners Club** (☎800/234–6377 in the U.S. or 303/799–1504 collect from abroad ⊕www.diners-club.com). **Discover** (☎800/347–2683 in the U.S. or 801/902–3100 collect from abroad ⊕www.discover-card.com). **MasterCard** (☎800/627–8372 in the U.S. or 636/722–7111 collect from abroad ⊕www.master-card.com). **Visa** (☎800/847–2911 in the U.S. or 410/581–9994 collect from abroad ⊕www.visa.com).

▌ SAFETY

Crime against visitors isn't a major problem in either Barbados or St. Lucia, but take normal precautions. Lock your room, and don't leave valuables—particularly passports, tickets, and wallets—in plain sight or unattended on the beach. Use your hotel safe. For personal safety, avoid walking on the beach or on unlit streets at night. Lock your rental car, and don't pick up hitchhikers. Using or trafficking in illegal drugs is strictly prohibited throughout the Caribbean. Any offense is punishable by a hefty fine, imprisonment, or both.

On St. Lucia, the Rapid Response Unit is a special police brigade dedicated to visitor security in and around Rodney Bay.

■ TAXES & SERVICE CHARGES

IN BARBADOS

At the airport, each adult passenger leaving Barbados must pay a departure tax of $12.50 (Bds$25), payable in either Barbadian or U.S. currency; children 12 and under are exempt. Although it may be included in cruise packages as a component of port charges, the departure tax is usually not included in airfare and must be paid in cash by each traveler prior to entering the secure area of the airport.

A 7.5% government tax is added to all hotel bills. A 10% service charge is often added to hotel bills and restaurant checks in lieu of a tip. At your discretion, tip beyond the service charge to recognize extraordinary service.

A 15% V.A.T. is imposed on restaurant meals, admissions to attractions, and merchandise sales (other than duty-free). Prices are often tax inclusive; if not, the V.A.T. will be added to your bill.

IN ST. LUCIA

The departure tax is $26 (EC$68), payable in cash only (either EC or U.S. dollars). A government tax of 8% is added to all hotel and restaurant bills. There's no sales tax on goods purchased in shops. Most restaurants add a service charge of 10% to restaurant bills in lieu of tipping.

■ TIPPING

In both Barbados and St. Lucia, if no service charge is added to your bill, tip waiters 10% to 15% and maids $2 per room per day, although many all-inclusive resorts have a no-tipping policy. Tip bellhops and airport porters $1 per bag. Taxi drivers and tour guides appreciate a 10% tip.

■ WEDDINGS

IN BARBADOS

Barbados makes weddings relatively simple for nonresidents, as there are no minimum residency requirements. Most resorts, therefore, offer wedding packages and have on-site wedding coordinators to help you secure a marriage license and plan a personalized ceremony and reception. Alternatively, you may wish to have your wedding at a scenic historic site or botanical garden, on the grounds of a restored great house, or at sunset on a quiet beach.

To obtain a marriage license, which often can be completed in less than a half hour, both partners must apply in person to the Ministry of Home Affairs (in the General Post Office building, Cheapside, Bridgetown, open 8:15–4:30 weekdays) by presenting valid passports. If either party was previously married and widowed, you need to present a certified copy of the marriage certificate and a death certificate for the deceased spouse;

if either party is divorced, you need a certified copy of the official divorce decree. Nonresidents of Barbados must pay a fee of $75 (Bds$150) plus a stamp fee of $12.50 (Bds$25). Finally, you must make arrangements for an authorized marriage officer (a magistrate or minister) to perform the ceremony.

IN ST. LUCIA

St. Lucia may be *the* most popular island in all of the Caribbean for weddings and honeymoons. Nearly all of St. Lucia's resort hotels and most of the small inns offer attractive wedding–honeymoon packages, as well as coordinators to handle the legalities and plan a memorable event. Sandals properties offer complimentary weddings to couples booking a minimum-stay honeymoon. Rendezvous, another couples-only resort, is also a popular wedding venue. The most striking setting, though, is probably smack between the Pitons at either Ladera or the Jalousie Plantation.

You can marry on the same day you arrive in St. Lucia if you apply for a "special" marriage license, pay the $200 fee, and have all the necessary documents. You must present valid passports, birth certificates, a decree absolute if either party is divorced, an appropriate death certificate if either party is widowed, and a notarized parental consent if either party is under the age of 18. Most couples opt for the standard marriage license, which costs $125 and requires two days of residence on the island prior to the wedding ceremony. After two days, a local solicitor can apply for a license on your behalf. In either case, special or standard, you can expect additional registrar and certificate fees amounting to about $40. Resort wedding coordinators will help you put together the correct paperwork and, if you wish, will arrange photographer, flowers, musicians, church or other locations for the ceremony, and food and beverage for a reception.

INDEX

NOTES

NOTES

NOTES

NOTES

NOTES

ABOUT OUR WRITER

Jane E. Zarem characterizes herself as a globe-trotting writer, intrepid researcher, fastidious editor, and curious soul with a positive outlook, mature view, and big-picture perspective. Notwithstanding the sheer enthusiasm for her work, she loves the chance to kick back in the Caribbean each year on her updating missions to Barbados, St. Lucia, and several other islands for *Fodor's Caribbean.*

Jane's love affair with the Caribbean began several decades ago, when she joined a 10-day Windjammer cruise that called on islands that, at the time, she never knew existed: Tortola, Virgin Gorda, Nevis, St. Kitts, St. Maarten, Saba, St. Barth's. Tourism hadn't yet hit those island paradises, and most claimed more goats than people. Times have changed.

She has since made more than 75 trips to the Caribbean and has visited Barbados and St. Lucia—two of her favorite islands—more than a dozen times each. She has stared at the awesome east coast of Barbados and swum between the Pitons in St. Lucia. She has visited historic great houses and wandered through St. Lucia's Diamond Botanical Gardens. She has explored shops and markets in both Bridgetown and Castries, off-roaded along the northern tip of Barbados and sailed along the west coast of St. Lucia. She's also met wonderful people on both islands, who have welcomed her back with a big hug and a broad smile on each subsequent visit.

Jane has been a freelance travel writer for more than 25 years. Her very first travel-writing assignment involved updating the Connecticut chapter of Fodor's *New England* in the late 1970s. Since then, she has worked on many Fodor's guides, contributed travel articles to various newspapers and magazines, written travel and other business-related newsletters, and contributed numerous articles and research reports to trade magazines and other organizations. Most significantly, she has been a contributor to *Fodor's Caribbean* since 1994, writing and updating the Grenada and St. Vincent & the Grenadines chapters, along with Barbados and St. Lucia.

ACKNOWLEDGMENTS

Writing this first edition of *In Focus Barbados & St. Lucia* was a natural assignment for her and, she will tell you, "a labor of love." She could not have accomplished it, though, without the assistance of the good people at the Barbados Tourism Authority and the St. Lucia Tourist Board, who have coordinated her trips to the respective islands over the many years that she has focused on these wonderful destinations.